fork + chopsticks

A Melting Pot of Asian American Recipes

Mei Liu and Kyong Han

DK

Publisher Mike Sanders
Editorial Director Ann Barton
Art & Design Director William Thomas
Senior Editor Brook Farling
Copy Editor Megan Douglass
Proofreaders Melissa Haskin, Claire Safran
Indexer Celia McCoy
Recipe Tester Lovoni Walker

First American Edition, 2026
Published in the United States by DK Publishing
1745 Broadway, 20th Floor, New York, NY 10019

The authorized representative in the EEA is Dorling Kindersley
Verlag GmbH. Arnulfstr. 124, 80636 Munich, Germany

26 27 28 29 30 10 9 8 7 6 5 4 3 2 1
001–357705–NOV2026

A catalog record for this book
is available from the Library of Congress.
ISBN 979-8-2173-0399-1

DK books are available at special discounts when purchased in bulk for sales promotions, premiums, fund-raising, or educational use. For details, contact SpecialSales@dk.com

Printed and bound in China

www.dk.com

MIX
Paper
FSC™ C018179

To our family & friends,
for your love and support.

To our culinary instructors & chefs,
for educating and guiding us.

To our amazing community,
for loving our recipes and
making our dreams come true.

Contents

6 • NOODLES + PASTAS 139

7 • SOUPS + STEWS + BRAISES 173

8 • BAKERY + SWEET THINGS 193

9 • SAUCES + CONDIMENTS 235

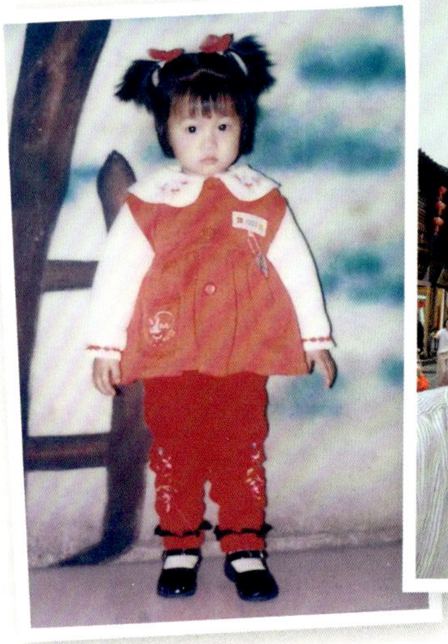  

MEET MEI

Mei grew up surrounded by the smells and sounds of her parents' Chinese restaurant. It wasn't just where her family worked—it was where she spent most of her childhood, and where her love-hate relationship with food began.

Mei's family moved a lot—five times, actually—and she even spent time living in China with her grandparents. But no matter where they landed, food was always at the center of life. She was constantly pulled into the action, soaking up different food cultures along the way.

From a young age, Mei did a little bit of everything: running the register, helping out in the kitchen, and cooking over a blazing-hot wok controlled with a tap of the knee. It was exhausting, both physically and mentally, and it made her swear she'd never work in restaurants when she grew up. Still, she couldn't ignore how powerful food was—not just because it tastes good, but because it brings people together, sparks laughter, and creates memories.

Eventually, that pull was too strong to resist. Even though she said she'd never go back, Mei found herself drawn right back into the world of food. So, against her parents' wishes, she enrolled in culinary school, ready to turn something she once avoided into something she truly loved.

Food has a way of bringing people together, and for Mei, culinary school is where that really clicked—especially the day she met a tall, Asian upperclassman in chef whites with an easy, confident smile. He said, "Hey there, I'm Kyong!"

MEET KYONG

Growing up in New Orleans, food and family always came first for Kyong. At home, Korean flavors filled the kitchen, mixed with the easygoing warmth of Southern hospitality. Even though his parents worked long hours running their dry cleaning business, dinnertime was nonnegotiable—it was when everyone came together.

For Kyong, food was never just about eating. It was about the moments around the table, the stories shared, and the memories being made. He watched his mom, grandma, and aunts cook, learning that meals had the power to connect generations.

He had originally planned to study architecture, but life had other plans. After his parents separated and his mother returned to South Korea, he found himself back where he felt most grounded—the kitchen. He traded blueprints for cutting boards and discovered that cooking was how he could hold onto his roots while creating something meaningful.

Today, Kyong's food blends Korean tradition with Southern comfort, shaped by family, heritage, and years in professional kitchens. Every dish tells a story—of where he came from, who raised him, and the joy of sharing a meal with people you care about.

THE START OF TWO PLAID APRONS

After graduating from culinary school, Mei and Kyong's careers pulled them in opposite directions. Kyong worked long nights on the hot line in restaurants, while Mei left home before sunrise to work in bakeries. Though they shared a roof and the same passion, they rarely had time to share meals, have conversations, or spend time in each other's company. It became clear that they were sacrificing their relationship for their careers, and they knew something had to change.

The start of that change came unexpectedly one day while they were researching holiday recipes. They stumbled upon a food blogger's story about turning her blog into a full-time career. To them, blogging was just an online trend for stay-at-home parents or retired grandparents to share their stories—like a public journal. They never imagined it could be an actual career. They thought: Why don't we do the same with our culinary training and experience?

So, in the winter of 2019, Two Plaid Aprons was launched as a side hobby to test how blogging worked and to share recipes with family and friends. Then, in 2020, the pandemic hit. Like many in the service industry, they were let go from their jobs and were left with little savings and a great deal of uncertainty. Before they could really start building their dream of a life around food, it was already slipping away.

Thankfully, their families welcomed them home, and they were able to get back on their feet by starting a Korean catering business. All the while, they continued posting recipes on their blog and began dabbling in filming and sharing cooking videos on social media.

About half a year later, they struck luck when one of their recipes went viral. Their Korean cream cheese garlic bread reached millions of readers, and suddenly the blog began earning more than it ever had—soon surpassing their catering income. This was proof that the food blogger's story wasn't just a tale that inspired false hope, but something achievable and real.

Shortly after, their very first video went viral. This breakthrough felt like the world nudging them to make a choice: continue catering, or take a leap of faith into food blogging—a world full of potential but even greater risk. They felt incredibly blessed to even have this choice, but it was terrifying nonetheless.

But as you've probably guessed, they chose the leap.

What followed was a constant learning curve, countless recipe tests and experiments, long days, sleepless nights, and more than a few breakdowns. It made them deeply resonate with the proverb, "Rome wasn't built in a day."

TODAY

We are proud to say that we've created a space where we can share approachable, trusted recipes with easy-to-follow instructions and content that reflects calmness and appreciation for food. In doing so, Two Plaid Aprons steadily gained followers and became more than a blog—it became a community.

While planning this cookbook, we often went on walks to brainstorm. We asked ourselves: As professionally trained chefs with experience in many different cuisines, why do we mainly focus on Asian-inspired recipes? After talking it through, the answer was simple—our roots.

From Kyong tasting kimchi straight from his grandmother's hand to Mei folding enough dumplings to feed a whole village with her family, our earliest food memories began in Korean and Chinese kitchens. These flavors are familiar and tell stories of how our families stayed true to authentic tastes while blending traditional flavors with new ingredients to create something nostalgic and delicious.

Fork & Chopsticks is a reflection of everything we value: heritage and creativity, tradition and adaptability, comfort and curiosity. It's a collection of dishes we grew up eating, modern and fun interpretations of flavors we love, and recipes that bring family and friends together—whether through cooking or eating. There are recipes in this cookbook for everyone. Some are simple, comforting dishes that you can whip up in less than 30 minutes and others are a bit more hands-on for days when you want to take on a little more challenge. Most importantly, it's an invitation: to cook more and make memories, to explore unfamiliar flavors, and to build confidence in the kitchen.

So, if this book inspires you to cook one more meal at home, try one new ingredient, or feel a little more connected to the people you feed, then it has done exactly what we hoped it would.

Welcome to our table!

Mei + Kyong

CHAPTER 1 Introduction

Stocking a Diverse Pantry

The first and most important component of cooking in a culturally diverse kitchen is building a diverse pantry. It can feel quite overwhelming when the ingredients are unfamiliar, especially when there's a plethora of choices—sometimes literally a whole wall. So, to simplify the process and get you started, we've listed here pantry items that we use often, if not daily. For consistency, the brands we've listed are all popular and widely available at all Asian markets and at most chain grocery stores. Having stocked your pantry, now you'll be much more confident when navigating through a new recipe.

SAUCES & SEASONINGS

Sauces and seasonings are the backbone of many Asian dishes. With just a few pantry staples, you can create layers of salty, sweet, savory, spicy, and aromatic flavors that turn simple ingredients into satisfying meals. They're often what make the difference between a dish that tastes flat and one that feels balanced and complete. Below are the core sauces and seasonings we use again and again—the building blocks behind many of our stir-fries, braises, marinades, soups, and sauces.

Regular/light soy sauce

Regular or "light" soy sauce (not to be confused with low-sodium) refers to the everyday soy sauce. It's thin, salty, slightly umami, and is used to season dishes. There are so many different types of soy sauce, from Japanese, to Korean, Chinese and more. They even come in premium, low-sodium, and ones specifically made for soups. To create a baseline, we use Kikkoman's All-Purpose Soy Sauce (regular sodium) for all of our recipes. You can find it in most stores or online.

Dark soy sauce

This is commonly used to add more color to dishes like stir-fries and braises, and in meat marinades. It's slightly thicker and darker, a little sweet and not as salty as regular soy sauce. We usually go between Pearl River Bridge brand's Superior Dark Soy Sauce or Lee Kum Kee's Premium Dark Soy Sauce.

Oyster sauce

Oyster sauce is a thick, savory sauce used in most Asian cuisine. Although it's made from cooked oyster extract, it's not fishy at all. Instead, it adds a nice, umami flavor to whatever dish it's added to. We like to use it in sauces, marinades, fried rice, and sometimes even with just some boiled vegetables. Our go-to is Lee Kum Kee's Premium Oyster Sauce.

Hoisin sauce

Popularly known as the condiment used in Vietnamese restaurants, hoisin sauce is also great for marinades, glazes, and commonly used in Chinese BBQ dishes because of its distinct five-spice flavors and sweet and salty profile. The Lee Kum Kee brand is what we usually use.

Fish sauce

If you're new to fish sauce, it can be quite intense and funky, but don't let that deter you from using it! It's made from fermented fish (usually anchovies) and salt that brings a world of deliciously addictive salty and savory but umami-packed flavors to your dishes. Also, after cooking and combining with other ingredients, the funkiness of fish sauce tends to mellow a lot. We love to use it in our Rotisserie Chicken Larb (page 33), and it's a must in our Lemongrass Chicken Thighs (page 99) and Kimchi (page 236). The Three Crab Brand is our go-to for price and versatility.

Shaoxing rice wine, soju, and sake

Rice wine, plain soju, and sake are great for marinating proteins to remove unwanted gamey/chicken-y flavors. A small amount added to your braising liquid could accomplish the same thing. These cooking wines are also great for stir-frying. A drizzle will make your stir-fry dishes extra aromatic.

Chicken bouillon powder

It's essentially granulated chicken-flavored stock powder. We call it "chicken magic" at home because a generous pinch of it will round out and complete the flavor missing in any savory dish you're making. We usually use the Totole brand. An alternative for chicken bouillon powder to keep a dish vegan/vegetarian is using mushroom bouillon powder. We like to use the one from Lee Kum Kee.

Dashi powder

While making homemade dashi is tasty, we find ourselves using instant dashi powder 90 percent of the time because it's so convenient and also shelf-stable. We like to use Ajinomoto brand's Hondashi Bonito Soup Stock. It's easy to find online and in most Asian grocery stores.

Gochugaru

Gochugaru is a Korean red chili powder used in a wide variety of Korean recipes. It's usually offered as fine powder or coarse flakes, but you'll likely only need the coarse flakes, which can be used in soups, stir-fries, and or making marinade for Kimchi (page 236). When shopping for gochugaru, we recommend that you choose varieties that look vibrant and are bright red. You should also look at the pepper flakes to see whether they're coarse or fine because the labels can sometimes be misleading and categorize both types of gochugaru as powders. To preserve its freshness, it's best to purchase smaller bags of gochugaru or store leftovers in the freezer. You can keep an airtight container in your spice cabinet for everyday use.

Five-spice powder

This fragrant spice blend is usually made of star anise, cloves, cinnamon, fennel, and ginger. It's often used in marinades and sauces, and associated with Chinese BBQ. Our favorite ways to use it is in our Asian Sticky Ribs (page 108) and Air-Fried Crispy Pork Belly (page 104).

Sichuan peppercorn

Known for its signature numbing sensation on the tongue and lips, Sichuan peppercorn also tastes subtly citrusy and floral. It's an important flavor profile in classic Sichuan dishes like mapo tofu, and also the sauce for our Sichuan Pepper Steak au Poivre (page 123). We like to crush our Sichuan peppercorns with a mortar and pestle for most recipes to get a more even distribution of flavor, but you can keep the peppercorns whole if you prefer.

CONDIMENTS

These condiments are essential to keep stocked in your kitchen, as they add brightness, depth, heat, and aroma—and sometimes simply help complete a dish.

Rice vinegar

It's a versatile vinegar that's milder, less acidic, and has a light sweetness compared to distilled white vinegar, making it perfect for sushi rice, dressings, and dipping sauces. Kikkoman rice vinegar is what we usually use. Note that there's also a seasoned version, which has sugar and salt added.

Distilled vinegar

Distilled vinegar can be pungent, but it really makes dishes that require bold acidity shine, like in our Restaurant-Style Hot and Sour Soup (page 183) and Sweet & Sour Fish (page 128). Any brand is perfect.

Chinese black vinegar

It goes by a few different names, including Chinkiang vinegar, black rice vinegar, and Zhenjiang vinegar. Chinese black vinegar is full bodied, less acidic than distilled vinegar, and tastes malty and slightly sweet, almost like Worcestershire sauce. It's commonly used for dressings and for dipping sauce for wontons.

Chinese chili oil

This, in many recipes, is like the cherry on top of an ice cream sundae. Not only does chili oil add spiciness to dishes, good chili oils are flavorful and aromatic, giving dishes an extra boost. We make our own Chinese Chili Oil (page 240) at least two to three times a year, but when we're in a pinch, Lao Gan Ma brand chili oil is our go-to.

Toasted sesame oil

Toasted sesame oil is usually used in soups, stir-fries, and fillings to add that iconic, nutty, slightly smoky flavor. It is known as a finishing oil, which means it can burn quickly, as its smoking point is low, and makes it not suitable for cooking over high heat. Instead, add it to dishes at the very end or cook over medium heat so that its toasted fragrance can be maximized. Kadoya is our go-to brand.

Extra-virgin olive oil (EVOO)

Although we don't use EVOO in a lot of our cooking, a small bottle comes in handy for pasta dishes, dressings, and as a finishing oil or condiment for bread.

PASTES

Pastes are some of the most powerful flavor builders you can keep in your pantry, forming the backbone of countless Asian dishes. Just a spoonful can add depth, heat, sweetness, and rich umami that would otherwise take hours to develop. Having a few of these staples on hand makes it easy to create bold, complex sauces, soups, stews, and marinades with minimal effort.

Miso paste

Miso is a Japanese fermented soybean paste made with three basic ingredients: soybeans, salt, and koji (a type of culture derived from rice and grains). It can be fermented and aged for months or years to develop and deepen the savory, umami flavor. In the US, miso is generally categorized into white, yellow, and red. For this cookbook, any recipes that call for miso refer to white miso, which is slightly sweet and the mildest and least salty of the three.

Gochujang

Also known as Korean fermented red chili paste, it's slightly sweet, savory, and spicy and is most often used in sauces, soups, stews and marinades. O'Food and CJ Foods are the two most common brands we see, but most brands are all fairly equal for cooking. However, do watch out for gochujang marked as extra spicy!

Doubanjiang paste

Doubanjiang is also known as Chinese fermented broad bean chili paste, and it's the soul of many Sichuan savory recipes. It's spicy, savory, and the main seasoning for mapo tofu or twice cooked pork. Our favorite brand is Juan Cheng Pai (鹃城牌). It's available online and at most Asian markets. Other brands with labels that say Pixian (郫县) are also a good choice. Pixian refers to Pixian, Sichuan, meaning the doubanjiang is from the region and is authentic, just like how a sparkling wine can only be labeled as champagne if it's made in Champagne, France.

Thai red curry paste

Our go-to is the red curry paste from Mae Ploy. It's flavorful and perfect for making quick red curries with coconut milk.

Japanese curry

This is technically not a paste, but we do love the convenience of having Japanese curry cubes on hand. All you have to do is dissolve the cubes in a proper amount of liquid, and it'll thicken and make a sauce with whatever you add it to. The cubes come in different levels of spiciness, and we usually go for the mild ones from S&B.

NOODLES AND RICE

Noodles and rice are the heart of so many Asian meals and our dinner table at home, serving as the comforting base for everything from quick weeknight stir-fries to our favorite clay pot rice dishes. Keeping a variety of dried, fresh, and frozen noodles—as well as the right type of rice—on hand gives you the flexibility to create different textures and styles of dishes whenever you want.

Bean thread/mung bean vermicelli

These noodles are made with mung bean starch and cook quickly. We like to soak them in hot water to soften them first before using. They are great for hot pots, soups, and for bulking up fillings, like in our Whole Shrimp Mandu (page 61).

Knife-sliced noodles

You can find knife-sliced noodles both fresh or dried. They are wide, bouncy, and chewy with ruffled edges, making them great for saucy dishes and stir-fries. It is also a great substitute for homemade hand-pulled noodles in our Cumin Lamb Noodles (page 162). We usually get the Wei-Chuan or Yi Feng brand dried noodles.

Instant ramen noodles

Not only are instant ramen noodles great midnight snacks, the noodles themselves are great for soups and creamy sauces. Some of our favorite instant ramen brands are Nongshim's Shin Ramen, Nissin's Chu Qian Yi Ding (出前一丁), and Indomie's Mie Goreng (although it's technically not a ramen).

Sweet potato glass noodles (vermicelli)

As the name suggests, these noodles are made with sweet potato starch. They're a grayish purple color before and after cooking, with a chewy, bouncy texture. They are usually available as long, thin sticks or flat, wide noodles and are often added to soups, used to bulk up fillings, like in our Bulgogi Mandu (page 57), and to make Korean glass noodle stir-fry (aka Japchae, on page 145). For all of our recipes, the long, thin sticks are the ones you want to use. We like the sweet potato noodles from Wang Food and Ottogi.

Frozen udon noodles

Frozen udon noodles are probably our favorite noodles to have on hand, next to instant ramen and dry wheat noodles because of how quick, easy, and versatile they are to use. All of the frozen udon brands we've tried so far are equally good, but Shirakiku is always a good choice.

Dry wheat noodles

Having a couple of dry wheat noodle choices in your pantry will always come in handy. We always have a bag of thin, round noodles for soups and a bag of wide, flat ones for saucy or dry noodle dishes, like our Fujianese-Style Creamy Peanut Noodles (page 169).

Rice

There are a lot of varieties of white rice, but generally speaking, white rice comes in long-, medium-, and short-grain varieties, which all are great for everyday meals. However, the different grain sizes make one more suitable for certain recipes than another. For example, medium- and short-grain white rice are starchier and stickier than long-grain white rice, making them good for sushi rice, while long-grain white rice is not suitable for recipes that call for sushi rice but is great for fried rice. If you eat rice daily like us and have the storage space, purchasing larger sacks of rice can be more cost effective than purchasing small bags. Also, if you need a quick guide on cooking white rice, you can learn more on page 22.

OTHER INGREDIENTS

Beyond sauces and noodles, there are a handful of versatile pantry ingredients that quietly support many recipes. These ingredients help create signature textures—whether chewy, crispy, silky—and add depth and body to dishes. The best part is that these are easy to find and shelf stable, making them perfect pantry staples.

Rice flours

Rice flours are divided into regular and glutinous. Regular rice flour packaging is usually labeled with red printing and is ground from regular white rice. It can be used for frying, as a gluten-free substitute in baking, as a thickener in soups and sauces, and for making noodles and some traditional Asian cakes. Glutinous rice flour, also known as sweet rice flour or mochiko, is usually labeled with green printing. It's milled from glutinous rice (sweet rice) and is most commonly used for making mochi, but can also be used for frying and for thickening sauces and soups. Our favorite brand for both is the Erawan and can be found at most Asian markets and online.

Cornstarch

This is probably one of the most used ingredients in our pantry. When used in batters and for frying, it gives the final product extra crunch. If you mix equal parts or a little less water with cornstarch, you get a slurry that can be used to thicken soups and sauces. Cornstarch is also an important ingredient used for velveting, a Chinese marinating technique that tenderizes and keeps marinated proteins juicy. Any brand is fine.

Dried mushrooms

Fresh shiitake and wood ear mushrooms can be difficult to find. Instead, we like to keep dried ones on hand. They are widely available online and at Asian markets, and since they are dried, the mushrooms are shelf stable and much easier to store. To use them, simply rehydrate the mushrooms in boiling hot water for about 15 minutes.

Essential Equipment

If having a well-stocked pantry is the most important component of building your culturally diverse kitchen, having proper equipment follows right behind, because having the right equipment can elevate a dish from 4 stars to 5 stars and make cooking more convenient and fun. Here is a list of basic tools that will make great additions to your kitchen if you don't already have them.

Knives

Knives are an extension of your arm in the kitchen, so it's important to choose ones that feel comfortable in your hand and are suitable for certain tasks. If you don't already have a collection of knives, we recommend starting with a chef's knife, a paring knife, a serrated knife, and a cleaver. A chef's knife is for general cutting and chopping; it's the most versatile, must-have knife. A paring knife is great for peeling and coring fruits, trimming produce, deveining shrimp, and other tasks that require precision. A serrated knife is mostly used for slicing cakes, bread, and roasts, but it's also great for cutting tomatoes. A cleaver is a general utility knife that can be substituted for a chef's knife, although you may need to get used to not chopping with the rocking motion used with a chef's knife. The flat sides of a cleaver are also great for crushing things like aromatics and shrimp.

Mise en place bowls

Mise en place is a French phrase that loosely translates to "everything in its place." Mise en place bowls can be any bowls or containers that can be used to hold prepped ingredients, seasonings, and other components. Having a variety of bowl sizes keeps cooking organized, clean, and efficient. You can never have too many.

Strainers and sieves

Strainers and sieves bring a lot of convenience to your kitchen. Spider strainers are ideal for blanching foods and safely lifting items from hot oil. For finer things, you can layer cheesecloth in the mesh strainers or use a chinois to filter out fine particles for a smoother final product. Mesh strainers are great for sifting dry ingredients like flour and draining boiled foods like noodles, dumplings, and vegetables. Then there are fine mesh sieves, which are great for skimming impurities off the surface of liquids.

Thermometers

A digital probe thermometer is a versatile tool for checking ingredient temperatures in general and the internal temperatures of proteins and bread for doneness. Using a clip-on thermometer when frying keeps your hands free and helps make temperature control easier and more efficient. Ovens all heat up at different speeds, and most of the time when an oven's preheat setting is complete, the oven is usually not yet heated to the temperature you actually need. So, having an oven thermometer in your oven will ensure your oven is truly at the correct temperature before you bake or roast. This small tool can make a big difference in achieving consistent, reliable results.

Kitchen scale

While a kitchen scale isn't a must, it's especially important for baking. It provides accuracy and consistency, which is essential for baked goods to turn out properly.

High-power blender

A high-power blender is a versatile piece of equipment for making sauces, soups, and general blending. You can even make sorbets with it, like our Mandarin Orange Calpico Sorbet (page 231).

Stand mixer & hand mixer

Generally speaking, you can usually use either a stand mixer or hand mixer for any recipe that calls for a mixer, unless you're making bread dough. We prefer using the hand mixer in our kitchen because it's easier to handle and you aren't limited to using only one mixing bowl. But at the end of the day, you can use whichever mixer you feel most comfortable using.

Basic baking tools

A rolling pin, pastry brush, rubber spatula, and bowl scraper are the basic tools you'll need for most baking projects. Outside of the basics, we like to have a few full-size sheet pans that fit in standard home ovens to maximize output and time, cookie scoops for portioning, a silicone pastry mat for working with doughs, a ruler for measuring the thickness and size of the dough/pastry, and toothpicks for testing the doneness of cakes.

Wok

A wok is great for stir frying and cooking with high heat. It's also great for steaming, as you can sit a bamboo steaming basket directly in it. Good quality woks are usually made of carbon steel, and when properly seasoned and maintained, they can become naturally nonstick and last for years. Unless you have a wok station, flat-bottom woks are the most practical ones to get because they provide better stability and heat contact on most standard cooktops.

Clay pot

Clay pots heat up more slowly than metal, but they maintain and spread heat more evenly. Those qualities are what make it ideal for simmered recipes, such as braises for meat where the juices create self-basting steam. They're also perfect for simmering soups and cooking rice. Some of our favorite clay pot recipes are our Hainanese-Style Chicken Clay Pot Rice (page 115) and Clay Pot Soy-Braised Chicken (page 188). Just make sure to follow the maintenance instructions for your clay pot before using it so that it lasts a long time!

Rice cooker

Although you can cook perfect white rice on the stovetop by following our guide on page 22, we love having a rice cooker because you can just turn it on and forget about it, then return to perfectly cooked rice after you've completed other tasks. Although rice cookers can be a little pricey, most of them are multifunctional appliances, allowing you to also steam food, make congee, soup, and more. They also come in a variety of sizes ranging from 3 to 10 cups, so you can choose one that best fits your needs. Since we eat rice nearly every day, we have a 10-cup rice cooker.

Steam basket

Steam baskets are typically made of bamboo or stainless steel and can be found at most Asian markets or online. Steaming is a method that cooks food with moist heat and is ideal for gently cooking delicate proteins like fish or dumplings and buns, or for just keeping dishes light and clean-tasting. To make a steamer setup with a steam basket, all you need is a pot that fits nicely under the baskets, or a wok that's big enough for the basket to sit in. Fill the pot or wok with a couple of inches of water and refill as needed during the steaming process. If you're using bamboo baskets in a wok, make sure to fill the wok with enough water so that the bottom edge of the basket (not the steaming platform) is submerged and the water is at least a couple inches or more from the bottom of the steaming platform. Make sure the water is always at a high simmer unless otherwise indicated by the recipe. You can also steam by placing a rack in a wok or pot and filling it with enough water so that there's about a half inch gap between the water and the top of the rack. Place what you're steaming on the rack (in a heatproof container) and cover the wok/pot with a lid. Keep the water at a gentle simmer.

Seasoning and caring for your wok

When seasoning a brand new wok, start by washing it thoroughly with hot, soapy water to remove the protective factory oil. Dry it off and place the wok over high heat, preferably outdoors (because it will smoke a lot) and on a gas burner or a butane burner, until it begins to smoke and the metal changes color—shifting from silver or dark gray to blue and sometimes yellow. Next, carefully rub a thin, even layer of high-smoke-point oil (like grapeseed, canola, or peanut) onto the entire interior and exterior metal surfaces with a paper towel and tongs. Wipe off any excess oil with a clean paper towel and let it cool before repeating this process one or two more times so that the oil can polymerize and create a dark, nonstick patina. There's a common myth that you can't scrub a wok without ruining the seasoned coating and scratching the surface, but you can definitely wash your wok after each use. Simply scrub the wok with hot water and a dishcloth or soft sponge, but if you need to, you can wash with dish soap and scrub with steel wool as well. If doing so, you'll just need to repeat the seasoning process after the wash. You'll also want to re-season the wok occasionally, even if you don't wash with soap.

Fundamental Techniques You Should Know

Getting better at cooking all starts with being familiar with the fundamentals. So we've listed and expanded on some cooking terminologies and techniques here that we think will make following a recipe and cooking easier and more fun.

BASIC KNIFE CUTS

These are the basic knife cuts that you will see mentioned throughout this cookbook:

- **Julienne:** Thin matchsticks, approximately ⅛″ × ⅛″ × 1–2″ (3mm × 3mm × 2.5-5cm). Commonly used for carrots and other firm vegetables.
- **Mince:** Finely chopped pieces with no defined shape. Often used for aromatics such as garlic, ginger, lemongrass, and similar ingredients.
- **Half-moons (Ds):** Usually for round, cylinder-shaped vegetables. Cut the vegetables lengthwise, then slice them into half-moon D shapes. The thickness will vary depending on the recipe.

MIS EN PLACE (PRONOUNCED MEEZ-AHN-PLAHS)

Mis en place is a French culinary phrase meaning "everything in its place." It's a practice of preparing and organizing all necessary ingredients and equipment before you start cooking. This also includes reading through the recipe so that you understand the general process before you start. Doing so will make the entire cooking process smoother, more efficient, and less error prone.

TASTING AS YOU GO

Tasting your food throughout the cooking process is a good practice for building flavor and ensuring proper seasoning. By sampling the food at different stages of the cooking process, you can make small seasoning adjustments to the dish as it becomes more concentrated or mellows. It will also give you an idea of how much more seasoning you'll need when you're finishing up the dish.

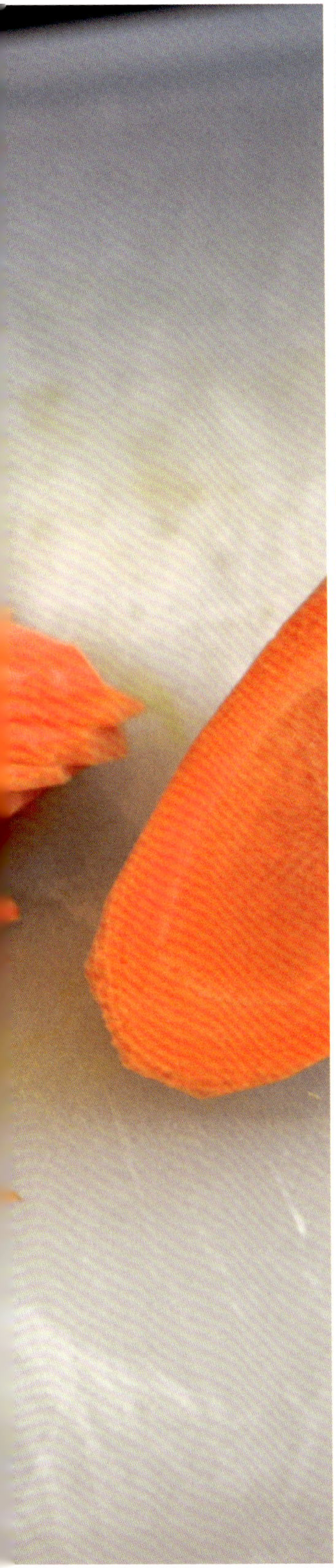

CONTROLLING HEAT

Heat control is one of the most essential skills for successful cooking, as it directly affects texture, flavor, and doneness. Too high heat can burn food before it's cooked through, but if the heat is too low, it can prevent proper browning and affect texture and flavor development. It's also important to understand your cooktop. Gas burners respond instantly but are likely to create hot spots, while electric stovetops tend to retain residual heat, heat up slower but more evenly, and are prone to constant temperature fluctuation. Knowing how your stovetop behaves will help you adjust the heat more confidently.

MAINTAINING OIL TEMPERATURE WHEN FRYING

Frying at the temperature the recipe calls for gives a final product and texture the recipe is intended to achieve. However, depending on how cold the food is, how much food you're frying at a time, and how much oil you're frying in, the oil temperature will immediately decrease by a varying amount when you first add the food. How fast the oil comes back to the target temperature will depend on how powerful your stovetop is. To combat the fluctuations in oil temperature, we recommend heating your oil about 15 to 25°F (8 to 14°C) above the target temperature. Starting with slightly hotter oil will let the oil settle back to the ideal frying temperature after the food is added.

BLANCHING AND SHOCKING

Blanching is a technique aimed to bring out the vibrancy and preserve the crispness and/or color of an ingredient, typically vegetables and herbs, by briefly cooking them in a pot of water. It can also be used in the beginning steps of making a soup to draw out and remove impurities from bones or meats. This is a common process in Asian cooking to keep soups clear and clean tasting. After blanching, sometimes it's necessary to "shock" the ingredient in a bowl of ice water to stop the cooking process so that the ingredient stays vibrant and doesn't become overcooked from the residual heat.

DEGLAZING

This is a cooking technique in which a liquid—such as water, stock, or alcohol—is added to a hot pan to dissolve the flavorful browned bits, known as fond, that are left behind after searing or sautéing. This process captures concentrated flavor and forms the base for rich pan sauces, gravies, and reductions. It's also helpful when a pan needs an "intermediate" deglazing when caramelizing an ingredient or cooking with an ingredient that can get easily caramelized, like a paste.

VELVETING

This is a Chinese cooking technique that involves marinating delicate proteins and thin slices of meat with water, egg whites (sometimes), cornstarch, and oil. This process protects the proteins and keeps them juicy after cooking. For less delicate or chewier cuts of meats (e.g., chicken breast and beef flank), a little baking soda is often added to help tenderize the cuts and promote moisture retention. Shaoxing rice wine is also often added to the marinade to help remove any undesirable, gamey flavors. Velveting is great for proteins that are quickly boiled/blanched, flash fried, and stir-fried.

PROPERLY MEASURING FLOUR (FLUFF, SPOON, AND LEVEL)

When baking, measuring in grams using a kitchen scale is highly recommended so that the end product stays consistent. Just measuring ingredients, specifically flour, using US customary measuring cups can result in variations in weight by more than 30 grams, which is about ¼ cup. If you've ever baked a cake or cookies that came out denser than expected, that could be the likely reason. So, in order to measure more accurately if you are only using measuring cups, you should first fluff up your flour really well with a spoon, then scoop the flour into the measuring cup until it overflows, and finish by scraping off the excess with the flat edge of a knife to level the flour. Make sure to not tap or shake the cup in the process so that the flour doesn't become compacted. This process will reduce the weight discrepancy to around 10 grams per cup.

THE WINDOW-PANE TEST

This is a method you can use to determine how much gluten a dough has developed. Although some recipes do not require the dough to pass the window-pane test, most recipes do. This will help ensure the dough develops a light texture and is able to hold its structure. To test the dough, pinch off a small piece and gently stretch it between your fingers. If it stretches thin enough that you can see your fingers' silhouette through it and light passes through—like a little windowpane—without tearing, the dough has developed enough gluten and is ready for the next step. If it tears before you can get it thin enough, the dough will require more kneading.

How to Make Perfect White Rice

No meal is complete without rice at our table, so here's a quick overview of cooking the perfect white rice, whether it's regular long grain, medium grain, or short grain.

MEASURING WHITE RICE

If you're making white rice using a rice cooker, use the plastic measuring cup that comes with the rice cooker to measure the rice. The rice cooker's inner pot will have markings that will show you how much water you need to add based on how many cups of raw white rice you're cooking.

If you're making white rice on the stovetop, it's important to note that all of our rice measurements are based on US customary cup measurements, not the measuring cup that comes with rice cookers. For all white rice, the ratio is 1 cup of rice to 1¼ cup (300ml) of water.

- **Long-grain rice (190g per cup):** The rice grains are long and skinny and have the least amount of starch, which makes it great for everyday meals and fried rice, like our Vegetable Fried Rice (page 83).
- **Medium-grain rice (200g per cup):** As the name suggests, the rice grains here are in between long- and short-grain rice in terms of size. Sometimes, it's also labeled as "Calrose" rice. Medium-grain rice is starchier and stickier than long grain rice, but it's still great for everyday meals. It's actually our go-to rice at home. One of our favorite recipes using it is our Salmon Sushi Bake (page 131).
- **Short-grain rice (210g per cup):** Also known as "sushi rice" or labeled as "Koshihikari," it shouldn't be confused with sweet rice or glutinous rice. When compared to medium- and long-grain rice, you'll see how short and almost round the short-grain rice looks. Between the three, short-grain rice is the starchiest and stickiest, but it is still great as an everyday rice.

COOKING WHITE RICE

1. Before cooking your rice, wash the rice to remove any excess starch by placing the rice in a large bowl and filling it with water. Swish the rice around and gently rub it between your fingers for a few seconds, then drain the water and repeat this process 2 to 3 more times until the water is mostly clear. Drain well.

2. After washing, transfer the rice and the appropriate amount of water into a suitable size heavy-bottomed pot. Bring to a boil over medium-high heat. When it comes to a boil, reduce the heat to low so that the rice is at a low simmer and then cover the pot with the lid.

3. Let the rice cook for 20 minutes, then turn off the heat and let it steam for another 10 minutes without opening the lid. If you're cooking on an electric stovetop, take the pot off the heat. When the 10 minutes are up, uncover the pot and fluff the rice with a fork.

Tips from our kitchen: Sometimes we like to soak our rice before cooking. This is to encourage more even cooking and to produce soft, fluffy rice, especially when cooking a larger amount of rice. It's also helpful when cooking rice in the clay pot. To soak rice, wash the rice as you normally would, but after the final wash, cover the rice with the amount of water needed for cooking and set it aside to soak at room temperature for 30 minutes, then cook the rice as is.

How to Boil Perfect Eggs

Boiling eggs is a skill we think everyone should learn, simply because it's an easy way to add more substance to any dish. Boiled eggs are also perfect to use as a garnish that instantly upgrade a visually bland dish to something much more interesting and enticing. Here is how to make the perfect boiled eggs using large-size eggs.

1. Bring a pot of water to a boil over high heat. The water should be able to fully submerge the eggs, and the pot size should be relative to how many eggs you're boiling.

2. Gently add cold eggs straight from the fridge into the boiling water, then reduce the heat to medium or to a level that keeps the water at a good, constant simmer.

3. Cook the eggs according to your desired doneness and immediately transfer them to an ice bath to stop the cooking process. While the eggs are cooling, lightly crack the shells all around to help separate the shell from the egg white and make peeling easier. Continue to let them soak in the ice water until they're cooled.

SOFT-BOILED (5–6 MINUTES)
The whites are set but the yolk is still runny.

MEDIUM-BOILED (7–8 MINUTES)
The whites are firm and the yolk is jammy.

HARD-BOILED (10–12 MINUTES)
The whites are firm and the yolk is set and fully cooked.

CHAPTER 2

Shareable Bites

Grandma's Spring Rolls

As a child, I lived in China for a few years with my grandparents. During those years, I was a super picky kid with very little interest in food, which is a total surprise now that I look back. My grandma would try different methods to coax me into eating my veggies, and these spring rolls were the only successful strategy for a little while, likely because they were fried and super flavorful. Because what child doesn't love fried food?! Grandma would make her spring rolls using whatever vegetables she had purchased that morning from the market: green cabbage was always the base, shiitake mushrooms added umami flavor, vermicelli noodles made them more filling, and wood ear mushrooms added some additional texture.
— Mei

Prep time: **1 hour 30 minutes**
Cook time: **5–7 minutes per batch**
Makes: **30–32 spring rolls**

- 2 bundles (3oz/85g) mung bean vermicelli
- 5 (20g) dried shiitake mushrooms
- ¼ oz (7g) dried wood ear mushrooms
- 2 tbsp (30ml) neutral cooking oil, plus more for frying
- 1 tbsp (9g) minced garlic
- 2 stalks green onion, sliced (whites and greens separated)
- 1 large (3oz/85g) carrot, peeled and julienned
- 1½ lb (680g) green cabbage, diced
- 2 tbsp (38g) oyster sauce
- 2 tbsp (30ml) soy sauce
- ½ tsp kosher salt
- ¼ tsp ground white pepper
- 1 tsp toasted sesame oil
- 30–32 8-inch (200mm) spring roll pastry wrappers
- Sweet chili sauce, for serving (optional)

1. **Rehydrate the dried ingredients.** Bring a pot of water to a boil and place the vermicelli, shiitake mushrooms, and wood ear mushrooms each into a separate heatproof bowl. Pour enough hot water over each of the dried ingredients to cover by at least 1 inch (2.5cm). Let each ingredient soak for about 15 minutes or until fully rehydrated, then drain well. Cut the vermicelli noodles into 1 to 2-inch (2.5 to 5cm) pieces. For the mushrooms, rinse them well to remove debris and cut them into thin slices. Set aside.

2. **Cook and cool the filling.** Heat a large nonstick pan over medium-high heat and add the oil. Once hot, add the garlic and the white parts of the green onions and sauté for about 15 seconds, or until fragrant. Add the carrot and shiitake mushrooms and cook briefly, about 30 seconds. Then add the cabbage and sauté until wilted. Reduce the heat to medium-low, and add the vermicelli and wood ear mushrooms, tossing well to combine. Season the filling with oyster sauce, soy sauce, salt, and white pepper, mixing thoroughly. Finish with a drizzle of sesame oil and the remaining green onions, and stir until evenly incorporated. Remove from the heat and let the filling cool completely. To speed up the cooling process, transfer it to a large sheet pan and stir occasionally.

3. **Prepare the wrapping station and assemble the spring rolls.** Once the filling has almost completely cooled, carefully separate the spring roll wrappers by gently peeling them apart. Keep the wrappers covered with a damp towel when not in use to prevent them from drying out. Prepare a clean, flat surface for wrapping (I like to use a cutting board for easier cleanup), a sheet pan lined with plastic wrap, and a bowl of room-temperature water. Then follow the instructions to assemble the spring rolls.

4. **Fry the spring rolls.** In a pot, heat about 2 inches (5cm) of oil to 350°F (175°C). While the oil heats, prepare a sheet pan fitted with a cooling rack or line a plate with paper towels. Also have a spider strainer or a pair of tongs at the ready. Once the oil is ready, carefully lower the spring rolls into the oil and fry for 5–7 minutes, or until golden brown. Do not overcrowd the pot; fry in batches as needed. Remove the spring rolls and let them drain on the rack or paper towels for a few minutes before serving.

5. **Serve.** Enjoy as is or with sweet chili sauce. Store any leftovers in an airtight container in the refrigerator for up to 3 days.

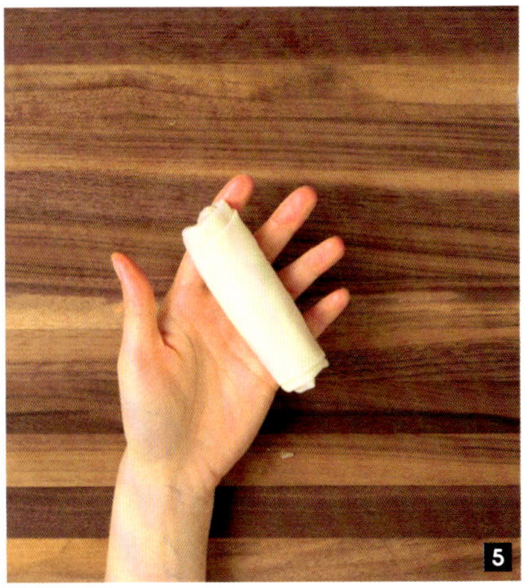

Assembling the spring rolls

1. Place a sheet of spring roll wrapper in front of you like a diamond, and place 3–4 tablespoons of the filling on the lower center half of the wrapper (photo 1).

2. Mold the filling into a 1-inch-thick (2.5-cm-thick) log. Fold the bottom flap of the wrapper over the filling, making sure to tuck the filling tightly (photo 2).

3. Fold the side flaps over each other (photo 3).

4. Using your fingers or a brush, wet the top flap of the wrapper with some water (photo 4).

5. Tightly roll the spring roll upwards to seal (photo 5). Place the finished spring roll in the prepared sheet pan and cover with a damp towel as you work on the rest of the spring rolls.

Tips from our kitchen: These spring rolls are perfect for feeding a crowd, but they also make great emergency freezer appetizers. To store, arrange them on a sheet pan, making sure to leave a small gap between each to prevent sticking. If they do stick, give them a firm tap on the counter to separate. Freeze the spring rolls for a few hours or overnight, until solid. Then transfer them to freezer-safe, airtight containers and store for up to 3 months. When ready to cook, fry them straight from frozen at 350°F (175°C) for 9–10 minutes, or until golden and heated through.

SUGAR

Crab Rangoons

Crab rangoons, also known as crab wontons or cheese wontons, are, without question, one of the most popular appetizers ordered at Chinese restaurants. This is also true for my parents' Chinese takeout restaurant—some customers would order two to three orders of crab rangoons at one time—that's eight per order! My parents' crab rangoons are beloved for two reasons: texture and flavor. Unlike many other Chinese restaurants that fold their crab rangoons into triangle-shaped dumplings, my parents fold theirs into four-point flower shapes, giving their crab rangoons extra real estate for that delicious crunch, which pairs so perfectly with the rich and tangy cream cheese filling. In terms of flavor, the secret lies with the addition of onion, carrot, and celery to the cream cheese mixture—they add so much flavor to the cream cheese, making the rangoons extra fragrant and savory. — Mei

---

Prep time: **1 hour**
Cook time: **about 2 minutes per batch**
Makes: **40–45 wontons**

- ¼ small (1oz/28g) yellow onion, cut into small chunks
- ⅓ medium carrot (1oz/28g), peeled and cut into small chunks
- ½ rib celery (1oz/28g), cut into small chunks
- 16 oz (454g) cream cheese, softened
- 4 (3oz/85g) imitation crab sticks, cut into ¼-inch (6mm) pieces
- ½ tsp kosher salt
- 40–45 square wonton wrappers
- Neutral cooking oil, for frying
- Sweet chili sauce, for serving (optional)

1. **Prepare the vegetables.** Blend the onion, carrot, and celery in a food processor until minced, then transfer the mixture into a double layer cheese cloth. Squeeze firmly to remove most of the moisture from the vegetables. Discard the juice.
2. **Make the filling and assemble the wontons.** In a mixing bowl, add the softened cream cheese, the vegetable mixture, imitation crab, and salt. Mix until well combined. Set aside until ready to use or cover and refrigerate for up to 3 days. Follow the instructions for assembling the rangoons.
3. **Prepare the fry station.** In a pot, heat about 3 inches (7.5cm) of oil to 350°F (175°C). While the oil is heating, prepare a sheet pan fitted with a rack or a plate lined with paper towels. Also have a spider strainer or a pair of tongs and a fine-mesh strainer.
4. **Fry the wontons.** Once the oil is hot, gently lower the wontons into the oil and fry until they're golden brown, about 2 minutes. Don't overcrowd the pot, and fry in batches as necessary. The cream cheese will leak slightly, but it's totally normal. Remove the wontons and let them cool and drain on the rack or plate. After frying each batch, use the fine-mesh strainer to remove all the debris in the oil.
5. **Serve.** Enjoy while hot with some sweet chili sauce, if desired.
6. **Storage.** This is a great emergency freezer appetizer. To store, arrange the uncooked crab rangoons on a sheet pan that'll fit in your freezer. If you have room, leave gaps between the wontons; if you can't, that's okay. Freeze the wontons for a few hours or overnight until they are solid, no covering needed. Once frozen, quickly transfer them to clean plastic bags or freezer-safe containers. They will be good for up to 3 months. When the craving hits, just fry them straight from frozen until golden, about 3 minutes. If any get stuck together, give them a firm tap on the countertop to pop them apart.

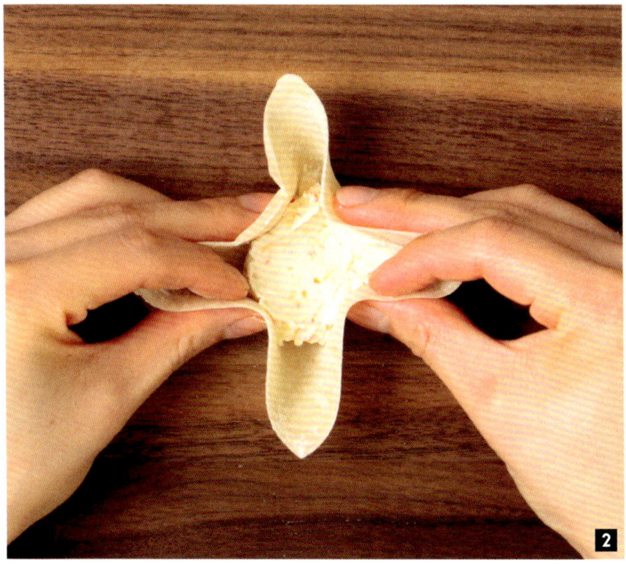

Assembling the wontons

1. Using the back of a spoon, smear about 1 tablespoon of the cream cheese filling onto the center of the wonton wrapper (photo 1).

2. Bring the middle of each edge of the wrapper to the center (photo 2).

3. Pinch gently to seal (photo 3). The cream cheese mixture will act as glue, so try to squeeze a little of the cream cheese mixture up as you're bringing edges up to help adhere the wrappers together. If any extra cream cheese is pushed out, just scrape it off and add it back into the bowl.

4. When you're done, it should look like a pointed four-leaf flower (photo 4). Place the finished crab rangoon onto a sheet pan and repeat the process with the remaining filling and wrappers.

Tips from our kitchen: Crab rangoons tend to float on the oil after a few seconds, so you'll need to push them down with a strainer or tongs to keep them submerged for even color. If it's difficult, you can doctor the color by holding the wonton upside-down in the oil so that you can fry just the tips of the wonton. If you're frying for a crowd, we recommend a double basket electric fryer. You can stack the baskets to keep the wontons submerged without having to manually hold them down.

Rotisserie Chicken Larb

Between Kyong and I, a whole rotisserie chicken is always too much to finish, so we like to get creative with the leftovers. Our favorite hack? A quick and tasty, Lao-inspired larb that's ready in under 30 minutes. It's perfect for lettuce wraps or simply with some rice. — Mei

Prep time: **15 minutes**
Cook time: **10 minutes**
Makes: **3 servings**

- 1 tbsp (15ml) neutral cooking oil
- 1¼ lb (570g) rotisserie chicken, shredded and roughly chopped (about 3 cups)
- ¼ cup (60ml) fresh lime juice
- 1½ tbsp (23ml) fish sauce
- ¼ large (3.5oz/100g) red onion, sliced
- 1 cup (30g) roughly chopped cilantro
- 1 stalk green onion, sliced
- Buttercup or green leaf lettuce, for serving

1. **Sauté the rotisserie chicken.** Add the oil into a small or medium pot and heat over medium heat. Once hot, add the rotisserie chicken and cook until warmed through, stirring frequently, about 3 minutes. Add the lime juice and fish sauce and mix well. Cook the rotisserie chicken for 30 seconds, until hot, then take the pan off the heat.
2. **Finish and serve.** Add the red onion, cilantro, and green onion and stir well to combine. Enjoy it warm over rice or with lettuce. Refrigerate leftovers in an airtight container for up to 2 days. Note that the cilantro and green onion may become brown due to the lime juice.

Tips from our kitchen: If you aren't fond of the red onion's spiciness, add them to the pot with the rotisserie chicken. The onion will taste sweeter and still maintain a slight crisp.

Bulgogi Meatballs

I always looked forward to making meals for Mei, but when I was a college student on a tight budget, expensive cuts of meat and decadent ingredients were a rarity. I often felt that what I made at home couldn't compare to the food I prepared and served in restaurants. Still, Mei always thanked me and reassured me that the meals I cooked for her tasted just as good—and meant far more—than anything we could have eaten out. One of her favorite dishes was these simple bulgogi meatballs, made with ground beef, coated in a glossy bulgogi sauce, and served over hot white rice (page 22) with a side of steamed vegetables or lightly seasoned cucumber slices. It may sound cliché, but this dish proves that a simple, inexpensive meal can also exceed expectations. — Kyong

---

Prep time: **15 minutes**
Cook time: **20 minutes**
Makes: **about 25 meatballs**

Neutral cooking oil, for greasing
1 lb (454g) ground beef (preferably a 70/30 ratio)
¾ cup (180ml) bulgogi sauce, divided (store-bought or homemade [page 244])
⅓ cup (2oz/60g) yellow onion, finely chopped
¼ cup (30g) plain breadcrumbs
1 stalk green onion, finely sliced, plus more for garnish
¼ tsp cracked black pepper
Toasted sesame seeds, for garnish

1. **Preheat the oven to 425°F (220°C).** Also, prepare a sheet pan lined with aluminum foil and lightly grease the foil with oil.

2. **Make the meatballs.** To a mixing bowl, add the ground beef, ½ cup (120ml) of bulgogi sauce, yellow onion, breadcrumbs, green onion, and black pepper. With gloved hands, mix well until everything is evenly incorporated, then portion with a 1½ tablespoon-size cookie scoop and roll each portion into a 1-inch (2.5cm) ball. Arrange the meatballs on the prepared sheet pan.

3. **Bake the meatballs.** Bake the meatballs on the middle rack for 10 minutes, then remove them from the oven. Brush with the remaining ¼ cup (60ml) of bulgogi sauce and return to the oven for another 5–10 minutes, until the internal temperature reaches 165°F (74°C) and the sauce is sticky on the outside. If you'd like some extra color or char on the meatballs, broil the meatballs on high until a desired amount of char develops.

4. **Serve.** Garnish the meatballs with green onions and sesame seeds. Enjoy while hot as appetizers or in a rice bowl. Refrigerate any leftovers in an airtight container for up to 4 days.

Gyoza-Stuffed Chicken Wings

These gyoza-stuffed chicken wings were created out of our love for anime, Korean fried chicken, and *anju*, or beer snacks, because they are great as late night snacks and even better with some cold, bubbly beer while you binge your favorite shows! The idea originally came to us after watching *Food Wars!*, a food-themed anime. Turning chicken wings into gyoza, one of our favorite foods, is such a genius idea, so it was a no-brainer that we had to recreate it with our own twist. These gyoza chicken wings are stuffed with a flavorful dumpling filling, coated in starch, double fried for maximum crisp, then tossed in a sticky, Sweet & Spicy Gochujang Sauce (page 47). They're perfect appetizers to wow a crowd. — Kyong

---

Prep time: **1 hour**
Cook time: **about 15 minutes**
Makes: **16–20 stuffed chicken wings**

- 8 oz (227g) ground pork
- ½ cup (2oz/57g) green cabbage, finely chopped
- 2 stalks green onion, thinly sliced
- 1 tbsp (15ml) soy sauce
- 1 tbsp (15ml) water
- ½ tbsp (8ml) Shaoxing rice wine
- ½ tbsp (5g) minced ginger
- 1 tsp toasted sesame oil
- ¼ tsp kosher salt
- 16–20 chicken wings (flats with wingtip only)
- ½ cup (90g) potato starch
- ¼ cup (32g) cornstarch
- Neutral cooking oil, for frying
- 1 batch Sweet & Spicy Gochujang Sauce (page 47)
- Sliced green onion, for garnish (optional)
- Toasted sesame seeds, for garnish (optional)

1. Make the filling. Add the ground pork, cabbage, green onion, soy sauce, water, Shaoxing rice wine, ginger, sesame oil, and salt to a mixing bowl. Mix vigorously until well combined and paste-like. Set aside.

2. Debone and stuff the chicken wings. See instructions for deboning the chicken wings. Once all the wings have been deboned, stuff each wing cavity with about 1–1½ tablespoons of the prepared filling, depending on the size of the wing. You can use your fingers to help pack the filling, but don't overstuff the wings. The filling will expand and the wings will tighten and shrink when fried.

3. Dredge the wings. Make the fry dredge by combining the potato starch and cornstarch in a wide mixing bowl or on a large plate. Mix well. Coat each wing thoroughly with the starch mixture, then give them a light tap to dust off the excess. Place the dredged wings on a plate as you get ready to fry.

4. Perform the first fry. Add about 2–3 inches (5–7.5cm) of oil to a pot and heat to 325°F (160°C). Prepare a sheet pan fitted with a rack or line a plate with paper towels. Also have a spider or a pair of tongs at the ready. Once the oil is ready, carefully lower the wings into the oil. Don't overcrowd the pot, and fry in batches if needed. Fry the wings for about 4–5 minutes. Remove the wings and let them drain and cool on the prepared rack or plate for about 5 minutes.

5. Perform the second fry. While the wings are resting, increase the oil temperature to 375°F (190°C). Carefully return the wings into the oil and fry until the wings are crispy on the outside and the filling is cooked through with the internal temperature registering 165°F (74°C), another 3 minutes.

6. Serve. Remove and toss the wings with some Sweet & Spicy Gochujang Sauce (page 47). Garnish with sliced green onion and sesame seeds if desired.

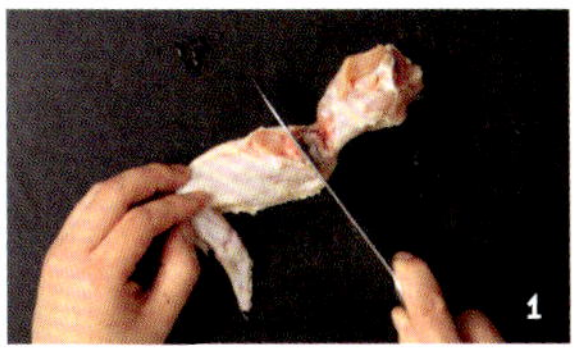

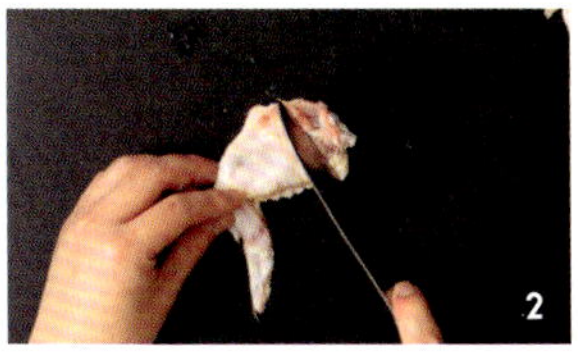

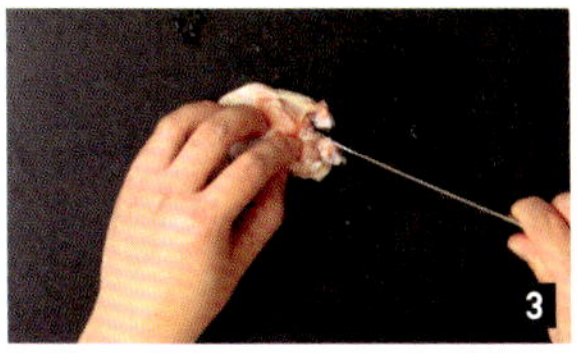

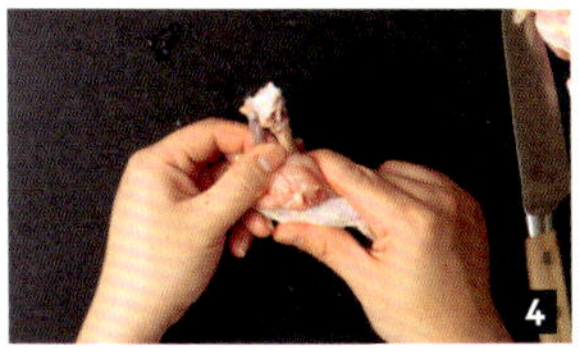

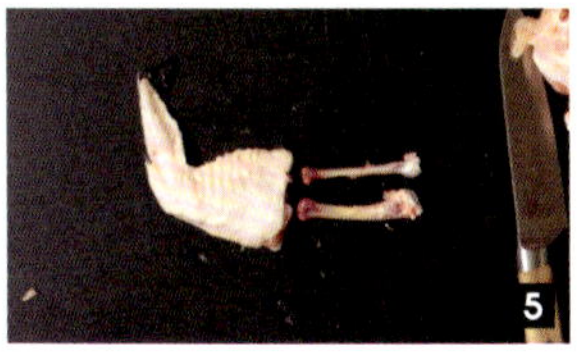

Deboning the Chicken Wings

1. If you can only purchase whole wings, separate the drumettes from the flats by cutting the wings at the joint (photo 1). (The drumettes can be dredged, fried, and enjoyed or stored for another use.)

2. Working with one wing at a time, use a knife to cut around the bones of the wing (the open ended side) to disconnect the meat from the bone (photo 2).

3. Cut in between the two bones to separate them (photo 3).

4. Use your fingers to push the meat off the bones (photo 4).

5. Once the bones are completely exposed and separated from the meat, twist the bones to pop them off the wingtip joint (photo 5). Repeat this process with the remaining wings.

Burrata with Gochujang Bacon Jam

If you haven't tried bacon jam, it's like the best sweet and savory spread ever! To make it, you render bacon, then cook onion in the bacon fat, season with a sweetener and vinegar, then stew down the mixture to create a flavor explosion. In our version, we sautéed gochujang with the onions to add a subtle spiciness that makes this jam even more irresistible. We love it on burrata and toasted bread, but it's delicious with just about anything—pasta, burgers, and whatever else your heart desires! — Kyong

---

Prep time: **15 minutes, plus 15–30 minutes of assembly time**
Cook time: **1–1½ hours**
Makes: **8–12 servings**

Gochujang bacon jam

12 oz (340g) thick-cut bacon, cut into ¼-inch (6mm) strips
1 large (14oz/400g) yellow onion, thinly sliced
2 tbsp (36g) gochujang
1 tbsp (9g) minced garlic
⅓ cup (80ml) apple cider vinegar
¼ cup (55g) packed dark brown sugar
¼ cup (70g) maple syrup
⅛ tsp cracked black pepper

For serving

4–6 large slices of rustic or sourdough bread
Olive oil or neutral cooking oil, as needed
16 oz (454g) burrata (four 4-oz/113g balls)
5–6 oz (140–170g) cherry tomatoes, halved or quartered
Cracked black pepper
Chopped parsley, for garnish

1. **Render the bacon.** Place a medium stainless steel pan or a nonstick pan over medium-high heat. Once it's hot, add the bacon and cook until the bacon pieces are rendered but not crispy, about 5–10 minutes. Remove the bacon with a slotted spoon and keep about 3 tablespoons (45ml) of the bacon fat. Discard the rest of the bacon fat.

2. **Make the bacon jam.** In the same pan with the reserved bacon fat over medium-high heat, add the onion once the fat is hot. Sauté until the onion begins to turn translucent, about 1–2 minutes. Add the gochujang and garlic and cook, stirring until well combined. Return the bacon to the pan, along with the vinegar, brown sugar, maple syrup, and black pepper. Stir to combine and bring the mixture to a simmer. Reduce the heat to low to maintain a gentle simmer and cook for 1–1½ hours, or until the jam has reduced by about two-thirds and reached a syrupy consistency. Remove from the heat and let the bacon jam cool completely. Once cooled, store it in an airtight container in the refrigerator for up to 2 weeks.

3. **Toast the bread.** Preheat the oven to 400°F (205°C) and prepare a sheet pan lined with parchment paper. Cut the sliced bread in half and arrange them on the prepared sheet pan. Lightly spray or brush both sides of the bread with some oil, then bake on the middle rack for about 4 minutes. After 4 minutes, remove the pan and flip the bread. Return it to the oven and bake for another 3–4 minutes or until lightly golden. Remove and cool before using.

4. **Assemble and serve.** Spread 1–2 tablespoons of bacon jam onto each slice of toasted bread. Split the burrata and scatter about 2 ounces (57g) on top of the jam. You can spread a little more bacon jam on top of the burrata if desired, then top with some tomatoes, a couple of cracks of black pepper, and chopped parsley.

Kimchi Grilled Cheese

I'm just gonna say it: kimchi and cheese is a power couple that doesn't get nearly enough love. They're both salty and umami-packed flavor bombs, and when you melt them together? Magic. Now imagine all that goodness sandwiched between two slices of golden, crispy sourdough. It's a grilled cheese dream come true! But wait—there's a twist. Just when you think this sandwich can't get any better, add a swipe of fig spread. That little bit of sweetness brings everything into balance, like two big flavors learning how to dance together without stepping on each other's toes. And of course, no grilled cheese is complete without tomato soup. But not just any tomato soup (page 180)—ours has caramelized gochujang for a spicy, savory kick that plays perfectly with all that melty, funky, sweet-and-salty goodness.
— Kyong

Prep time: **5 minutes**
Cook time: **10 minutes**
Makes: **1 sandwich**

1 cup (220g) fermented kimchi
1 tbsp (15ml) neutral cooking oil
1 tbsp (13g) mayonnaise
2 large slices sourdough bread
2 tbsp (44g) fig spread
3 slices (70g) low-moisture mozzarella
3 slices (70g) medium-sharp cheddar

1. **Cook the kimchi.** If your kimchi pieces are large, give them a rough chop for easier eating. To a medium pan over medium heat, add the oil. Once the oil is hot, add the kimchi and sauté until most of the kimchi juice has evaporated, about 3–5 minutes. Set aside.

2. **Prepare the bread.** Thinly spread the mayonnaise onto one side of each slice of sourdough bread, then spread the other side of each slice of bread with the fig spread. On the fig spread side, top each slice of sourdough with three shingled slices of cheese. You can alternate the cheese if you'd like. Also, the sliced bread we usually use is from a large sourdough boule. If your sourdough bread slices are smaller, feel free to use less cheese.

3. **Toast the grilled cheese.** Place both slices of bread into a large nonstick pan, mayo side down. Heat the pan over medium-low to low heat and cover the pan with a lid. Let the bread slices toast for about 3 minutes or until they are starting to turn golden on the bottom and the cheese is gooey. Top one slice of bread with the prepared kimchi, making sure to spread it evenly, then sandwich with the other slice of bread. Give the sandwich a firm press to help the cheese and kimchi stick together. Toast on each side for another 2–3 minutes or until the bread is golden brown and crispy.

4. **Serve.** Let the sandwich cool for a moment before enjoying.

Tips from our kitchen: After spreading the mayo onto your bread, you can place them directly into the pan that you'll be using, mayo side down since the pan doesn't have to be preheated. Then you can continue to spread your fig jam without the mayo dirtying up your cutting board or plate.

Dynamite Shrimp

These shrimp are called dynamite shrimp because they are flavor bombs on their own. The shrimp are first seasoned, dredged, fried until golden and crispy, then tossed in a simple but addictive spicy mayo sauce. They are great for sharing as appetizers on their own or enjoyed in lettuce wraps for lunch or dinner. They also make great protein in a rice bowl, tortilla wraps, and subs. For this recipe, we like to use 60/80 size shrimp if you are curious. — Mei

---

Prep time: **20 minutes**
Cook time: **6–10 minutes**
Makes: **3–4 servings**

Sauce
½ cup (105g) mayonnaise
3 tbsp (45g) sriracha, more or less to your preference
1 tbsp (21g) honey

Shrimp
1 lb (454g) peeled and deveined raw small shrimp
¾ tsp fine salt, divided
¾ tsp cracked black pepper, divided
½ cup (90g) corn flour
½ cup (60g) all-purpose flour
¼ cup (32g) cornstarch
1 tsp garlic powder
1 tsp onion powder
Neutral cooking oil, for frying
2 large (100g) eggs, beaten

To serve (optional)
Lettuce of choice (red and green leaf, romaine, and butter are preferred)

1. **Make the sauce.** Combine the ingredients for the sauce in a large mixing bowl and mix well. Set aside until needed.
2. **Season the shrimp.** Make sure the shrimp are well drained and place them in a bowl and season with ½ teaspoon of salt and ¼ teaspoon of black pepper. Mix well and set aside.
3. **Prepare the dredge.** In a medium or large bowl, add the corn flour, all-purpose flour, cornstarch, garlic powder, onion powder, the remaining ¼ teaspoon of salt, and remaining ½ teaspoon of black pepper. Mix well.
4. **Prepare the fry station.** In a pot, heat 2–3 inches (5–7.5cm) of oil to 350°F (175°C). Also, prepare a sheet pan fitted with a rack or line a plate with paper towels, and have a spider strainer at the ready.
5. **Dredge the shrimp.** Pour the beaten eggs into the seasoned shrimp and mix well. Making sure to let some of the excess egg drip off and working in batches, transfer the shrimp into the dry dredge. Coat the shrimp well, then gently shake off the excess flour. Place the dredged shrimp on a plate or in a bowl. Repeat with the remaining shrimp.
6. **Fry the shrimp.** When the oil is ready, gently add the dredged shrimp and let them fry for 2–3 minutes or until the shrimp are golden and crispy. Remove and let them drain for a couple minutes on the prepared sheet pan or plate. Fry in batches as needed.
7. **Toss with sauce and serve.** Add the fried shrimp to the mixing bowl of prepared sauce and toss gently or mix with a spoon or a pair of tongs until evenly coated. Transfer the shrimp to a serving plate and enjoy. These dynamite shrimp are amazing on their own, but we also love making lettuce wraps with them. Leftover shrimp can be covered and refrigerated for up to 3 days.

Homemade Gua Bao Buns

These tender, steamed buns, are often shaped and eaten like small tacos and are traditionally filled with a slice of soy-glazed pork belly. However, nowadays, you'll also find them filled with crispy fried chicken, crispy pork belly, and a variety of other delicious options. Whatever filling you choose, gua baos make a perfect choice for a party or any meal! — Mei

---

Prep time: **30 minutes, plus 30–45 minutes proofing time**
Cook time: **15 minutes**
Makes: **12 buns**

- 1¼ cups (300ml) warm water (around 105°F/40°C)
- 2 tsp (8g) granulated sugar
- 2½ tsp (7g) active dry yeast
- 4 cups (480g) all-purpose flour (fluffed, spooned, and leveled), plus more for dusting
- 1 tsp (4g) baking powder
- Neutral cooking oil, for brushing

1. **Activate the yeast.** To the warm water, add the sugar and stir until the sugar has dissolved. Then sprinkle the yeast over the water and give it a good mix. Set it aside in a warm area to let the yeast dissolve and activate, about 5 minutes. It should form a foamy cap. Give it another stir before use.

2. **Make the dough.** To a mixer bowl, add the flour and baking powder. Give it a good mix with the dough hook attachment. Once the yeast is ready, add it to the flour mixture. Mix with the dough hook until a rough dough comes together, then knead with the stand mixer on medium to medium-high speed until the dough is smooth. There is no need to reach the window-pane stage. (See page 21 for details on the window-pane test.)

3. **Initial shaping.** Lightly dust your work surface with flour as needed while you work. Turn the dough out and divide it into 12 equal-size pieces. Shape each piece into a taut ball. Cover the dough balls with a clean kitchen towel and let them rest for 10–15 minutes. While waiting, prepare 16 squares of parchment paper, each about 4 × 4 inches (10 × 10cm) wide, and steam baskets.

4. **Finish shaping.** After resting, use a rolling pin to roll each dough ball into ovals that are twice as long as they are wide, about 6 × 3 inches (15 × 7.5cm). Flip each oval and give the other side a gentle roll to smooth it out. Lightly brush the top half of the oval with oil and fold the oval in half. Give the dough a gentle press to help keep it closed. Lightly dust the bottom of the dough with flour and place it on a prepared parchment square. Repeat with remaining dough and keep them covered as you work.

5. **Proof and cook the buns.** When all the dough balls are shaped, arrange them in the steam baskets, leaving about 1 inch of space in between each. Place the lid over the steam baskets and place the baskets over a pot of warm water. Let the buns proof until they have risen by 50 percent. Leaving the baskets over the pot, bring the pot of water to a boil over high heat. When steam is visibly coming out of the steam baskets, start a timer to steam for 12 minutes. Once the time is up, turn off the heat but do not open it yet! Keep the baskets covered for another 3 minutes.

6. **Use and storage.** After the 3 minutes, carefully take the steam baskets off the heat. If you don't have another batch of buns to steam, let the buns cool until comfortable to touch. Use immediately or cool completely before storing in a freezer-safe container. Keep frozen for up to 3 months. To reheat, give the buns a quick rinse, then shake off the excess water. Wrap 4 buns in damp paper towels and microwave for 45 seconds to 1 minute. Alternatively, you can steam thawed buns for 1–2 minutes and frozen buns for 5–8 minutes until warmed through.

Tips from our kitchen: If your steam baskets can't fit all your buns in one session, you can cover and proof the remaining buns in a warm area. Once the first batch of buns are done steaming, arrange the next batch of buns in the baskets. Cover and bring the water to a boil again. Once the steam is visible, steam the buns for 12 minutes and cover for 3 minutes.

Soy-Glazed Pork Bao

During our trip in China, one of the vendor stalls with the longest line in the bustling morning market was the gua bao stall. Those tender white steamed buns, folded like tacos, cradled slices of succulent braised pork belly simmered in a rich soy-based braising liquid. Topped with fresh cilantro and a light sprinkle of crushed peanuts, they're the ultimate handheld breakfast in the morning and street snack by night. When we make them at home, we usually make our own gua bao buns (page 43), but you can use store-bought buns that can be found at most Asian grocery stores in the frozen aisle, often labeled as "gua bao buns" or "steamed lotus leaf buns." Pair these baos with some Sesame Ginger Slaw (page 238) and they're sure to be a crowd-pleaser! — Mei

---

Prep time: **15 minutes**
Cook time: **1 hour 30 minutes**
Makes: **6–8 servings**

Soy-glazed pork belly

2 lb (907g) skin-on pork belly
1 tbsp (15ml) neutral cooking oil
⅓ cup (67g) granulated sugar, divided
2 cups (480ml) water
3 tbsp (45ml) soy sauce
1 tbsp (15ml) Shaoxing rice wine
½ tbsp (7ml) dark soy sauce
1-inch (2.5cm) (10g) knob of ginger, peeled and cut into slices
1 cinnamon stick
1 star anise
2 dried bay leaves

To serve

12–16 gua bao buns (homemade [page 43] or store-bought)
Sesame Ginger Slaw, optional (page 238)
Chopped cilantro (optional)
Crushed peanuts (optional)

1. **Prepare the pork belly.** Pat the pork belly dry with paper towels. If your pork belly is a whole piece, cut it into 2-inch-wide (5cm-wide) slabs first, then cut them into slices that are about ½-inch (1cm) thick. To a well-seasoned wok or a large nonstick sauté pan over medium heat, add the oil. Once the oil is hot, add the pork belly and sear until they are lightly golden, about 5–10 minutes. Sear in batches if necessary. Remove the pork belly and set aside. Reserve about 2 tablespoons (30ml) of fat in the pan and discard the rest.

2. **Caramelize the sugar.** To the same wok or pan over medium heat, add 3 tablespoons (38g) of sugar. Let the sugar cook in the fat, stirring occasionally, until it turns a rich amber color, about 3–5 minutes. Immediately, but carefully, add the water and increase the heat to medium-high and bring to a boil. Then add the soy sauce, remaining sugar, rice wine, dark soy sauce, ginger, cinnamon stick, star anise, and bay leaves.

3. **Braise.** When the braising liquid comes to a boil, add the pork belly and bring it back to a boil, then reduce the heat to medium-low to keep it at a simmer. Skim the surface using a spoon or a fine-mesh skimmer to remove any scum and excess fat. Cover and let the pork belly gently simmer for about 1 hour or until tender. Stir the pan and skim the surface occasionally as needed.

4. **Reduce sauce.** Once the pork belly is tender, remove and discard the cinnamon stick, star anise, and bay leaves. With the pan uncovered, bring the braising liquid to a high simmer over medium-high heat and reduce the sauce until it looks glossy, about 5–10 minutes, stirring occasionally. Toss to coat the pork belly evenly and transfer to a serving plate for self-assembly or assemble for serving.

5. **Assemble and serve.** Reheat the homemade or store-bought gua bao as instructed. Open the buns and stuff them with the braised pork belly and if desired, some Sesame Ginger Slaw, cilantro, and crushed peanuts. Leftover pork belly can be stored in an airtight container and refrigerated for up to 4 days.

KFC Bites

Not to confuse this with the Colonel's chicken, we're talking Korean fried chicken in shareable bite-size form. Juicy, well-seasoned chicken thighs are coated in seasoned fry batter and double fried until golden brown and irresistibly crispy. It's delicious on its own, but for sauce lovers, we recommend our Soy-Garlic Sauce—sweet, savory, and garlicky—or the gochujang sauce for those who love a spicy-sweet kick.
— Kyong

Prep time: **30 minutes**
Cook time: **about 15 minutes**
Makes: **4–6 servings**

Chicken

- 2 lb (907g) boneless, skinless chicken thighs, cut into 1-inch (2.5cm) chunks
- 1 tsp fine salt
- 1 tsp granulated sugar
- ½ tsp onion powder
- ½ tsp garlic powder
- Neutral cooking oil, for frying

Fry mix (makes 1¾ cup/240g)

- 1 cup (120g) all-purpose flour
- ½ cup (64g) cornstarch
- 1 tbsp (9g) onion powder
- 1 tbsp (9g) garlic powder
- 2 tsp (4g) fine gochugaru (optional)
- 2 tsp (8g) granulated sugar
- 2 tsp (4g) cracked black pepper
- 1½ tsp (11g) fine salt
- 1 tsp ground ginger
- 1 tsp baking powder

Fry batter

- 1¾ cups (240g) fry mix, divided (store-bought or homemade)
- ¼ cup (32g) cornstarch
- ½ cup (120ml) water

1. **Season the chicken.** Place the chicken into a large mixing bowl and season with the salt, sugar, onion powder, and garlic powder. Mix well and set aside to marinate for about 15 minutes, or cover and refrigerate overnight.
2. **Prepare the fry mix (if making).** In a medium or large bowl, mix together all the ingredients for the fry mix.
3. **Make the fry batter.** In another bowl, add ½ cup (70g) of the prepared or store-bought fry mix, cornstarch, and water. Whisk until smooth. Optionally, drizzle a couple of tablespoons of fry batter or water into the remaining fry mix, then mix with your fingers or a fork. This is called "seeding" and will give your fried chicken crispier bits and that iconic shaggy batter appearance.
4. **Prepare the fry station.** In a large pot, heat about 3 inches (7.5cm) of oil to 325°F (160°C). Also, prepare a sheet pan fitted with a rack or line a plate with paper towels, and have a spider strainer at the ready.
5. **Batter the chicken.** While waiting for the oil to heat up, start battering the chicken. Pour the prepared fry batter into the marinated chicken and mix until the chicken is evenly coated. Then, in batches, dredge the chicken in the bowl of fry mix. Gently pack the fry mix onto the chicken so that it is well coated, then shake to remove excess coating. Set aside on another plate or tray and repeat with the remaining chicken.
6. **Perform the first fry.** When the oil is ready, gently add the chicken to the oil and let it fry for 3–4 minutes. Remove the chicken and let it rest on the prepared sheet pan or plate for about 5 minutes. Fry in batches as necessary.
7. **Perform the second fry.** Bring the oil to 350°F (175°C). When the oil is ready, add the fried chicken back into the oil and fry for another 3–4 minutes or until the chicken is golden brown and crispy. Remove and let the chicken drain for a couple of minutes. Fry in batches as necessary.
8. **Serve or toss with sauce.** Feel free to enjoy the fried chicken bites as is, or toss them in Soy-Garlic Sauce or Sweet & Spicy Gochujang sauce. If coating with sauce, we recommend using a large mixing bowl for easy tossing.

Soy-Garlic Sauce
(per recipe of chicken)

Makes: **about 1½ cup (360ml)**

- ½ cup (120ml) soy sauce
- ½ cup (150g) light corn syrup
- ½ cup (100g) granulated sugar
- ½ cup (65g) chopped garlic

1. Mix together all the ingredients for the sauce in a wok or large pan and bring to a simmer over medium heat. Let the sauce cook for about 4–5 minutes, stirring often, until the sauce is a thin syrup.

Sweet & Spicy Gochujang Sauce
(per recipe of chicken)

Makes: **about 1 cup (240ml)**

- ⅓ cup (100g) gochujang
- ⅓ cup (112g) honey
- ¼ cup (50g) granulated sugar
- ¼ cup (60ml) soy sauce
- 3 tbsp (27g) minced garlic

1. Mix together all the ingredients for the sauce in a wok or large pan and bring to a simmer over medium heat. Let the sauce cook for about a minute, stirring often, until the sugar has melted.

CHAPTER 3

Dumplings + Mandu

Dumplings and Mandu Basics

When Kyong and I first started dating, we had our inevitable debate about which was superior: dumplings or mandu. If you're not familiar with them, both are flavorful fillings wrapped in thin sheets of dough. The main difference is that *dumplings* is a broad term often used in America to describe dumpling-shaped foods. More often than not, it refers to Chinese-style dumplings, typically filled with a combination of meat or seafood and vegetables, and wrapped in dough made from wheat flour and water. Mandu, on the other hand, are Korean. The fillings are usually vegetarian or a mixture of meat and vegetables, often with the addition of sweet potato glass noodles. The wrappers can be slightly larger than standard dumpling wrappers and are sometimes made with wheat flour, starch (usually rice flour), and water.

Ultimately, which is better comes down to personal preference. These days, we both love dumplings and mandu from each of our cultures. I especially love Kyong's Kimchi Mandu (page 58)—the tangy, spicy flavors are so different from what I grew up with. But no matter how delicious his kimchi mandu are, I will always welcome a plate of juicy Pork and Cabbage Dumplings (page 55). We hope you come to love these delicious parcels, no matter which culture they're from, just as we have. — Mei

GET THE PARTY STARTED!

To start any proper dumpling- or mandu-making party, it's very important to practice "mise en place," meaning get everything in place. This includes having your filling made, the wrappers thawed and ready to use, sheet pans lined with plastic wrap that'll fit in your freezer (if freezing), damp paper towels to keep the dumplings covered to prevent drying out, spoons or chopsticks for scooping up the filling, and a bowl (or multiple bowls) of water to wet the wrappers. This will ensure a smooth assembly process with minimal interruptions.

When you're diving into any dumpling or mandu recipe, it's a great opportunity to invite your friends and loved ones to participate, which makes it a dumpling wrapping party! It's the perfect time to catch up, gossip, and bond in the kitchen. If you need an incentive for participation, send your guests home with a bag of frozen dumplings!

FOLDING TECHNIQUES

Here are four simple folding techniques you can refer to when making dumplings and mandu, both within and beyond this cookbook. You may have already considered using different folds to distinguish between various fillings—but did you know that certain folding techniques are better suited to specific cooking methods than others?

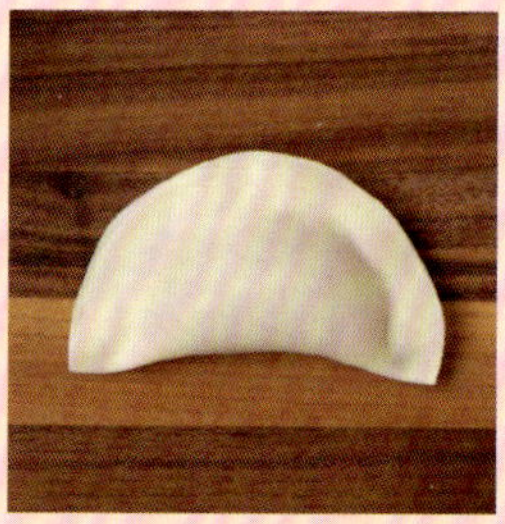

SIMPLE HALF-MOON

- Easiest fold
- Holds more filling
- Suitable for boiling, pan frying, and deep frying

PLEATED HALF-MOON

- A few bidirectional pleats
- Holds slightly less filling
- Suitable for steaming, boiling, pan frying, and deep frying

POTBELLY

- Simple but versatile fold
- Could hold more filling
- Best suited for boiling, but can also be pan fried

ROUND INGOT

- Resembles tortellini
- Normal amount of filling
- Suitable for steaming, boiling, and pan frying

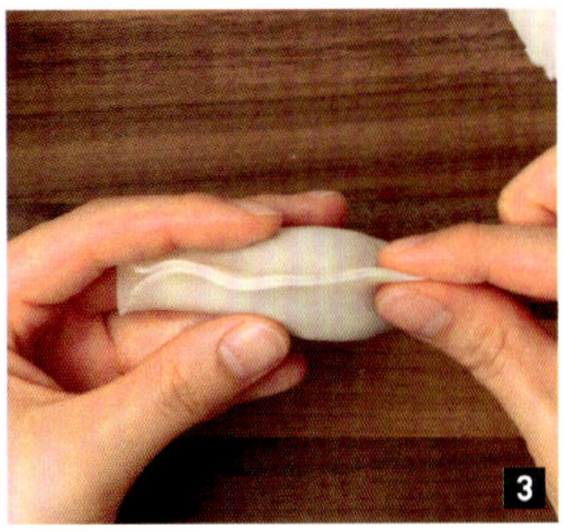

Simple half-moon

This is the easiest fold and is suitable for boiling, pan frying, and deep frying. Because it's such a simple fold, you can pack more fillings with this technique.

1. Place up to 1½–2 tablespoons of filling at the center of the wrapper and brush the outer ¼ inch (6mm) of the wrapper with some water with your fingers (photo 1).
2. Fold the wrapper in half and pinch at the top (photo 2).
3. Work your way left and right from the top, pinching along the way, to seal the filling (photo 3).
4. We like to go back along the edges again to make sure the dumpling is properly sealed (photo 4).

Pleated half-moon

This fold is basically a simple half-moon with a few bidirectional pleats. Because of the extra pleats, this fold holds a little less filling. It is suitable for steaming, boiling, pan frying, and deep frying.

1. Place about 1–1½ tablespoons of filling at the center of the wrapper and brush the outer ¼ inch (6mm) of the wrapper with some water with your fingers (photo 1).
2. Fold the wrapper in half and pinch at the top (photo 2).
3. Working on one side first, close to the center, fold the wrapper forward like a Z. Pinch the fold to make your first pleat. Repeat this a couple more times all the way to the end then repeat on the other side to seal (photo 3).

The potbelly

This fold will probably become your favorite once you master it because it's so simple! It holds a normal amount of filling, maybe a little more if you're feeling bold and your dumpling wrappers are pliable. This fold is most suitable for boiling but works for pan frying as well.

1. Place about 1–1½ tablespoons of filling at the center of the wrapper and brush the outer ¼ inch (6mm) of the wrapper with some water with your fingers (photo 1).
2. Fold the wrapper in half and pinch at the top. Hold the dumpling in your hands. With your pointing fingers overlapping each other behind the top of the dumpling, press down on the edge of the wrapper with your thumb and pointing finger to seal (photos 2 and 3).
3. While holding that position, gently squeeze inward so that the filling bulges out a little to give the dumpling a potbelly appearance (photo 4).

The round ingot

This fold somewhat resembles the making of tortellini and wontons and can hold a normal amount of filling. It's great for steaming, boiling, and pan frying.

1. Place about 1–1½ tablespoon of filling at the center of the wrapper and brush the outer ¼ inch (6mm) of the wrapper with some water with your fingers (photo 1).
2. Fold the wrapper in half and seal it completely by pinching all along the edge of the wrapper, like you would in the simple half-moon. Flip the dumpling so that the curved side is closer to you and dab a little water on the left corner of the wrapper (photo 2).
3. Bring the corners of the wrapper together, overlapping the right corner over the left (photo 3).
4. Pinch to seal (photo 4).

Storage

While you're making these dumplings and mandu, arrange them on sheet pans lined with plastic wrap, leaving a small gap between each. Cover the dumplings and mandu with plastic wrap and freeze them for a few hours until they are rock solid or leave them in the freezer overnight. Once they are frozen, transfer them into resealable freezer bags and keep frozen for up to 4 months. When you're ready for some dumplings or mandu, cook them from frozen.

COOKING METHODS

These four cooking methods can be applied to most dumplings and mandu. The cooking time suggested is for dumplings and mandu made with standard-size, store-bought dumpling wrappers (around 3½ inches/8.25cm). You'll need tongs or a spider strainer and a kitchen thermometer for each of these methods.

Steaming

For this method, you'll need a steamer basket and perforated parchment, steam cloth, or cabbage leaves to line the basket with.

Prepare your steaming set up with 1 inch (2.5cm) of water and bring to a boil. Line the basket(s) with perforated parchment, steam cloth, or cabbage leaves. Arrange the dumplings or mandu in the basket, leaving gaps between each. Steam fresh dumplings or mandu over boiling water for 10 minutes and frozen ones for 12 minutes or until the filling is cooked through with the internal temperature registering 165°F (74°C).

Boiling

Bring a pot of water suitable for the amount of dumplings or mandu you're cooking to a boil over high heat. Add the dumplings or mandu and give them a gentle stir to prevent them from sticking to the bottom of the pot. For both fresh and frozen dumplings/mandu, cook until they float to the top, stirring occasionally, then cook another 2–3 minutes or until the internal temperature registers 165°F (74°C).

Pan frying

Heat a nonstick pan fitted with a lid over medium heat, and add enough neutral cooking oil to lightly coat the bottom of the pan. While the oil is heating up, arrange the dumplings or mandu in the pan. Let them pan fry for 1–2 minutes or until the bottoms start to brown, then add 2 tablespoons (30ml) of room-temperature water for fresh dumplings and mandu or ¼ cup (60ml) room-temperature water for frozen ones. Cover the pan immediately and reduce the heat to medium-low. Let them cook until the water has mostly evaporated, about 3 minutes for fresh ones and 5–6 minutes for frozen ones. Uncover the pan and continue to cook the dumplings and mandu for another minute or until the bottom crust is golden brown and the filling is cooked through or until the internal temperature registers 165°F (74°C).

Deep frying

Line a plate with paper towels or prepare a sheet pan fitted with a rack. In a pot, heat 2 inches (5cm) of oil to 350°F (175°C). Once hot, lower the dumplings or mandu into the oil, then give them a gentle stir to prevent sticking. Fry fresh ones for about 3–4 minutes or frozen ones for about 6–7 minutes or until the outsides are golden brown and crispy and the filling is cooked through with an internal temperature registering 165°F (74°C).

Pork and Cabbage Dumplings

These pork and cabbage dumplings are my favorite because they are little dough pouches filled with juicy, comforting flavors of my childhood. My mom and I would sit down once every few months to make a few hundred of these pork and cabbage dumplings. The ones that survived our post-dumpling wrapping party meal would be frozen for emergency lunch or dinner when we didn't have time to cook, and when our dumpling supplies were depleted, it would be time for another dumpling wrapping party. — Mei

---

Prep time: **1 hour**
Cook time: **3–10 minutes**
Makes: **about 40 dumplings**

- 6 oz (170g) green cabbage, diced
- ½ tsp kosher salt
- 1 lb (454g) ground pork
- 3 stalks green onion, sliced
- 1 tbsp (10g) minced ginger
- 3 tbsp (45ml) water
- 3 tbsp (45ml) soy sauce
- 2 tbsp (30ml) toasted sesame oil
- ½ tbsp (8ml) Shaoxing rice wine
- 40 sheets round dumpling wrappers

1. **Salt the cabbage.** Place the diced cabbage into a large mixing bowl and season with salt. Mix well and set aside to salt for 5–10 minutes.

2. **Make the filling.** To the same bowl as the salted cabbage, add the ground pork, green onion, ginger, water, soy sauce, sesame oil, and rice wine. Mix well with gloved hands until well combined, then mix the filling vigorously in a circular motion until the filling becomes more paste-like and holds together well.

3. **Set up the dumpling assembly station.** Prepare a sheet pan lined with plastic wrap, damp paper towels to cover finished dumplings, a small bowl of water for wetting the wrappers, the dumpling wrappers, a spoon or chopsticks for the filling, and the dumpling filling.

4. **Fold the dumplings.** Refer to Dumplings and Mandu Basics—Folding Techniques (see page 50) for folding techniques, instructions, and photo reference. These pork and cabbage dumplings are suitable for all of the folds, but our personal favorites for this filling is the half-moon pleat. As you fold the dumplings, arrange them on the prepared sheet pan, making sure to leave a gap between each dumpling. Cover the dumplings with the damp paper towels as you work.

5. **Cook the dumplings.** Refer to Dumplings and Mandu Basics—Cooking Methods (see page 53). These dumplings will taste great using any of the four methods. We prefer them pan fried with a drizzle of Chinese Chili Oil (page 240) and a side of Dumpling Dipping Sauce (page 242).

Chicken and Mushroom Dumplings

In the world of dumplings where pork, beef, and shrimp often take center stage, chicken-filled dumplings are often overlooked. Maybe it's because people assume chicken means less flavor or less juiciness compared to its counterparts, but we're here to change that. This dumpling, packed with juicy chicken and umami-packed shiitake mushrooms, is one of our absolute favorites. Whether steamed, pan-fried, or boiled, it delivers every time—and we'd confidently put it up against any dumpling out there. — Mei

---

Prep time: **1 hour 10 minutes**
Cook time: **3–10 minutes**
Makes: **30–40 dumplings**

- 4 (16g) dried shiitake mushrooms
- ¼ oz (7g) dried wood ear mushrooms
- 1 lb (454g) ground chicken
- 3 stalks green onion, sliced
- 3 tbsp (57g) oyster sauce
- 2 tbsp (30ml) soy sauce
- 1 tbsp (10g) minced ginger
- 1 tbsp (15ml) Shaoxing rice wine
- 1 tbsp (15ml) toasted sesame oil
- Generous dash of white pepper
- 30–40 round dumpling wrappers

1. **Rehydrate the mushrooms.** Place the shiitake mushrooms and the wood ear mushrooms each into separate heatproof bowls and pour enough hot water over them to cover by at least 1 inch (2.5cm). Let the mushrooms soak for about 15 minutes or until fully rehydrated. Reserve 2 tablespoons (30ml) of the shiitake mushroom soaking water for the filling and discard the rest. Rinse both sets of mushrooms thoroughly to remove debris, then finely chop them both.

2. **Make the filling.** To a large mixing bowl, add both types of mushrooms, the reserved mushroom water, ground chicken, green onion, oyster sauce, soy sauce, ginger, rice wine, sesame oil, and white pepper. Mix with gloved hands until evenly combined, then mix vigorously in a circular direction until the filling becomes more paste-like and holds together well.

3. **Set up the dumpling assembly station.** Prepare a sheet pan lined with plastic wrap, damp paper towels to cover finished dumplings, a small bowl of water for wetting the wrappers, the dumpling wrappers, a spoon or chopsticks for the filling, and the dumpling filling.

4. **Fold the dumplings.** Refer to Dumplings and Mandu Basics—Folding Techniques (see page 50) for folding techniques, instructions, and photo reference. These chicken and mushroom dumplings are suitable for all of the folds, but our personal favorite for this filling is the potbelly fold. As you fold the dumplings, arrange them on the prepared sheet pan, making sure to leave a gap between each dumpling. Cover the dumplings with the damp paper towels as you work.

5. **Cook the dumplings.** Refer to Dumplings and Mandu Basics—Cooking Methods (see page 53). These dumplings are suitable for any of the four cooking methods, but the best and also our favorite way to enjoy these dumplings is to simply boil them, then top with some cilantro and Chinese Chili Oil (page 240). We also love to add them to our Chicken and Mushroom Dumpling Noodle Soup (page 191).

Bulgogi Mandu

As crazy as it sounds, I feel like I could eat dozens of mandu and never get tired of them. Growing up, I tried a variety of flavors, but bulgogi mandu has always been in my top three—especially when it's fried. It's actually one of the few types I prefer fried, paired with some cold, tangy Kimchi (page 236) between each bite. — Kyong

---

Prep time: **1 hour 20 minutes**
Cook time: **3–10 minutes**
Makes: **about 60 mandu**

- 2 oz (57g) dry sweet potato glass noodles
- 1 lb (454g) ground beef (preferably a 80/20 ratio)
- 1 medium (3oz/85g) carrot, finely chopped
- ¼ large (3.5oz/100g) yellow onion, finely chopped
- 3 stalks green onion, sliced
- 1½ cup (360g) Bulgogi Sauce (page 244)
- 1 tbsp (15ml) toasted sesame oil
- ½ tsp cracked black pepper
- 60 round dumpling wrappers

1. **Cook the sweet potato noodles.** Bring a small pot of water to a boil over high heat and add the sweet potato glass noodles. Cook according to the package instructions or until the noodles are tender and easy to chew but still bouncy. Once cooked, drain the noodles and rinse thoroughly with cold water until the noodles are completely cooled. Then drain the noodles really well and either cut them with kitchen shears or on a cutting board with a knife into pieces no longer than 1 inch (2.5cm).

2. **Make the filling.** To a large mixing bowl, add the prepared sweet potato noodles, ground beef, carrot, both onions, bulgogi sauce, sesame oil, and black pepper. Mix with gloved hands until evenly combined, then vigorously mix in a circular motion until the filling becomes more paste-like and holds together well.

3. **Set up the mandu assembly station.** Prepare a sheet pan lined with plastic wrap, damp paper towels to cover finished mandu, a small bowl of water for wetting the wrappers, the dumpling wrappers, a spoon or chopsticks for the filling, and the mandu filling.

4. **Fold the mandu.** Refer to Dumplings and Mandu Basics—Folding Techniques (see page 50) for folding techniques, instructions, and photo reference. These bulgogi mandu are most suitable for the simple half-moon and the pleated half-moon folds, and our personal favorite for this filling is the simple half-moon fold. As you fold the mandu, arrange them on the prepared sheet pan, making sure to leave a gap between each mandu. Cover the mandu with the damp paper towels as you work.

5. **Cook the mandu.** Refer to Dumplings and Mandu Basics—Cooking Methods (see page 53). These mandu are suitable for any of the four cooking methods. Although they definitely taste the best deep fried, with the boiling method following closely as the second best option. They are delicious on their own.

Tips from our kitchen: It is very important for this mandu filling to get vigorously mixed in a circular direction so that the ground beef turns paste-like. The ground beef is basically the glue that binds all the loose bits of veggies and noodles together.

Kimchi Mandu

When I was younger, one of the things I looked forward to was Thanksgiving with all my family. I remember all of us at different stages in our lives, laughing, bickering, and sharing stories as we sat around a table covered with old newspapers, folding Kimchi Mandu by hand. In between our mandu-folding party, with our fingers still dusted with starch, we'd race for bites of freshly steamed mandu while my grandpa sipped makgeolli (Korean rice wine) and quietly watched his grandkids gathered together. To me, Kimchi Mandu is more than just a dish—it's an homage to some of my favorite memories growing up, a symbol of family, tradition, and love. — Kyong

---

Prep time: **1 hour 10 minutes**
Cook time: **3–10 minutes**
Makes: **50–60 mandu**

- 2 oz (57g) dry sweet potato glass noodles
- 2 oz (57g) Asian chives
- 1 lb (454g) ground pork
- 2 cups (14oz/400g) finely chopped fermented, sour kimchi, drained
- 2 tbsp (30ml) soy sauce
- 1 tbsp (10g) minced ginger
- ½ tbsp (5g) minced garlic
- 50–60 round dumpling wrappers

Tips from our kitchen: This mandu has lots of small loose bits in the filling, so make sure to really mix the filling in a circular direction vigorously until the ground pork becomes paste-like. This will ensure your filling holds together while you're assembling the mandu and after they are cooked.

1. **Cook the sweet potato noodles.** Bring a small pot of water to a boil over high heat and add the sweet potato glass noodles. Cook according to the package instructions or until the noodles are tender and easy to chew but still bouncy. Once cooked, drain the noodles and rinse thoroughly with cold water until the noodles are completely cooled. Then drain the noodles really well and either cut them with kitchen shears or on a cutting board with a knife into pieces no longer than 1 inch (2.5cm).

2. **Prepare the Asian chives.** Asian chives can sometimes hold dirt in between the leaves at the bottom of the stalk. Make sure to rinse it well. Also, because the bottom of the Asian chives can be quite woody, cut and discard the bottom 1 inch (2.5cm) of the chive. Cut the chive into ¼-inch (6mm) pieces.

3. **Make the filling.** To a large glass mixing bowl, add the prepared sweet potato noodles, ground pork, chopped kimchi, Asian chives, soy sauce, ginger, and garlic. With gloved hands, mix the filling until evenly combined, then mix vigorously in a circular motion until the filling becomes more paste-like and holds together well. If your kimchi isn't fermented and sour enough, you can add white vinegar (1–2 tbsp/15–30ml at a time) to give your kimchi mandu their tangy, iconic sharpness. You can taste-test your filling by cooking a tiny patty in the microwave.

4. **Set up the mandu assembly station.** Prepare a sheet pan lined with plastic wrap, damp paper towels to cover finished mandu, a small bowl of water for wetting the wrappers, the dumpling wrappers, a spoon or chopsticks for the filling, and the mandu filling.

5. **Fold the mandu.** Refer to Dumplings and Mandu Basics—Folding Techniques (see page 50) for folding techniques, instructions, and photo reference. These kimchi mandu are most suitable for the simple half-moon and the round ingot folds, and our personal favorite for this filling is the round ingot fold. As you fold the mandu, arrange them on the prepared sheet pan, making sure to leave a gap between each mandu. Cover the mandu with the damp paper towels as you work.

6. **Cook the mandu.** Refer to Dumplings and Mandu Basics—Cooking Methods (see page 53). These kimchi mandu can be cooked using any of the four cooking methods. However, they do taste the best steamed or boiled and are pretty good pan fried too. These are very delicious on their own or with a side of classic Dumpling Dipping Sauce (page 242).

Whole Shrimp Mandu

Dinnertime is usually when we catch up on our ever-growing list of TV shows and dramas—and when some of our favorite recipe ideas come to life. These addictive whole shrimp mandu were one of those creations. Similar to traditional Chinese potstickers, these mandu are open-ended. Each mandu is wrapped around a whole shrimp and filled with a juicy, flavorful shrimp paste mixed with vermicelli and Asian chives, creating a satisfyingly bouncy, snappy texture. — Mei

---

Prep time: **1 hour**
Cook time: **6–8 minutes**
Makes: **18–20 mandu**

- 2 lb (32oz/907g) jumbo shrimp, divided
- 1¼ tsp kosher salt, divided
- ¼ tsp cracked black pepper
- 1 bundle (1.5oz/42g) mung bean vermicelli
- 1 oz (28g) Asian chives
- ¼ large (3.5oz/100g) yellow onion, cut into small chunks
- 2 tbsp (16g) cornstarch
- 1 tbsp (15ml) Shaoxing rice wine
- 1 tbsp (15ml) toasted sesame oil
- ⅛ tsp ground white pepper
- 18–20 jumbo Korean mandu wrappers
- Neutral cooking oil, for pan frying

1. **Prepare the shrimp.** Peel and devein all of the shrimp. For presentation, you may leave the tails on 18–20 of them—these will be used whole in the mandu. For those shrimp, make 5–6 shallow crosswise cuts along the underside to prevent them from curling (photo 1). Season with ½ teaspoon of salt and ¼ teaspoon of black pepper, then set aside until needed. Reserve the remaining shrimp for the filling.

2. **Prepare the vermicelli.** Bring a small pot of water to a boil over high heat. Once boiling, take it off the heat and add the vermicelli. Make sure the water is covering the noodles by about 1 inch (2.5cm) and let soak for 5–10 minutes or until completely rehydrated and doubled in thickness. Drain well and roughly cut into shorter pieces.

3. **Prepare the Asian chives.** Asian chives can sometimes hold dirt in between the leaves at the bottom of the stalk. Make sure to rinse it well. Also, because the bottom of the Asian chives can be quite woody, cut and discard the bottom 1 inch (2.5cm) of the chive. Cut the chive into ¼-inch (6mm) pieces.

4. **Make the filling.** Add the shrimp (the ones without the crosswise cuts), onion, cornstarch, rice wine, sesame oil, the remaining ¾ teaspoon of salt, and white pepper to a food processor. Blend until the mixture is well combined and paste-like. Fold in the prepared vermicelli noodles and Asian chives, then transfer the filling to a piping bag or resealable bag to make assembly easier.

5. **Assemble.** Pipe about 2 tablespoons of filling vertically down the center of a wrapper (photo 2). Spread it evenly with a spoon, keeping the center slightly thicker and the left and right edges thinner (photo 3). Place a whole shrimp, belly-side down, on top of the filling (photo 4). Fold the left and right sides of the wrapper over the shrimp (photo 5). Press firmly to seal (photo 6). Repeat with the remaining mandu, keeping them covered with a damp towel as you work. Refer to our dumplings and mandu basics for storage (see page 53).

6. **Pan fry the mandu.** Heat a large nonstick pan over medium-low heat and add enough oil to generously coat the bottom. Once the oil is hot, arrange the shrimp mandu flap-side down and pan-fry for 1–2 minutes, or until golden brown. Turn and cook the remaining sides, browning each one, about 5–6 minutes total. If cooked frozen, the mandu will take about 8–10 minutes total. Once fully cooked, transfer to a plate to drain and cool for a couple of minutes. Serve hot with sweet chili sauce or a classic Dumpling Dipping Sauce (page 242).

Tips from our kitchen: If jumbo Korean mandu wrappers aren't available, you can substitute with regular-size dumpling wrappers. You'll need about 30–35 wrappers and more whole shrimp, and will need to decrease the cook time by 2–3 minutes.

Air Fryer Garlic Eggplant

If you're craving a side dish that's bursting with flavor and also ridiculously easy to make, you've got to try this eggplant! Although it's not much of a looker, the garlicky punch in every bite, paired with the mild heat of the spicy doubanjiang, makes this eggplant good enough to be an entrée. — Mei

---

Prep time: **5 minutes**
Cook time: **20 minutes**
Makes: **2–4 servings**

- 1 large (1.5 lb/680g) American (globe) eggplant
- 2½ tbsp (38ml) neutral cooking oil, divided
- ¼ cup (36g) minced garlic
- 2 bird's eye chilis, sliced (more or less to your preference)
- 1 tbsp (19g) oyster sauce
- 1 tbsp (15ml) soy sauce
- 1 tbsp (20g) Chinese spicy bean paste (spicy doubanjiang)
- ½ tsp granulated sugar
- Sliced green onion, for garnish (optional)

1. **Air-fry the eggplant.** Trim off both ends of the eggplant and rub the outside with about ½ tablespoon (8ml) of oil. Place it into the air fryer and air-fry at 400°F (205°C) for 15 minutes. (No need to flip midway through.)
2. **Make the sauce.** To a heatproof bowl, add the garlic and chili pepper. Heat the remaining 2 tablespoons (30ml) of oil in a pan over high heat until it just starts to smoke, then pour it over the garlic and chili pepper. Add the oyster sauce, soy sauce, spicy bean paste, and sugar. Mix well.
3. **Finish the eggplant.** After 15 minutes, the eggplant should be very tender and the skin should be able to be easily pierced with a knife. Keeping the eggplant in the air fryer, cut it vertically down the middle to split it in half. Open the eggplant so it's lying flat and spread the prepared sauce evenly over both sides. Air-fry the eggplant for another 5 minutes at 400°F (205°C).
4. **Serve.** Once the eggplant is cooked, use a spatula to carefully transfer it onto serving plates and garnish with green onion, if desired. When ready to eat, stir the sauce into the tender eggplant flesh and enjoy hot. The skin is also edible but can be a little chewy. Refrigerate leftovers in an airtight container for up to 4 days.

Tips from our kitchen: If you can't find spicy doubanjiang, you can substitute with a tablespoon (20g) of Korean doenjang (fermented soybean paste) mixed with two teaspoons of spicy chili oil. The amount of chili oil can be adjusted to your preference, depending on how spicy you like it. Of course, this is not the perfect substitute, but it's fine in a pinch.

Garlic Bok Choy Stir-Fry

We're always in need of a vegetable side that's quick to make and pairs well with any meal, and this garlic bok choy stir-fry is just that! There are many different types and sizes of bok choy, but we prefer Shanghai bok choy because they're just the right size, milder, sweeter, and more tender than regular bok choy, a.k.a. their larger and greener counterparts. If you need an alternative, regular baby bok choy are fine too.
— Mei

Prep time: **10 minutes**
Cook time: **5 minutes**
Makes: **4 servings**

2 lb (907g) Shanghai bok choy
3 tbsp (45ml) neutral cooking oil
8–10 garlic cloves, sliced
2 tbsp (30ml) Shaoxing rice wine
¾ tsp kosher salt
1 tsp chicken bouillon powder
2 tsp (10ml) sesame oil (optional)
Chinese Chili Oil (page 240) (optional)

1. **Prepare the bok choy.** Cut and discard about ½ inch (1cm) of the bottom of the bok choy to separate the leaves. If needed, pull apart the leaves in the inner section by hand. Wash the leaves by placing them in a large bowl of water. Let the leaves soak for a few minutes, then swish them around with your hands. Fish out the bok choy, drain the water, and fill the bowl with fresh water to rinse the bok choy again. Some bok choy leaves may be dirtier than others, especially around the base. Give those an extra thorough rinsing. Drain well and set aside.

2. **Stir-fry the bok choy.** To a well-seasoned wok or large sauté pan over medium-high heat, add the oil. When the oil is hot, add the garlic and sauté until fragrant and the garlic slices start to turn golden. Then add the bok choy and stir-fry briefly to coat evenly with oil. Drizzle the rice wine around the wok and give it a couple of tosses. Cover with a lid and let the bok choy steam for about 1–2 minutes or until the leaves have wilted.

3. **Season.** Once the bok choy leaves have wilted, uncover and season with salt and bouillon powder. Stir-fry briefly until well combined. Finish by drizzling in the sesame oil (if using) and giving everything a few mixes.

4. **Serve.** Transfer to a serving plate and enjoy while hot. Optionally, top the bok choy with your desired amount of chili oil. Leftovers can be stored in an airtight container for up to 4 days.

Mixed Vegetable Stir-Fry

Got random vegetables in the fridge that need using up and no idea what to make? We've got you covered with this mixed vegetable stir-fry recipe! Our fridge is always stocked with broccoli, carrots, mushrooms, zucchini, bell peppers, and onion, so that's what our vegetable stir-fries usually look like. But what makes it special is the sauce—it's reminiscent of your favorite Chinese takeout brown sauce, inspired by the stir-fry dishes with brown sauce from my parents' Chinese takeout restaurant. — Mei

---

Prep time: **15 minutes**
Cook time: **10 minutes**
Makes: **3 servings**

- ¾ cup (180g) water
- 2½ tbsp (38ml) soy sauce
- ¼ tsp dark soy sauce
- 1½ tbsp (19g) granulated sugar
- 1 tsp chicken bouillon powder
- 2 tbsp (16g) cornstarch
- 1½ lb (24oz) fresh mixed vegetables of your choice, cut into bite-size pieces
- 1 tsp sesame oil
- 1 tbsp (15ml) neutral cooking oil
- 1 tbsp (9g) minced garlic
- 1 tbsp (10g) minced ginger

1. **Prepare the sauce.** To a bowl or measuring cup, add the water, both soy sauces, sugar, chicken bouillon powder, and cornstarch. Mix until the sugar has dissolved and the cornstarch is no longer clumpy. Finish by mixing in the sesame oil. Set aside.
2. **Blanch the mixed vegetables.** Bring a large pot of water to a boil over high heat. Add the vegetables in order of hardiness. For example, we would add our broccoli florets and carrots first and let them cook for 1–2 minutes, then add the mushrooms, zucchini, bell peppers, and onions for another 30 seconds. If we have canned vegetables like baby corn or water chestnuts, we'd add them next and cook for 15–30 seconds, then finish with the most tender veggies, like snow peas, which you can just let cook for 15 seconds or until they turn bright green. Once the veggies are all blanched, drain them well.
3. **Finish the stir-fry.** To a well-seasoned wok or large pan over medium-high heat, add the cooking oil. Once the oil is hot, add the garlic and ginger. Sauté until fragrant, about 15–30 seconds. Give the prepared sauce a good stir and add it to the wok. Stir the sauce constantly until it thickens and becomes glossy. Add the blanched mixed vegetables and stir-fry briefly until the vegetables are evenly coated with sauce.
4. **Serve.** Serve immediately and enjoy while hot. Refrigerate leftover mixed vegetables in an airtight container for up to 3 days.

Tips from our kitchen: Feel free to change out the mixed veggies to your preference because this recipe is a great clean-out-your-fridge opportunity. Vegetables that have high water content will usually take no time to cook at all, so they can be added last. Also, if you prefer some vegetables to maintain a little more crunch, you can blanch them at the end as well.

Miso Maple-Glazed Carrots

Maple syrup and miso might sound like an unlikely duo, but trust me—you'll be hooked from the very first bite. The sweet maple syrup balances the savory miso perfectly and creates a glossy glaze that slightly caramelizes while the carrots roast. Top these tender roasted carrots with some crunchy, toasted pecans, and you've got a side dish that'll be requested on repeat for holidays and dinners. —Mei

---

Prep time: **10 minutes**
Cook time: **30 minutes**
Makes: **5–6 servings**

2 lb (907g) carrots, washed, peeled, and trimmed
2 tbsp (30ml) olive oil
½ tsp kosher salt
¼ tsp cracked black pepper
¼ cup (70g) maple syrup
2 tbsp (36g) white miso
½ cup (60g) pecan pieces

1. **Roast the carrots.** Preheat the oven to 425°F (220°C). On a sheet pan lined with foil, toss the carrots with olive oil, salt, and pepper. Arrange the carrots so that they are in a single layer and not overlapping. Roast the carrots for about 20–25 minutes or until they are just about tender. Use a pairing knife to test. The knife should go through with almost no resistance.

2. **Make the glaze.** Add the maple syrup and miso paste to a bowl and mix well with a whisk.

3. **Glaze the carrots.** When the carrots are nearly tender, remove them from the oven and brush with half of the glaze. Flip them, then sprinkle on the pecan pieces. Brush both the carrots and pecans with the remaining glaze. Return the carrots to the oven and roast for about another 5–10 minutes or until the glaze is bubbly and sticky. If desired, broil the carrots to add some char.

4. **Serve.** Transfer the carrots to a serving plate and enjoy while hot. Leftover carrots can be stored in an airtight container and refrigerated for up to 4 days.

Tips from our kitchen: We like to use heirloom carrots—the thin ones with the tops still attached—because the carrot tops turn crispy and incredibly delicious when roasted. Plus, they're beautiful! You can also use rainbow carrots, baby carrots, or even large, thick carrots. If using larger carrots, cut them so they're no thicker than ½ inch (1cm) to ensure quicker, more even roasting.

Wood Ear Mushroom Salad

Flavor, flavor, flavor—that's really the only way to describe this side dish! This salad is bursting with bold flavors and fun textures. You've got the kick from aromatics and chili, the zingy tang of Chinese black vinegar, and that signature snappy crunch from the wood ear mushrooms. It's cold, refreshing, and so delicious; you'll find your chopsticks going back for more before you even realize it. — Kyong

---

Prep time: **25 minutes, plus 30 minutes marinating time**
Cook time: **none**
Makes: **4 servings**

- 1 oz (28g) dried wood ear mushrooms
- 2 tbsp (30ml) Chinese black vinegar
- 2 tbsp (30ml) soy sauce
- 1 tbsp (19g) oyster sauce
- 1 tbsp (9g) minced garlic
- 2 bird's eye chilis, sliced (more or less to your preference)
- 1 tsp granulated sugar
- ¼ large (3.5oz/100g) red onion, thinly sliced
- ½ cup (15g) roughly chopped cilantro
- 2 tbsp (18g) roasted peanuts , roughly chopped (optional)
- 1 tbsp (8g) toasted sesame seeds

1. **Rehydrate the mushrooms.** Place the dried wood ear mushrooms into a heatproof bowl and cover with boiling water. Make sure the water covers the mushrooms by at least 2 inches (5cm). Let the mushrooms soak for about 15 minutes or until completely rehydrated. Once ready, rinse them well to remove any debris and dirt.
2. **Make the dressing.** While the mushrooms are rehydrating, add the black vinegar, soy sauce, oyster sauce, garlic, chilis, and sugar to a medium or large serving bowl. Mix until the sugar has dissolved. Set aside.
3. **Blanch the mushrooms.** Bring a small or medium pot of water to a boil and prepare a bowl of ice water. Once the water is boiling, add the rehydrated wood ear mushrooms and cook for 1 minute. Drain well, then transfer the mushrooms to the ice water and let them chill completely. Drain thoroughly using a salad spinner or paper towels, then add the mushrooms to the bowl with the dressing.
4. **Assemble and serve.** To the bowl of wood ear mushrooms, add the onion, cilantro, peanuts (if using), sesame seeds, and the dressing. Toss well, cover, and refrigerate for at least 30 minutes to let the salad marinate for better flavor. Serve chilled. Leftover salad can be stored in an airtight container and refrigerated for up to 3 days.

Tips from our kitchen: If you're not a fan of the spiciness from the onion, soak the slices in a bowl of ice water for about 10 minutes. This will make the onion less pungent. Just make sure to drain well before using.

Cold Shrimp Avocado Cucumber Salad

I like a typical leafy greens-style salad, but to be honest, I'm more of a good cucumber salad fan. Mei had thrown together a quick dinner one evening using leftover boiled shrimp, chunks of avocado, smashed cucumber, sliced cherry tomatoes, and a generous handful of cilantro in a simple soy and chili oil dressing. And let me tell you—it was so good, it instantly became one of my top three favorite salads! According to Mei, the secrets are the avocado, which adds a creamy texture, and using a flavorful chili oil that brings the whole dish together. — Kyong

---

Prep time: **25 minutes**
Cook time: **none**
Makes: **4 servings**

Shrimp

Kosher salt, for boiling the shrimp

8 oz (227g) jumbo shrimp, peeled and deveined

2 thick slices of ginger

Salad

1 (11oz/312g) English cucumber

½ tsp kosher salt

1 large (7oz/200g) ripe Hass avocado, cut into large chunks

½ pint (5oz/140g) cherry tomatoes, halved

½ cup (15g) roughly chopped cilantro

Dressing

2 tbsp (30ml) Chinese Chili Oil (page 240)

2 tbsp (30ml) soy sauce

1 tbsp (15ml) lime juice

2 tsp (12g) honey

1 tsp sesame oil

1. **Prepare the shrimp.** Bring a medium pot of water to a boil over high heat and season with salt. We recommend adding 2 teaspoons of salt per 4 cups (about 1L) of water. Also, prepare a bowl of ice water. Once the water comes to a boil, add the shrimp and ginger slices. Boil the shrimp until just cooked, about 2 minutes. The shrimp should be bright orange and curled like a C. Drain the shrimp and shock them in the ice water until completely chilled. Drain well and set aside until needed.

2. **Salt the cucumber.** Cut off and discard the ends of the cucumber. Using the flat side of a cleaver or a rolling pin, smack the cucumber until it cracks. It doesn't have to be completely broken. Cut the cucumber into 1-inch (2.5cm) chunks and place it into a mixing bowl. Season with salt and toss to evenly coat. Set the cucumber aside to salt for 5 minutes to draw out excess moisture. You can prepare the other ingredients in the meantime.

3. **Make the dressing.** To a large mixing bowl, add all the ingredients for the dressing and mix until well combined.

4. **Assemble and serve.** Once the cucumber is done salting, drain it well then add it to the bowl with the dressing, along with the shrimp, avocado, tomato, and cilantro. Gently mix until evenly coated. Enjoy immediately. Leftovers can be stored in the fridge for 2–3 days.

Tips from our kitchen: This salad really benefits from having all the salad ingredients chilled ahead of time so that the salad is cold when served. Also, if the dressing is too spicy you can replace half of the chili oil with a neutral oil like avocado oil.

Soft Tofu Salad

Kyong ranks this among the top three side dishes he's ever had. I know cold tofu as a side might be new to many, but in China, it's common to enjoy a simple block of fresh, soft tofu drizzled with soy sauce. Our take adds layers of flavor and texture that makes it seriously addictive. It's one of our favorite cold sides, guaranteed to impress anyone. — Mei

---

Prep time: **10 minutes**
Cook time: **none**
Makes: **2 servings**

- 2 tbsp (18g) minced garlic
- 1 stalk green onion, sliced
- 1 bird's eye chili, sliced (optional)
- 1½ tbsp (23ml) neutral cooking oil
- 2 tbsp (30ml) soy sauce
- 1 tbsp (19g) oyster sauce
- 1 tbsp (15ml) rice vinegar
- 1 tsp granulated sugar
- 1 tsp sesame oil
- 1 tube extra soft tofu (about 11oz/312g)
- ¼ cup (8g) chopped cilantro

1. **Make the dressing.** To a heatproof bowl, add the garlic, green onion, and chili (if using). Heat the oil in a small pan over high heat until the oil just starts to smoke. Pour the hot oil evenly over the bowl of aromatics. Give the aromatics a stir, then add the soy sauce, oyster sauce, rice vinegar, sugar, and sesame oil. Stir to combine and set aside.

2. **Prepare the tofu.** Cut open one end of the tofu tube and push the tofu onto a serving plate. Drain the tofu if there's visible liquid on the dish. The ends of the tofu are usually not as pretty, so feel free to serve them or just snack on them. Gently cut the tofu into ½-inch (1cm) slices, then shingle and spread them out.

3. **Dress and serve.** Give the prepared dressing a good stir and spoon it over the tofu. Top with the chopped cilantro and enjoy it at room temperature or chilled. Leftovers can be stored in an airtight container in the refrigerator for up to 3 days.

Tips from our kitchen: If the tube-packaged, extra soft tofu is not available, you can substitute it with regular silken tofu.

Sweet Chili Broccolini

Back when I was cooking in Baton Rouge, one of our top-selling sides wasn't anything fancy. It was just broccolini tossed in a hot pan with sweet chili sauce. The truth is, sides don't need to be complicated. With a few simple ingredients from your fridge, you can whip up something delicious in minutes. I still make this one at home when we need a quick veggie that goes well with any protein. — Kyong

---

Prep time: **10 minutes**
Cook time: **10 minutes**
Makes: **2 servings**

- 2 tbsp (30ml) neutral cooking oil
- 2 (8g) garlic cloves, sliced
- ½ tsp crushed red pepper
- 1 lb (454g) broccolini, washed and ends trimmed
- ¼ cup (60ml) water
- ¼ cup (60ml) sweet chili sauce
- ½ tsp kosher salt
- Fried shallot or fried onion, for garnish (optional)

1. **Sauté the aromatics.** To a large sauté pan fitted with a lid, add the oil and heat the pan over medium heat. Once the oil is hot, add the garlic and red pepper flakes and sauté until fragrant, about 15 seconds.

2. **Cook the broccolini.** To the pan, add the broccolini and sauté for 1 minute, or until they start to turn bright green, then add the water and cover with the lid. Let the broccolini steam for about 5–6 minutes or until the thick stalks are just tender. If there is still water left in the pan, let it evaporate with the lid off. Season the broccolini with sweet chili sauce and salt, then sauté until they are evenly coated.

3. **Finish and serve.** Serve the broccolini hot and garnish with fried shallot or fried onion, if desired. Leftovers can be stored and refrigerated in an airtight container for up to 3 days.

Tips from our kitchen: I always cut the ends of the broccolini at a slant instead of a straight cut to give them a pointy look. This way they look more elegant and prettier for presentation.

Caramelized Kabocha Squash

This roasted kabocha squash is super easy to make and perfect for making ahead and stashing in the fridge. The squash gets roasted in a sticky-sweet glaze of maple syrup, soy sauce, and cinnamon, turning into creamy, caramelized wedges that are delicious all on their own and pair well with just about anything. If a whole kabocha is too much, feel free to halve the recipe. — Mei

---

Prep time: **15 minutes**
Cook time: **35–45 minutes**
Makes: **6–8 servings**

- 1 (3–4 lb/1.3–1.8kg) kabocha squash
- 3 tbsp (38g) granulated sugar
- 2 tbsp (35g) maple syrup
- 2 tbsp (30ml) soy sauce
- 2 tbsp (30ml) olive oil
- 1 tsp ground cinnamon
- ⅛ tsp fresh cracked black pepper

1. **Preheat the oven to 425°F (220°C).** Also, line a large sheet pan with parchment paper.
2. **Prepare the kabocha squash.** Wash and scrub the squash well and pat dry with a clean kitchen towel. Using a chef's knife or a cleaver, cut the squash in half and scoop out and discard the seeds. Cut the squash into 1-inch (2.5cm) wedges. Cut and discard the woody core. If there are any gnarly bumps, you can trim those off as well.
3. **Season the squash.** To a large mixing bowl, add the sugar, maple syrup, soy sauce, olive oil, cinnamon, and black pepper. Mix until the sugar has dissolved. Add the kabocha wedges and toss until evenly coated.
4. **Bake.** Transfer the seasoned kabocha squash onto the prepared sheet pan. Arrange them so that they are in a single layer. Bake on the middle rack for 35–45 minutes or until the squash can be easily pierced with a fork. Flip the squash midway through baking for even color.
5. **Serve.** Once cooked, remove the tray of kabocha squash from the oven and allow them to cool for a moment. Enjoy while warm. Leftover squash can be stored in an airtight container and refrigerated for up to 4 days.

Celery and Egg Stir-Fry

Kyong will eat just about anything I make and rarely requests a specific dish, but without fail, he'll ask for my celery and egg stir-fry once a week. Honestly, I was surprised at how much he liked it since we rarely eat celery except with hot wings and peanut butter. But hey, I won't complain at all because this is probably the easiest minimal-prep stir-fry you can whip up in less than 15 minutes, and it tastes amazing!
— Mei

Prep time: **5 minutes**
Cook time: **5 minutes**
Makes: **2 servings**

3 large (150g) eggs
¼ tsp plus a generous pinch of kosher salt, divided
2 tbsp (30ml) neutral cooking oil, divided
3–4 ribs (7oz/200g) of celery, ends trimmed and cut at an angle into ¼-inch (6mm) slices
½ tbsp (8ml) Shaoxing rice wine
½ tsp chicken bouillon powder

1. **Scramble the eggs.** To a medium bowl, add the eggs and a generous pinch of salt. Beat until well combined. To a nonstick pan over medium-high heat, add 1½ tablespoons (23ml) of oil. When the oil is just starting to smoke, add the egg and scramble until just cooked, breaking up the egg in the process. Remove the eggs from the pan and set aside.

2. **Stir fry the celery.** If your celery is wet, make sure to dry it with paper towels first before stir frying. To the same pan over medium-high heat, add the remaining ½ tablespoon (8ml) of oil. Once the oil is hot, add the celery and stir fry for 1 minute or until the celery turns bright green and the thinner parts start to brown lightly.

3. **Finish and serve.** Add the scrambled eggs and drizzle the rice wine around the pan. Stir fry briefly to cook off the alcohol, about 15 seconds. Season with the bouillon powder and the remaining ¼ tsp of salt and stir fry for another 30 seconds to incorporate. Serve hot. Store any leftovers in an airtight container in the refrigerator for up to 3 days.

Vegetable Fried Rice

Pork fried rice and other meat-based fried rice dishes are really tasty, but this vegetable fried rice is an underdog that doesn't get enough appreciation. Even though it's meatless, it's still incredibly flavorful and aromatic thanks to the eggs and the vegetables, which add extra texture and freshness to each bite. — Mei

---

Prep time: **10 minutes**
Cook time: **10 minutes**
Makes: **2–3 servings**

- 3 oz (85g) broccoli, cut into small florets
- ½ medium (1oz/28g) carrot, peeled and cut into thin slices
- 2 oz (57g) baby bella mushrooms, sliced
- 3 tbsp (45ml) neutral cooking oil, divided
- 2 large (100g) eggs, beaten
- ¼ large (3.5oz/100g) yellow onion, diced
- 2 cups (300g) day-old cold white rice, loosened up
- 1 tbsp (15ml) Shaoxing rice wine
- 2 tbsp (30ml) soy sauce
- 2 tbsp (38g) oyster sauce
- 1 stalk green onion, sliced
- 1 tsp sesame oil

1. **Blanch the vegetables.** Bring a small pot of water to a boil over high heat. Add the broccoli and carrot first and blanch for about 1 minute, then add the mushrooms and blanch for 15 seconds more. You can always cook the veggies longer to suit your texture preference. Drain the veggies well and set aside.
2. **Scramble the eggs.** To a well-seasoned wok or large nonstick pan, add a tablespoon of oil and heat over medium-high heat until the oil just starts to smoke. Add the beaten egg and scramble until just cooked, breaking up the egg in the process. Remove from the pan and set aside.
3. **Stir-fry the fried rice.** To the same wok or a large pan over medium-high heat, add the remaining oil. Once hot, add the onions and stir fry briefly, about 5–10 seconds. Then add the fried rice and stir fry briefly while breaking up any clumps of rice in the process. Add the blanched vegetables and scrambled egg and drizzle the rice wine around the wok or pan. Stir fry everything until well combined and the alcohol is cooked off, about 30 seconds. Season with soy sauce and oyster sauce and stir fry until the rice is evenly colored.
4. **Finish and serve.** Add the green onion and sesame oil, and give the fried rice a final few tosses. Serve while it's hot. Any leftovers can be stored in an airtight container and kept refrigerated for up to 3 days.

Tips from our kitchen: Fried rice is cooked on pretty high heat and is such a fast recipe to prepare, so make sure to have all the ingredients and seasonings ready and nearby. It's also very helpful to loosen up the day old white rice ahead of time before you start cooking. You can rub the rice between your hands to easily break it up. If you're cooking fresh white rice to make fried rice, make the white rice a little on the drier side to prevent it from becoming soggy.

Cabbage Stir-Fry with Pork Belly

This cabbage stir-fry is one of those back-pocket recipes we rely on when we need a quick, simple, and delicious vegetable side. When we shared it on social media, we were surprised by how many people asked for the recipe, even though it's such a humble dish. So, here's the secret that takes this simple dish to the next level: *wok hei*—the irresistible charred flavor resulting from cooking the cabbage in a really hot pan.
— Mei

Prep time: **10 minutes**
Cook time: **10 minutes**
Makes: **2–3 servings**

- 1 lb (454g) green cabbage (about ½ of a medium head)
- 1 tbsp (15ml) neutral cooking oil, or as needed
- 5 oz (140g) pork belly, cut into ¼-inch (6mm) strips
- 2 stalks green onion, cut into 2-inch (5cm) pieces (keep the greens and whites separated)
- 1 tbsp (15ml) Shaoxing rice wine
- 2 tbsp (38g) oyster sauce
- 1 tbsp (15ml) soy sauce

1. **Prepare the cabbage.** Cut the cabbage into 1-inch (2.5cm) pieces and discard the core. Find all the leaves with the thick "stems" and use the flat side of your knife's blade to crush them. This step is a little tedious, but it'll ensure a more even cook on the cabbage.

2. **Render the pork belly.** To a well-seasoned wok or a large sauté pan over medium heat, add the oil. When the oil is hot, add the pork belly strips and cook until they are golden and well rendered, about 3–5 minutes, stirring occasionally. Remove the pork belly from the wok or pan and set it aside.

3. **Stir fry the cabbage.** In the same wok or pan, reserve about 3 tablespoons (45ml) of the rendered pork fat. If there isn't enough, add a little more oil. Heat the wok over medium-high heat. Once hot, add the cabbage and the white parts of the green onions. Stir-fry briefly so the cabbage is coated in the fat, then let it sit in the wok for 10–15 second intervals before tossing or stirring again. This creates slight charring and caramelization on the leaves, mimicking the restaurant-style *wok hei* flavor. Repeat this process a few times until the cabbage is vibrant and wilted.

4. **Finish and serve.** Return the pork belly to the pan and drizzle in the rice wine. Stir-fry briefly to cook off the alcohol, then season with oyster sauce and soy sauce. Stir-fry for another 30 seconds, then finish by adding the remaining green onions and giving everything a few final tosses. Enjoy the cabbage stir-fry while it's hot. If you have leftovers, store them in an airtight container and keep refrigerated for up to 4 days.

Tips from our kitchen: If you want to keep this stir-fry meatless, skip the pork belly and use a neutral cooking oil.

Silky Steamed Eggs

With just four ingredients, you can make the silkiest steamed egg that melts in your mouth. It's one of our favorite side dishes for lunch and dinner—not only because it's incredibly simple, but also because it serves as the perfect blank canvas for a variety of toppings. From soy ground pork to fresh clams to shrimp with mushrooms, the possibilities are endless and effortlessly delicious. — Mei

---

Prep time: **5 minutes**
Cook time: **12 minutes**
Makes: **1–2 servings**

Steamed egg base
2 large (100g) eggs
1 cup (240ml) water
½ tsp kosher salt
½ tsp chicken bouillon powder

Sauce and garnish
½ tbsp (8ml) soy sauce
½ tbsp (8ml) water
1 tsp sesame oil
Chinese Chili Oil (page 240) (optional)
Sliced green onion, for garnish (optional)

1. **Set up the steamer.** Add about 1 inch (2.5cm) of water in your steamer set up and bring the water to a boil. If you are steaming with a steam basket, keep the heat on a medium-high. If you are steaming with a rack inside of a wok or pot, reduce the heat so that the water is at a medium simmer.

2. **Make the steamed egg base.** Crack the eggs into a bowl and beat well, then add the water, salt, and bouillon powder. Mix gently to combine.

3. **Extra preparation to keep the steamed egg silky.** Strain the egg mixture through a sieve into a shallow heatproof bowl or coupe that can hold 2 cups (480ml) of liquid. Skim off the foam on top of the mixture with a spoon. Turn a plate upside down to cover the bowl or wrap the bowl with plastic wrap and poke a few holes on top to vent.

4. **Steam the egg.** Carefully place the bowl in the steamer and steam for 12 minutes or until the egg is set, with only the center slightly wobbling when gently shaken. When you cut the center of the steamed egg, the juice should run clear. If it is cloudy, steam for a couple more minutes.

5. **Finish and serve.** While waiting on the steamed egg, make the sauce by mixing together the soy sauce, water, and sesame oil. When the egg is done, remove it from the steamer and top with the prepared sauce, chili oil (if desired), and sliced green onions (if desired). Enjoy it while it's hot.

Steamed Egg with Ground Pork

This steamed egg is topped with a simple, savory, soy-based pork topping full of flavors that are easily palatable for everyone. — Kyong

---

Prep time: **15 minutes**
Cook time: **12 minutes**
Makes: **1–2 servings**

Steamed egg base
- 2 large (100g) eggs
- 1 cup (240ml) water
- ½ tsp kosher salt
- ½ tsp chicken bouillon powder

Topping
- ⅓ cup (80ml) plus 1 tsp water, divided
- 1 tbsp (15ml) soy sauce
- ½ tsp dark soy sauce
- ½ tsp sesame oil
- ¼ tsp granulated sugar
- ½ tsp cornstarch
- ½ tbsp (8ml) neutral cooking oil
- 1 tsp minced ginger
- 3 oz (85g) ground pork
- Sliced green onion, for garnish

1. **Set up the steamer.** Add about 1 inch (2.5cm) of water in your steamer set up and bring the water to a boil. If you are steaming with a steam basket, keep the heat on a medium-high. If you are steaming with a rack inside of a wok or pot, reduce the heat so that the water is at a medium simmer.
2. **Make the steamed egg base.** Crack the eggs into a bowl and beat well, then add the water, salt, and bouillon powder. Mix gently to combine.
3. **Extra preparation to keep the steamed egg silky.** Strain the egg mixture through a sieve into a shallow heatproof bowl or coupe that can hold 2 cups (480ml) of liquid. Skim off the foam on top of the mixture with a spoon. Turn a plate upside down to cover the bowl or wrap the bowl with plastic wrap and poke a few holes on top to vent.
4. **Steam the egg.** Carefully place the bowl in the steamer and steam for 12 minutes or until the egg is set, with only the center slightly wobbling when gently shaken. When you cut the center of the steamed egg, the juice should run clear. If it is cloudy, steam for a couple more minutes. While waiting, prepare the pork topping.
5. **Prepare the sauce and slurry.** In a bowl, mix together ⅓ cup of water, both soy sauces, sesame oil and sugar until the sugar has dissolved. In another bowl, mix together cornstarch and the remaining teaspoon of water until combined. Set both aside until needed.
6. **Make the pork topping.** To a small pan over medium heat, add the oil. Once hot, add the ginger and cook until fragrant, about 15 seconds. Next, add the ground pork and cook until it's no longer pink. Make sure to break it up as you're cooking. Then add the prepared sauce and let the pork simmer for 30 seconds to 1 minute, until cooked through. To finish, give the cornstarch slurry a good mix and drizzle it into the pork mixture while stirring. Let the pork simmer for about 10–15 seconds, until the sauce thickens and becomes glossy. Keep warm and set aside.
7. **Finish and serve.** Once the steamed egg is ready, uncover and top with the ground pork and garnish with green onions. Enjoy while it's hot.

Silky Steamed Eggs

Steamed Egg with Ground Pork

Steamed Egg with Clams

Steamed Egg with Shrimp and Mushrooms

Steamed Egg with Shrimp and Mushrooms

This version of steamed egg is Kyong's favorite. He really enjoys the different textures imparted from the shrimp and mushrooms and also the natural juices released after steaming. If you're curious, we used 60/80-size small shrimp. — Mei

---

Prep time: **10 minutes**
Cook time: **12 minutes**
Makes: **1–2 servings**

Steamed egg base
2 large (100g) eggs
1 cup (240ml) water
½ tsp kosher salt
½ tsp chicken bouillon powder

The topping
2 oz (57g) peeled and deveined raw small shrimp
2 oz (57g) shimeji or enoki mushrooms

Sauce and garnish
½ tbsp (8ml) soy sauce
½ tsp toasted sesame oil
Sliced green onions, for garnish

1. **Set up the steamer.** Add about 1 inch (2.5cm) of water in your steamer set up and bring the water to a boil. If you are steaming with a steam basket, keep the heat on a medium-high. If you are steaming with a rack inside of a wok or pot, reduce the heat so that the water is at a medium simmer.

2. **Make the steamed egg base.** Crack the eggs into a bowl and beat well, then add the water, salt, and bouillon powder. Mix gently to combine.

3. **Extra preparation to keep the steamed egg silky.** Strain the egg mixture through a sieve into a shallow heatproof bowl or coupe that can hold 2 cups (480ml) of liquid. Skim off the foam on top of the mixture with a spoon. Turn a plate upside down to cover the bowl or wrap the bowl with plastic wrap and poke a few holes on top to vent.

4. **Steam the egg.** Carefully place the bowl in the steamer and steam for 8 minutes or until the egg is just setting. While waiting, prepare the shrimp and mushrooms.

5. **Prepare the toppings.** Rinse the shrimp thoroughly with cold water and drain well. Pat them dry with paper towels and set them aside. For the mushrooms, trim the ends and separate clumps. If you're using enoki mushrooms, cut it in half for easier eating.

6. **Add the toppings.** After 8 minutes, the steamed egg should be just setting. Remove and uncover the bowl, and top the egg with the shrimp and mushrooms. Return the bowl to the steamer, leaving it uncovered but with the steamer lid on, and steam for another 4 minutes, or until the shrimp are cooked through and the egg is set, with only the center slightly wobbling when gently shaken. When you cut the center of the steamed egg, the juice should run clear. If it is cloudy, steam for a couple more minutes.

7. **Finish and serve.** When the steamed egg is ready, uncover and top with soy sauce, sesame oil, and green onions. Enjoy it while it's hot.

Steamed Egg with Clams

If you love seafood, you'll love this version of steamed egg! In this recipe, we replace plain water with the reserved clam cooking liquid to enhance the sweet, briny flavor that makes clams so delicious. — Kyong

Prep time: **20 minutes, plus 1 hour of purging time**
Cook time: **12 minutes**
Makes: **1–2 servings**

The topping
- ½ lb (227g) littleneck clams
- 2 cups (480ml) water
- 2 tbsp (32g) kosher salt, for purging

Steamed egg base
- 2 large (100g) eggs
- ½ tsp kosher salt
- ½ tsp chicken bouillon powder

Sauce and garnish
- ½ tbsp (8ml) soy sauce
- ½ tbsp (8ml) water
- ½ tsp sesame oil
- Chinese Chili Oil (page 240) (optional)
- Sliced green onion, for garnish

1. **Purge the clams.** Inspect the clams and discard ones with cracked shells or ones that remain open. Scrub the clam shells under cold running water if needed to remove debris, then place them in a quart (about 1L) of cold water dissolved with the 2 tablespoons of salt. Let the clams purge in the water for about 1 hour. After purging, rinse the clams well with cold water.

2. **Precook the clams.** To a saucepan, add 2 cups of water and bring to a boil. Once the water is boiling, add the cleaned clams and cook them, shaking the saucepan occasionally, until they pop open, about 1–2 minutes. Remove the clams and reserve 1 cup (240ml) of the cooking liquid, discarding the last bit at the bottom if there's debris.

3. **Set up the steamer.** Add about 1 inch (2.5cm) of water in your steamer set up and bring the water to a boil. If you are steaming with a steam basket, keep the heat on medium-high. If you are steaming with a rack inside of a wok or pot, reduce the heat so that the water is at a medium simmer.

4. **Make the steamed egg base.** Crack the eggs into a bowl and beat well, then add the reserved clam cooking liquid, salt, and bouillon powder. Mix gently to combine.

5. **Extra preparation to keep the steamed egg silky.** Strain the egg mixture through a sieve into a shallow heatproof bowl or coupe that can hold 2 cups (470ml) of liquid. Skim off the foam on top of the mixture with a spoon then scatter the clams (with their shells intact) into the egg mixture. Turn a plate upside down to cover the bowl or wrap the bowl with plastic wrap and poke a few holes on top to vent.

6. **Steam the egg.** Carefully place the bowl in the steamer and steam for 12 minutes or until the egg is set, with only the center slightly wobbling when gently shaken. When you cut the center of the steamed egg, the juice should run clear. If it is cloudy, steam for a couple more minutes.

7. **Finish and serve.** While waiting on the steamed egg, make the sauce by mixing together the soy sauce, water, and sesame oil. When the steamed egg is ready, uncover and top with the prepared sauce, Chinese Chili Oil (if desired), and sliced green onions. Enjoy it while it's hot.

CHAPTER 5

Mains

Juicy Soy-Roasted Chicken

This roasted chicken has a couple of quirks—it's brined in a soy-based mixture and poached before roasting, with each step serving a purpose: The soy-based brine infuses the meat with rich, savory depth while imparting a beautiful golden-brown color to the skin, and the additional step of poaching before roasting ensures the chicken remains exceptionally juicy throughout. — Mei

---

Prep time: **30 minutes, plus 6 hours or more for cooling and marinating**
Cook time: **1 hour 15 minutes**
Makes: **4–6 servings**

1 (5 lb/2.25kg) whole chicken
¼ cup (60ml) Shaoxing rice wine
3-inch (7.5cm) (30g) knob of ginger, peeled and sliced
2 stalks green onion
Neutral cooking oil, for brushing (or cooking spray)

Marinade
1 cup (240ml) water
¾ cup (180ml) soy sauce
¼ cup (50g) granulated sugar
1 tbsp (15ml) dark soy sauce
5–7 (18g) garlic cloves, crushed
2-inch (5cm) (20g) knob of ginger, peeled and sliced

1. **Poach the chicken.** Rinse the chicken and discard or save the giblets for another use. We also like to trim and discard the excess fat around the chicken's bottom cavity area. Place the chicken into a large pot, such as a stock pot, and fill it with enough water to cover the chicken, then add the rice wine, ginger, and green onions. Bring the pot to a simmer over high heat, and once it's simmering, reduce the heat to keep the water at a gentle simmer. Poach the chicken for 20 minutes.
2. **Make the marinade.** In a bowl, combine all the ingredients for the marinade and mix until the sugar has completely dissolved.
3. **Chill and marinade the chicken.** After 20 minutes, carefully drain the chicken, making sure there is no water left in the cavity. Transfer it to a large mixing bowl and pour the prepared marinade over the chicken, including inside the cavity. Let it cool in the marinade at room temperature, turning it every 30 minutes or so, for about 2 hours. Once the chicken has cooled to room temperature, transfer it to a gallon-size resealable bag along with the marinade. Squeeze out as much air as possible to ensure the chicken is fully in contact with the marinade. Refrigerate for at least 4 hours, preferably overnight.
4. **Roast the chicken.** Preheat the oven to 400°F (205°C) and adjust the rack so the chicken will be centered while roasting. Prepare a roasting pan or a sheet pan fitted with a rack. Remove the chicken from the marinade (reserve the marinade) and pat the skin dry with paper towels. Place it breast-side up on the rack. Roast for 1 hour to 1 hour 15 minutes, or until the internal temperature reaches 165°F (74°C). After the first 15 minutes, remove the chicken from the oven and brush the outside with some of the marinade. Return it to the oven for another 15 minutes, then remove it again and brush or spray it with oil. Continue roasting until fully cooked. If the tips of the legs or wings begin to darken too much, loosely cover them with aluminum foil.
5. **Serve.** Once cooked, remove the chicken from the oven and let it rest for 10–15 minutes. Be careful of the juice collected in the cavity. Drain if necessary. Carve the chicken and serve with your favorite sides. One of our favorite condiments for this soy-roasted chicken is the ginger scallion sauce used for our Hainanese-Style Chicken Clay Pot Rice (page 115). It's simple, super easy to make, and a perfect addition if you like an aromatic, savory sauce for your roasted chicken!

Orange Chicken

This classic Chinese takeout dish features golden, crispy fried chicken coated in a spicy, savory, sweet sauce full of orange flavor. A key tip when making this dish is to taste the sauce if you're using freshly squeezed orange juice, as the sweetness of orange juice can vary. You can adjust the sugar to achieve the perfect balance. Also, check out our Sesame Chicken (page 103) for tips on frying and storing chicken to save you time, effort, and extra oil. — Mei

---

Prep time: **20 minutes**
Cook time: **15 minutes**
Makes: **4 servings**

Chicken

- 2 lb (907g) boneless, skinless chicken thighs, cut into 1-inch (2.5cm) chunks
- ¼ cup (60ml) water
- 1 tsp (5g) kosher salt
- ½ tsp baking soda
- 1 large (50g) egg
- ½ cup (64g) cornstarch
- 1 tbsp (15ml) neutral cooking oil, plus more for frying

Sauce

- 1 cup (240ml) orange juice (carton or freshly squeezed)
- ¼ cup (68g) ketchup
- 2 tbsp (25g) granulated sugar (or as needed if using freshly squeezed orange juice)
- 1 tbsp (15ml) white vinegar
- 1 tbsp (8g) cornstarch
- 1 tbsp (15ml) neutral cooking oil
- 6–8 pieces orange peels, thumb-size pieces peeled using a vegetable peeler
- 1 stalk green onion, sliced (green and white parts separated)
- ½ tbsp (4g) minced garlic
- ½ tsp Chinese chili flakes or crushed red pepper

1. **Marinate the chicken.** To a large mixing bowl, add the chicken, water, salt, and baking soda. Mix well until the water has been mostly absorbed. Add the egg and mix well, then add the cornstarch and mix until evenly combined. To finish, mix in the oil. Set the chicken aside and let it marinate as you prepare the other ingredients, or cover the bowl and marinate in the fridge overnight.

2. **Make the sauce.** Combine the orange juice, ketchup, sugar, vinegar, and cornstarch in a bowl and mix well with a whisk. Set aside until needed.

3. **Prepare the frying station.** To a large pot, add 2–3 inches (5–7.5cm) of oil and heat it to 375°F (190°C). Prepare a sheet pan with a rack or line a large plate with paper towels. Have a spider strainer and a pair of tongs at the ready.

4. **Perform the first fry.** When the oil is ready, gently add the marinated chicken one piece at a time, using gloved hands, until there's an even layer. Do not overcrowd the pot; fry in batches if necessary. Cook for 4–5 minutes, stirring occasionally and separating any pieces that stick together with tongs. Remove the chicken with a spider strainer and let it cool and drain on the prepared rack or plate for about 5 minutes before proceeding to the second fry.

5. **Perform the second fry.** Keeping the oil at 375°F (190°C), add the chicken pieces for their second fry. Fry in batches as necessary, and this time let the chicken fry for 5–6 minutes or until the outside is golden brown and crispy. Remove the chicken with the spider strainer and let it drain while you prepare the sauce.

6. **Finish the sauce.** Add the oil to a well-seasoned wok or large nonstick pan over medium heat. When the oil is hot, add the orange peels, the white parts of the green onions, garlic, and chili flakes (or crushed red pepper). Sauté until fragrant, about 15–20 seconds, then immediately add the prepared sauce, stirring it well before adding. Bring the sauce to a simmer, stirring constantly. Once it begins to simmer, cook for 30 seconds to 1 minute, or until it thickens and becomes glossy.

7. **Toss the chicken and serve.** Take the sauce off the heat for a moment as you add all the fried chicken, then place the pan back on to the heat and toss and mix until the chicken is evenly covered with the sauce.

8. **Serve.** Garnish with the green parts of the green onion, and enjoy the orange chicken while it's hot. Leftover orange chicken can be refrigerated in an airtight container for up to 3 days.

Tips from our kitchen: Feel free to use less orange peel if you prefer a milder orange flavor. Use about 2–4 thumb-size pieces of orange peel instead.

Lemongrass Chicken Thighs

We know how hard it can be to find a main protein that's flavorful, quick to make, and perfect for meal prep. That's why we had to share our lemongrass chicken thighs—marinated in a fragrant blend of lemongrass, shallots, soy sauce, sugar, and fish sauce. No matter if you grill it, pan-sear it, air-fry it, or bake it in the oven, the chicken thighs will be bursting with bold flavors in every bite. — Mei

---

Prep time: **10 minutes, plus 2 or more hours for marinating**
Cook time: **8–15 minutes**
Makes: **4 servings**

2 lb (907g) skinless, boneless chicken thighs

Marinade

1 cup (4oz/113g) shallot, thinly sliced
⅓ cup plus 1 tsp (75g) granulated sugar
¼ cup (32g) minced lemongrass (about 2 fresh stalks)
2 tbsp (18g) minced garlic
¼ cup (60ml) soy sauce
¼ cup (60ml) fish sauce
¼ cup (60ml) neutral cooking oil, plus more for cooking
2 tsp (4g) black pepper

1. Marinate the chicken. Make the marinade by combining all the ingredients in a large mixing bowl. Mix until the sugar dissolves, then add the chicken thighs and mix well to evenly cover the chicken. Cover and let the chicken marinate for at least 2–3 hours in the fridge, but it's best overnight and up to 3 days. You can also marinate the chicken in a resealable bag for the most optimal coverage and to save room in your fridge.

2. Choose a cooking method to cook your chicken. Personally, we like to cook it in our air fryer because it gets decent char with minimal work and mess, but pan searing and grilling are definitely where the flavor is at.

Air fryer: Grease the bottom of the air fryer basket with oil, then arrange the marinated chicken into the basket in a single layer. Cook in batches if needed. Air fry the chicken at 400°F (205°C) for about 10–11 minutes or until the chicken is cooked through to an internal temperature registering 165°F (74°C). Flip the chicken midway through.

Oven: Preheat the oven to 450°F (230°C). Line a sheet pan with aluminum foil and lightly grease it with oil. Let any excess marinade drip off the chicken, then arrange the chicken on the pan in a single layer. Bake the chicken on the center rack for about 13–15 minutes or until cooked through to an internal temperature registering 165°F (74°C). Then broil the chicken to get some char. Make sure to keep an eye on the chicken when you turn on the high broil function.

Stovetop: Remove the chicken thighs from the marinade and scrape off the aromatics (shallot, lemongrass, and garlic). To a large nonstick pan over medium heat, add enough oil to lightly coat the pan. Once the pan is hot, arrange the chicken in the pan in a single layer and sear each side for about 3–4 minutes with the pan covered until the chicken is nicely charred and cooked through to an internal temperature registering 165°F (74°C).

Grill: Preheat your grill until hot (350°F/175°C). Grease the grates with oil, then grill the chicken thighs on both sides until cooked through to an internal temperature registering 165°F (74°C).

3. Serve. Enjoy the lemongrass chicken thighs while they're hot with some steamed white rice and veggies of choice. Leftovers can be refrigerated for up to 4 days in an airtight container.

Tips from our kitchen: We like to top our lemongrass chicken thighs with some scallion oil for an extra pop of flavor and color. To make the scallion oil, heat up ¼ cup (60ml) of a neutral cooking oil on medium heat and add 4–5 stalks of sliced green onions (green parts only). Cook for a few seconds until the greens turn more vibrant. Use immediately or refrigerate for up to 5 days.

Gochujang BBQ Baked Chicken

Back in a small town in Georgia, my parents owned a Chinese dine-in restaurant that also served classic Southern country food. One of our sweetest cooks, Mrs. Pearl, made the best BBQ chicken you could imagine. Inspired by her unforgettable cooking, we've recreated the dish with a twist using our tangy, mildly spicy Gochujang BBQ Sauce (page 245). — Mei

---

Prep time: **5 minutes, plus 4 or more hours for brining**
Cook time: **about 40 minutes**
Makes: **4–5 servings**

- 2½ lb (1.1kg) bone-in chicken thighs
- 2 cups (480ml) water
- 2 tsp (10g) kosher salt
- 1 tsp onion powder
- 1 tsp garlic powder
- 1½ cups (360ml) Gochujang BBQ Sauce, divided (page 245)

1. **Brine the chicken.** To a gallon-size resealable bag, add the chicken thighs, water, salt, onion powder, and garlic powder. Mix well and seal. Try to push out as much air as possible as you seal up the bag. Let the chicken brine in the fridge for at least 4 hours or overnight. You can also brine the chicken in a mixing bowl. Try to use a bowl that's more tall than wide, or double the brine so the chicken can be fully submerged.
2. **Bake the chicken.** Preheat the oven to 425°F (220°C) and line a sheet pan with aluminum foil. Remove the chicken from the brine and pat it dry with paper towels. Toss the thighs with ¾ cup (180 ml) of the BBQ sauce, then arrange them on the prepared sheet pan. Bake on the middle rack for 25 minutes.
3. **Brush with BBQ sauce.** After 25 minutes, remove the pan from the oven and generously brush the tops of the thighs with about half of the remaining BBQ sauce. Return the chicken to the oven and bake for another 10 minutes, or until just cooked through and the internal temperature reaches 165°F (74°C). Remove the pan from the oven and switch the oven to high broil.
4. **Broil.** Brush the top of the thighs with the remaining gochujang BBQ sauce and broil on the middle rack for 3–5 minutes or until the top of the chicken is charred to your preference.
5. **Serve.** Remove the pan from the oven and let the chicken cool for a moment before serving. Enjoy while it's hot. Leftover chicken can be refrigerated for up to 4 days in an airtight container.

Tips from our kitchen: If you're an extra saucy person, you can heat up some extra gochujang BBQ sauce in a saucepan until it's bubbly and serve it on the side.

Sesame Chicken

Call us predictable, but Kyong and I still believe that sesame chicken is *the* ultimate Chinese takeout dish. Every time we visit Louisiana and stop by my parents' restaurant, it's impossible to resist a plate of sesame chicken with a side of fried rice. The chicken is double-fried until crispy and golden, then tossed in a glossy, sweet, tangy, and savory ketchup-based sauce. Just writing this makes us crave it all over again, especially when you roll a piece of the sauce-coated chicken in some fried rice. Not sure if this gives an upgrade to the fried rice or the chicken, but either way, it's A-MA-ZING! — Mei

---

Prep time: **20 minutes**
Cook time: **15 minutes**
Makes: **4 servings**

Chicken

- 2 lb (907g) boneless, skinless chicken thighs, cut into 1-inch (2.5cm) chunks
- ¼ cup (60ml) water
- 1 tsp (5g) kosher salt
- ½ tsp baking soda
- 1 large (50g) egg
- ½ cup (64g) cornstarch
- 1 tbsp (15ml) neutral cooking oil, plus more for frying

Sauce

- ½ cup (136g) ketchup
- ½ cup (120ml) water
- ½ cup (100g) granulated sugar
- 2 tbsp (30ml) white vinegar
- 1 tbsp (15ml) soy sauce
- 1 tbsp (8g) cornstarch
- ½ tsp dark soy sauce, for color (optional)
- ½ tbsp (8ml) neutral cooking oil
- 2 stalks green onion, sliced (white parts only)
- Toasted white sesame seeds, for garnish

1. **Marinate the chicken.** To a large mixing bowl, add the chicken, water, salt, and baking soda. Mix well until the water has been mostly absorbed. Add the egg and mix well, then add the cornstarch and mix until evenly combined. To finish, mix in the oil. Set the chicken aside and let it marinate as you prepare the other ingredients, or cover the bowl and marinate in the fridge overnight.
2. **Prepare the sauce.** Combine the ketchup, water, sugar, vinegar, soy sauce, cornstarch, and dark soy sauce (if using) and mix well with a whisk. Set aside until needed.
3. **Prepare the frying station.** To a large pot, add 2–3 inches (5–7.5cm) of oil and heat it to 375°F (190°C). Prepare a sheet pan with a rack or line a large plate with paper towels. Have a spider strainer and a pair of tongs at the ready.
4. **Perform the first fry.** When the oil is ready, gently add the marinated chicken one piece at a time, using gloved hands, until there's an even layer. Do not overcrowd the pot; fry in batches if necessary. Cook for 4–5 minutes, stirring occasionally and separating any pieces that stick together with tongs. Remove the chicken with a spider strainer and let it cool and drain on the prepared rack or plate for about 5 minutes before proceeding to the second fry.
5. **Perform the second fry.** Keeping the oil at 375°F (190°C), add the chicken pieces for their second fry. Fry in batches as necessary, and this time let the chicken fry for 5–6 minutes or until the outside is golden brown and crispy. Remove the chicken with the spider strainer and let it drain while you prepare the sauce.
6. **Finish the sauce.** Heat the oil in a well-seasoned wok or large nonstick pan over medium-high heat. Once hot, add the white parts of the green onions and stir-fry until fragrant, about 10 seconds. Stir the prepared sauce, then add it to the pan. Bring the sauce to a simmer, stirring constantly. Once simmering, cook for about 30 seconds, or until thickened and glossy with a deep red color.
7. **Toss the chicken and serve.** Take the sauce off the heat for a moment as you add all the fried chicken. Place the pan back on to the heat and toss the chicken until it's evenly covered with sauce. Top with sesame seeds and enjoy while hot. Leftover sesame chicken can be refrigerated in an airtight container for up to 3 days.

Tips from our kitchen: To forgo having to fry chicken every time you crave sesame chicken, you can fry extra chicken to freeze for later. To do so, let the chicken drain and cool completely after the first fry. Then transfer them onto a sheet pan and freeze the chicken until solid. Store the chicken in an airtight, freezer-safe bag for up to 2–3 months. When you're ready for sesame chicken, just pop the frozen chicken into the air fryer at 400°F (205°C) for 15–20 minutes or until hot and crispy. You can do this for Orange Chicken (page 96) as well.

Air-Fried Crispy Pork Belly

After testing this crispy pork belly recipe countless times and experimenting with various temperatures and drying techniques, we've finally perfected it! Our version requires a little bit of prep the day before, but it's well worth the effort because you'll get a juicy, pork belly with puffy, crispy skin that's not hard or chewy. The meat is also seasoned with a fragrant five-spice blend, making it impossible to not snack on before it makes it to the dining table! — Kyong

---

Prep time: **20 minutes, plus minimum 8 hours drying time**
Cook time: **1 hour 5 minutes**
Makes: **4 servings**

1 tbsp (15g) packed dark brown sugar
1 tbsp (6g) five-spice powder
3½ tbsp (53g) kosher salt, divided
½ tsp ground cumin
½ tsp onion powder
½ tsp garlic powder
½ tsp cracked black pepper
2½ lb (1.1kg) skin-on pork belly
White vinegar, as needed for brushing
Neutral cooking oil, as needed for brushing

Tips from our kitchen: To get the most even bubbling on the skin, it is very important that the pork belly is level all the way across. If needed, trim the meaty part of the pork belly so that the skin lays flat. If needed, you can also stuff some rolled-up paper towels under dipped areas before you start drying the pork belly in the fridge to fix an isolated dip.

1. **Prepare the seasoning.** In a bowl, mix together the brown sugar, five-spice powder, ½ tablespoon (8g) of salt, cumin, onion powder, garlic powder, and black pepper until well combined. Set aside until needed.

2. **Prepare the pork belly.** Prepare a sheet of aluminum foil that's a bit larger than the pork belly, a sheet pan or plate, and a meat tenderizer or a bundle of toothpicks or skewers tied together. Place the pork belly skin-side up on a cutting board and pierce the entire surface of the skin using the meat tenderizer or toothpick/skewer bundle. This is to help the skin dehydrate better. Next, flip the pork belly and make vertical and horizontal cuts halfway through the pork belly's meaty side, with each cut about 1 inch (2.5cm) apart. Make sure to not pierce the skin. Rub the prepared seasoning in between the cuts and on the meaty parts of the pork belly, avoiding the skin. Flip the pork belly back to skin-side up and pat the skin dry with a paper towel.

3. **Dehydrate the pork belly skin.** Place the pork belly onto the prepared foil, still skin-side up, and wrap with the foil around the pork belly while keeping the skin exposed. We like to fold each edge of foil up toward the pork belly so that the foil covers the sides of the pork belly. Then pinch and fold the corners to hold the sides up, like a makeshift box. Brush the pork belly skin with a layer of white vinegar, then carefully transfer the foil-wrapped pork belly onto the sheet pan or plate and place it into the refrigerator uncovered. Let the skin dry for 8–12 hours.

4. **Further dry the pork belly skin.** After 8–12 hours, remove the pork belly from the fridge and brush the skin with another layer of white vinegar, then make sure your hands are dry and sprinkle the remaining 3 tbsp (45g) of salt evenly over the skin. Carefully place the foil-wrapped pork belly into the air fryer basket and air fry at 340°F (170°C) for 40 minutes.

5. **Finish cooking.** After 40 minutes, scrape off and discard the salt. The salt at this point will have turned into a sheet, so if you're gentle enough, you can use a fork or spatula to help you remove the salt in sheets and pieces. Dab the skin dry with paper towels, then brush it with a layer of oil. Place the basket back into the air fryer and air fry on 425°F (220°C) for another 20–25 minutes or until the skin is bubbly and the meat is cooked through with the internal temperature registering 165°F (74°C). Be careful during this whole process as both the air fryer basket and pork belly will be hot. Also, the pork belly will have rendered a decent amount of fat into the foil box, so be careful while moving the air fryer basket.

6. **Cut and serve.** When the pork belly is cooked, carefully remove it from the foil box with tongs. Let the pork belly rest for 5–10 minutes before cutting it into bite-size pieces. We like to get the job done with a sharp cleaver and cut the pork belly on its side to prevent breaking up the crispy skin too much or making it soggy. Enjoy while it's hot. Leftovers can be stored in an airtight container and refrigerated for up to 4 days.

Korean BBQ Pulled Pork

I'm a big fan of slow-cooked *anything*. I really don't mind the wait, especially when it comes to pulled pork. My love for it started after reading and making Chef Sean Brock's recipe for pulled pork with tomato gravy. After that, I was hooked. There's just something satisfying about taking a big slab of meat and slowly cooking it until it's tender enough to shred with the back of a spoon and yet still juicy. This Korean-inspired version of pulled pork is slowly roasted with bulgogi sauce and onions that melt right into the pan juices, creating a savory base that gets mixed back into the meat for even more flavor. Sandwich it between some homemade Milk Bread Rolls (page 202) and top it with Gochujang BBQ Sauce (page 245) and Kimchi Pickles (page 239), and you've got sliders no one can resist. — Kyong

---

Prep time: **15 minutes**
Cook time: **8 hours, plus 30 minutes to 1 hour of resting**
Makes: **8–10 servings**

- 5 lb (2.25kg) boneless pork shoulder or Boston pork butt
- ½ large (7oz/200g) yellow onion, thinly sliced
- 1 cup (240ml) Bulgogi Sauce (homemade [page 244] or store-bought)
- 1 tbsp (16g) kosher salt
- 1 tbsp (6g) coarsely cracked black pepper

1. **Preheat the oven to 275°F (135°C).** Also, prepare a baking dish and line it with aluminum foil. For extra protection, you can double-line the dish.
2. **Season the pork.** Drain the pork shoulder (or butt) and place it into the prepared baking dish. Add the onion, bulgogi sauce, salt, and pepper, then rub the seasonings and onion evenly over the surface of the pork. Tightly wrap the baking dish with foil.
3. **Cook.** Place the baking dish onto the middle rack and roast the pork shoulder for 8 hours. After 8 hours, remove the dish from the oven. At this point, the pork will be so tender, you'll be able to easily pull it apart with a fork. Keep the pork covered and let it rest for 1 hour.
4. **Shred.** Uncover the baking dish and, if needed, skim the fat from the surface of the pan juices. Shred the pork with forks directly in the dish—it will likely still be hot, so be careful! Toss the shredded pork well and let it soak in the juices to keep it moist. Before serving or using, drain any excess liquid from the pork.

Tips from our kitchen: Leftover pulled pork is perfect for meal prepping. You can keep it refrigerated in an airtight container for up to 4 days or frozen for up to 2 months. We like to portion the pulled pork to single-portion sizes for when we crave an easy rice bowl, burritos, or tacos.

Asian Sticky Ribs

Everyone has a go-to rib recipe they swear by for game days and gatherings, and this Asian sticky ribs recipe is ours. These ribs are juicy, fall-off-the-bone tender, yet they still have a satisfying texture. The sauce is perfectly sticky, sweet, savory, and spiced—it's flavorful without being overpowering. Serve with Milk Bread Rolls (page 202), Sesame Ginger Slaw (page 238), and Kimchi Pickles (page 239) to complete the experience. — Kyong

---

Prep time: **20 minutes**
Cook time: **2½–3 hours**
Makes: **4 servings**

1 rack (2.5–3 lb/1.1–1.4kg) St. Louis or baby back ribs

Dry rub

½ cup (110g) packed dark brown sugar
1 tbsp (16g) kosher salt
1 tsp five-spice powder
1 tsp ground paprika
1 tsp garlic powder
1 tsp onion powder
½ tsp cracked black pepper

Glaze

½ cup (120ml) soy sauce
½ cup (110g) packed dark brown sugar
¼ cup (84g) honey
¼ cup (60ml) rice vinegar
1-inch (2.5cm) (10g) knob of ginger, peeled and cut into a few slices
2 (6g) garlic cloves, crushed
1 cinnamon stick
1 star anise
1 tsp toasted sesame oil
1 bird's eye chili, sliced (optional)

1. **Preheat the oven to 275°F (135°C) and line a sheet pan with aluminum foil.** Also, prepare an additional sheet of foil long enough to wrap the entire rack of ribs in. If you want an extra blanket of security to prevent the bones from poking a hole in the foil, prepare two sheets of foil and stack them together.

2. **Prepare the ribs.** Pat dry the rack of ribs with paper towels then flip it meat-side down on the sheet(s) of foil. Nudge a finger underneath the membrane and slowly start to peel it away. Once you have enough leverage, grasp the membrane with a dry paper towel and peel off the entire membrane lining. Removing the membrane ensures that you get tender, juicy ribs and also helps the dry rub penetrate the meat better.

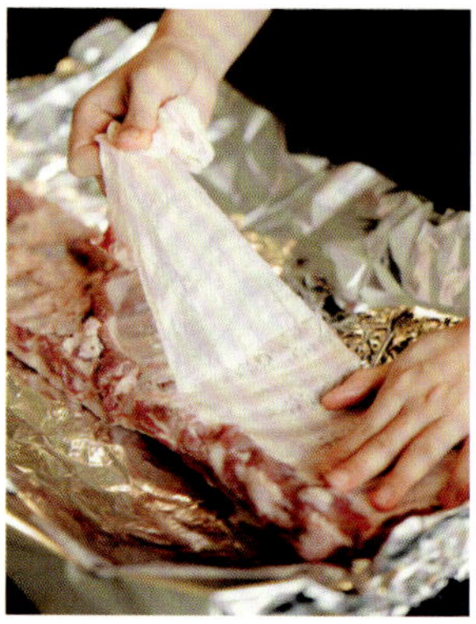

3. **Season the ribs.** In a bowl, make the dry rub by mixing together the brown sugar and all the spices until well combined. Sprinkle the dry rub over the entire surface of the ribs, both front, back, and the sides. Pack the seasoning onto the ribs so that it sticks.

4. **Bake the ribs.** Wrap the foil around the seasoned ribs, making sure to fold and crimp the edges of the foil together to create a tight seal. This turns the foil packet into a steamer and ensures the ribs stay juicy. Place the ribs onto the prepared sheet pan and bake on the center rack for 2½–3 hours. Start checking the doneness of the ribs around 2½ hours. The ribs are ready when the bone pulls away from the meat and a knife goes through the meat with little resistance.

5. **Make the glaze.** While the ribs are baking, make the glaze by combining all the ingredients along with the bird's eye chili (if using) in a saucepan. Bring it to a hard simmer over medium-high heat and let the glaze reduce by half and until it looks glossy, about 5–10 minutes. You can test it by pouring a spoonful of glaze onto a chilled plate. When the glaze cools, it should not be runny and should look glossy. When the glaze has reached the right consistency, use a spoon to remove and discard the ginger, garlic, cinnamon stick, and star anise. Set aside until needed.

6. **Broil the ribs with the glaze.** Once the ribs are ready, switch the oven to the broil function. Open the foil to expose the top of the ribs and brush on a layer of glaze. Place the ribs back on the center rack and broil for about 30 seconds to 1 minute or until the glaze starts to bubble vigorously and slightly caramelizes. Make sure to keep a careful eye on the ribs because the glaze can burn very easily! Repeat the glazing and broiling process a total of 2–4 times until you get your desired thickness of glaze and char. Remove the ribs from the oven and finish by brushing the ribs with another layer of glaze so that they're shiny and sticky. Warm up the remaining glaze for serving.

Pork Belly Rice Cake Stir-Fry

Rice cakes can be eaten for more than just Chinese New Year. In fact, this rice cake stir-fry is one of Kyong's favorites, and we make it often as an everyday meal. And as many ways as there are to enjoy rice cakes, they also come in many different shapes for different uses. For this stir-fry, we prefer the flat, oval-shaped rice cakes because they're thinner, cook faster, and stay softer. This style of rice cake is also available dry but more popularly "fresh" (vacuum packed and refrigerated). If you're using dry rice cake, you'll have to pre-boil it according to package instructions before using it for this recipe. If you're using "fresh" rice cake, you may need to soak and separate them in a bowl of water, then rinse and drain before use. — Mei

---

Prep time: **20 minutes**
Cook time: **15 minutes**
Makes: **3 servings**

Stir-fry

- 6 (24g) dried shiitake mushrooms
- 1 tbsp (15ml) neutral cooking oil, or as needed
- 6 oz (170g) skinless pork belly, cut into ½-inch (1cm) strips
- 2 cloves (7g) garlic, sliced
- 4 oz (113g) napa cabbage, washed and cut into 1-inch (2.5cm) chunks
- 4 oz (113g) baby bok choy, leaves separated and washed
- 1 stalk green onion, cut into 1-inch (2.5cm) pieces with whites and greens separated
- 1 tbsp (15ml) Shaoxing rice wine
- 1 lb (454g) sliced rice cake, rinsed and separated
- 1 tsp toasted sesame oil

Sauce

- ½ cup (120ml) water
- 2 tbsp (38g) oyster sauce
- 1 tbsp (15ml) soy sauce
- 1 tsp dark soy sauce
- 1 tsp granulated sugar

1. **Prepare the shiitake mushrooms.** Place the dried shiitake mushrooms into a heatproof bowl and pour enough boiling hot water over them to cover them entirely. Let the mushrooms soak for 10–15 minutes while you prepare the other ingredients. When ready to use, rinse the mushrooms to remove debris. Trim and discard the mushroom stems, then cut the mushroom caps into slices. Set aside until needed. For extra flavor, the mushroom water can be reserved to replace the regular water used for the sauce. Discard the bottom bits if there is debris.
2. **Prepare the sauce.** In a bowl, mix together all the ingredients until the sugar has dissolved. Set aside until needed.
3. **Render the pork belly.** To a well-seasoned wok or large nonstick pan over medium heat, add the oil. Once hot, add the pork belly and cook, stirring occasionally, until all the pieces are mostly golden and the fat is mostly rendered, about 3–5 minutes. When done, keep the pork belly and about 2 tablespoons (30ml) of fat in the pan. If needed, add more oil.
4. **Stir fry.** Keeping the heat on medium, add the garlic and stir fry until fragrant, about 10–15 seconds, then add the napa cabbage, bok choy, sliced shiitake, and whites of the green onion and drizzle the Shaoxing rice wine around the pan. Stir fry until the alcohol has evaporated, about 15 seconds, then spread the stir-fried mixture out and add the rice cakes on top. This is to prevent the rice cake from sticking while it softens up. Drizzle the prepared sauce over everything and cover with a lid. Increase the heat to medium-high and steam for about 5 minutes or until the rice cakes are tender.
5. **Finish and serve.** When the rice cakes are tender, uncover the pan and allow the excess moisture to evaporate, tossing and stirring frequently during the process. Once most of the moisture is cooked out and the sauce looks thickened and glossy, add the sesame oil and the rest of the green onion. Stir fry briefly to combine. Enjoy the rice cake stir-fry while it's hot. Leftovers can be refrigerated in an airtight container for up to 3 days.

Tips from our kitchen: Feel free to use only napa cabbage or baby bok choy if you prefer. Just substitute in equal amounts.

Braised Pork Over Rice

To me, anything braised over a bowl of rice is pure comfort, and this braised pork belly over rice checks all the marks. The secret that makes this dish so aromatic and magical is the caramelized shallots that are slowly braised with the pork belly until they nearly melt into the sauce, creating a deeply flavorful sauce and tender, gelatinous pork belly. — Mei

---

Prep time: **20 minutes**
Cook time: **1½–2 hours**
Makes: **3 servings**

- 2 cups (380–400g) raw long- or medium-grain white rice
- 3 large (150g) eggs, for serving (optional)
- 1 tbsp (15ml) neutral cooking oil
- 1½ lb (680g) skin-on pork belly, cut into ¼-inch (6mm) strips
- 8 oz (227g) shallot, thinly sliced
- 4 cups (960ml) water
- 3 tbsp (45ml) soy sauce
- ½ tbsp (8ml) dark soy sauce
- 2 tbsp (30ml) Shaoxing rice wine
- 2½ tbsp (32g) granulated sugar
- 1 tsp five-spice powder
- 1-inch (2.5cm) (10g) knob of ginger, peeled and cut into slices
- 1 cinnamon stick
- 2 bay leaves
- Shanghai or baby bok choy, halved and washed, for serving (optional)

1. **Prepare the rice.** Wash and cook the rice using your preferred method. You can also refer to page 22 for rice cooking instructions. Keep warm for serving.
2. **Boil the eggs (if adding).** Cook the eggs to medium-boiled. Soak in an ice bath, then peel and set aside. Refer to page 23 for more details and cook time.
3. **Render the pork belly.** To a wok or medium pot over medium-high heat, add the oil. Once the oil is hot, add the pork belly and cook until mostly golden brown and well rendered. Remove the pork belly with a slotted spoon and keep about 4 tablespoons (60ml) of fat in the pot. Discard the rest.
4. **Caramelize the shallot.** Heat the pot until the fat is hot again, then reduce the heat to medium or medium-low. Add the sliced shallots and cook, stirring frequently, until the shallots are golden brown and caramelized, about 10 minutes.
5. **Braise the pork belly.** To the caramelized shallots, add the rendered pork belly along with the water, both soy sauces, rice wine, sugar, five spice powder, ginger, cinnamon stick, and bay leaves. Give everything a stir and bring it to a boil, then reduce the heat to medium-low or low to keep it at a gentle simmer. Skim the surface to remove impurities and excess fat. Add the boiled eggs, cover, and braise until the pork belly is tender, about 1–1½ hours, stirring occasionally.
6. **Reduce.** Once the pork belly is tender, uncover the wok or pot and remove the eggs. Set them aside for serving. Skim the surface again if needed to remove excess fat, and also remove and discard the ginger slices, cinnamon stick, and bay leaves. Keeping the lid off, turn the heat to medium-high and reduce the braised pork belly by about two thirds of the original amount. Stir often.
7. **Blanch the bok choy (optional).** Bring a pot of water to a boil over high heat. When the water is at a boil, add the bok choy and cook for 30 seconds to 2 minutes, depending on how tender you like them. Drain well.
8. **Serve.** Enjoy the braised pork belly hot over a bowl of rice along with a braised egg and some bok choy, if desired. Leftover braised pork and eggs can be refrigerated in an airtight container for up to 4 days.

Tips from our kitchen: Overcooked eggs have a very particular flavor and are understandably not on everyone's favorite list. But, in our opinion, the overcooked flavor is essential to the authentic experience of certain Chinese dishes, and braises in particular. If you prefer your eggs not overcooked, add them toward the last 30 minutes of braising to still infuse flavor without overcooking the eggs.

Skin-on pork belly is desired here because the gelatin present in the skin makes the sauce sticky. Plus, the collagen in the pork belly skin is great for your skin! If you can't find skin-on pork belly, you can use skinless pork belly or supplement with pork skin. Sometimes grocery stores and butcher shops sell pork skin on its own. If doing so, use about 3 ounces (85g) of pork skin per recipe. To use, simmer the pork skin in a pot of water with a generous splash of Shaoxing rice wine for about 5–10 minutes, then cut it into small dices and add it to the braise when you add the water and seasonings.

Hainanese-Style Chicken Clay Pot Rice

We love the traditional version of Hainanese chicken, but sometimes convenience is king. For this easy version of Hainanese chicken rice, we're using boneless chicken thighs that are marinated and steamed on top of the rice to infuse flavor. Aromatics are also added to the rice to make it really fragrant. While that's happening, we whip up an addictive ginger-scallion sauce that's salty and full of flavor, perfect for both the chicken and rice. We like to make this in a clay pot because clay pots are supposed to make extra-tasty rice, but if you don't have a clay pot, you can also make it in a regular pot. — Mei

---

Prep time: **15 minutes, plus 30 minutes for marinating**
Cook time: **35–40 minutes**
Makes: **2 servings**

Chicken

- 8 oz (227g) boneless chicken thighs (preferably with skin)
- ½ tbsp (7ml) Shaoxing rice wine
- ½ tsp fine salt
- ⅛ tsp turmeric powder, for color (optional)

Sauce

- 2–3 stalks scallion, thinly sliced
- 1 tbsp (10g) minced ginger
- ½ tsp chicken bouillon powder
- ¼ tsp fine salt
- 2 tbsp (30ml) neutral cooking oil

Rice

- 1 cup (200g) raw long-grain white rice
- 1½ tbsp (22ml) neutral cooking oil
- ½ (30g) shallot, finely chopped
- ½-inch (1.25cm) (5g) knob of ginger, peeled and sliced
- 1 stalk lemongrass, cut in half and bruised
- 1¼ cup (300ml) water
- 1 tsp chicken bouillon powder
- ¼ tsp kosher salt

1. **Marinate the chicken.** In a bowl, season the chicken with rice wine, salt, and turmeric powder (if using). Mix well and let it marinate for 30 minutes.
2. **Make the sauce.** To a heatproof bowl, add the scallion, ginger, bouillon powder, and salt. Mix well. In a small pan, heat the oil over medium-high heat until it just starts to smoke. Carefully pour the hot oil over the scallion and ginger mixture, then stir to combine. Set aside to cool until needed. This can be made up to 3 days ahead of time and kept refrigerated.
3. **Wash the rice.** Wash and rinse the rice 2–3 times until the water is mostly clear. Drain well. If you have time, you can soak the rice for 30 minutes in the amount of water needed for cooking. Soaking the rice encourages the rice to cook more evenly. If you are soaking the rice, drain it well but reserve the soaking water for cooking, or measure the soaking water and replace it with fresh water in the same amount.
4. **Start the rice.** To a 40 ounce (1.2L) or larger clay pot, add the cooking oil and place over medium heat. When the clay pot and the oil are hot, add the shallot, ginger, and lemongrass and sauté until fragrant and the shallot just starts to turn golden, about 30 seconds to a minute. Add the prepared rice and sauté until well combined, then add the water, bouillon powder, and salt. Give everything a good stir and level out the rice as best as you can.
5. **Finish cooking.** Bring the rice to a simmer, and while waiting, spread the chicken thighs, skin-side up (if using skin-on chicken) over the rice in an even layer. Once at a simmer, place the lid over the clay pot and reduce the heat to low. Let the rice and chicken cook for 20 minutes, then turn off the heat and let it steam for another 10 minutes. At this time, the rice should be perfectly cooked and the chicken should be cooked through, with an internal temperature registering 165°F (74°C).
6. **Serve.** To enjoy, remove the chicken thighs and cut them into slices of your desired thickness. Fluff the rice with a rice paddle or a wooden spoon and remove the lemongrass and ginger slices. Portion the rice and chicken onto serving plates and top the chicken with your desired amount of the ginger scallion sauce. Taste the sauce first to decide how much to use. Leftovers can be stored in airtight containers and refrigerated for up to 3 days.

Tips from our kitchen: When purchasing fresh lemongrass, it can come in a whole stalk or just the bottom 4 inches (10cm) or so, which is the main usable part. If you purchased a whole stalk, you can cut and discard the top portion and use the bottom section, where it's whiter. Peel off a couple layers of outer leaves and chop it up, or, like this recipe, just bruise it with the side of a knife or a rolling pin.

Black Pepper Garlic Steak Stir-Fry

If you love the bold kick of black pepper, this dish is for you! The beef is marinated for maximum flavor, then stir-fried with butter for added richness, along with plenty of garlic, onion, and bell pepper for a crisp texture. It's an easy dish to throw together, yet so delicious that you'll keep going back for more with every bite. — Kyong

---

Prep time: **15 minutes, plus 15 minutes or more for marinating**
Cook time: **10 minutes**
Makes: **2 servings**

- 1 lb (454g) beef rib eye or tenderloin
- 1 tbsp (15ml) Shaoxing rice wine
- 2 tbsp (30ml) soy sauce, divided
- 1¾ tsp (3g) coarsely cracked black pepper, divided
- 1 tbsp (15ml) neutral cooking oil
- 2 tbsp (28g) unsalted butter
- 6 garlic cloves, sliced
- ½ large (7oz/200g) yellow onion, cut into 1-inch (2.5cm) chunks
- 1 (7oz/200g) bell pepper (any color), core discarded and cut into 1-inch (2.5cm) chunks
- 1 tbsp (19g) oyster sauce

1. **Prepare and marinate the steak.** Trim and discard the excess fat, if needed, then cut the steak into 1-inch (2.5cm) cubes. Place the steak in a bowl and season with rice wine, 1 tablespoon (15ml) of soy sauce, and ¼ teaspoon of black pepper. Let the steak marinate for at least 15–30 minutes or cover and refrigerate overnight.

2. **Stir fry the steak.** To a large sauté pan over medium-high heat, add the oil. When the oil is hot, add the marinated steak and stir fry for 3–5 minutes, depending on how well-done you like your steak. Remove it and set aside. If there's a lot of oil in the pan at this point, wipe it clean with paper towels.

3. **Finish the stir-fry.** To the same pan over medium-high heat, add the butter. Once the butter has melted, add the garlic and cook until it starts to turn golden brown. Add the onion and bell pepper and stir fry for about 30 seconds to 1 minute or until the onion just starts to turn translucent. Add the steak back to the pan along with the oyster sauce, the remaining tablespoon of soy sauce, and the remaining 1½ teaspoons of black pepper. Stir fry for about a minute or until everything is evenly coated and the steak is hot again.

4. **Serve.** Enjoy the steak stir-fry while it's hot. Leftovers can be stored in the fridge for up to 3 days.

Mongolian Beef

One of the most popular beef dishes at my parents' restaurant is their Mongolian beef. The beef is marinated using a velveting technique that uses a very small amount of baking soda—the method Chinese restaurants use to make beef incredibly tender. The beef is then stir-fried with sugar and soy sauce, along with plenty of green onions and yellow onions, creating a sweet and savory stir-fry dish that goes perfect with rice. — Mei

---

Prep time: **15 minutes**
Cook time: **15 minutes**
Makes: **4 servings**

Beef

- 1 lb (454g) beef flank, top sirloin, or tri-tip
- 2 tbsp (30ml) water
- 1 tbsp (15ml) Shaoxing rice wine
- ½ tsp kosher salt
- ¼ tsp baking soda
- 2 tbsp (16g) cornstarch
- 1 tbsp (15ml) neutral cooking oil

Rest of the dish

- 4 tbsp (60ml) neutral cooking oil, or as needed
- 1 tbsp (9g) minced garlic
- ½ large (7oz/200g) yellow onion, sliced
- 1 bunch (3oz/85g) green onion, cut into 2-inch (5cm) pieces with green and whites separated
- 1 tbsp (15ml) Shaoxing rice wine
- 3 tbsp (38g) granulated sugar
- 3 tbsp (45ml) soy sauce
- 1 tsp cracked black pepper

1. **Velvet the beef.** Cut the beef against the grain into slices no thicker than ¼ inch (6mm). Depending on the size of the cut of your beef, you may also want to cut it *with the grain* into 2–3 sections first so that the beef is bite-size. Add the beef, water, rice wine, salt, and baking soda to a medium bowl, then mix until most of the liquid is absorbed. Add the cornstarch and mix until well combined. Finish by mixing in the oil. Set the beef aside as you prepare the rest of the ingredients or cover and let it marinate in the fridge overnight.

2. **Stir fry the beef.** To a well-seasoned wok or a large nonstick pan over medium-high heat, add the oil and swirl it around the wok/pan. When the oil is hot, add half of the beef and stir fry until just cooked, about 3–4 minutes. Remove the beef and repeat with the other half.

3. **Bring the dish together.** Once the beef has all been cooked, keep about 2 tablespoons (30ml) of oil in the wok. Add more oil if needed. Keep the wok on medium-high heat and add the garlic. Stir fry briefly until the garlic is fragrant, about 10–15 seconds, then add the onion and whites of the green onion. Stir fry until the onion starts to look translucent. Then add the beef back into the wok and drizzle the rice wine around the wok. Stir fry until the alcohol is cooked off, about 30 seconds, then season with the sugar, soy sauce, and black pepper. Add the green parts of the green onions, then stir fry and toss until everything is evenly coated and seasoned.

4. **Serve.** Enjoy the Mongolian beef while it's hot. Leftovers can be stored in an airtight container and refrigerated for up to 3 days.

Curry Cottage Pie

This recipe may sound like an unexpected mash-up, mixing a classic Irish comfort dish with familiar Japanese flavors, but trust me: Just give it one bite and you'll see why this is one of our favorite recipes in this book. The ground beef and veggies are stewed in a gravy-like sauce, with subtle curry flavors woven throughout, then covered in a generous blanket of creamy mashed potatoes. It's a dish that will appeal to all palates. — Kyong

---

Prep time: **1 hour**
Cook time: **about 20 minutes**
Makes: **6–8 servings**

Mashed potatoes

- 4 lb (1.8kg) russet potatoes, peeled and cut into 2-inch (5cm) chunks
- 1¼ cup (300ml) heavy cream
- 1¼ sticks (141g) unsalted butter
- 2 tsp (10g) kosher salt

Filling

- 3 tbsp (42g) unsalted butter
- 2 tbsp (18g) minced garlic
- 1 tbsp (10g) minced ginger
- 2 lb (907g) lean ground beef
- 1 large (14oz/400g) yellow onion, diced
- 2 large (12oz/340g) carrots, peeled and cut into ½-inch (1cm) chunks
- 8 oz (225g) baby portobello mushrooms, sliced
- 2 cups (480ml) unsalted beef stock
- 1 (15oz/425g) can crushed tomatoes
- 4 cubes (3.8oz/110g) Golden Curry mild sauce mix
- 2 tsp (10g) kosher salt
- ½ tsp cracked black pepper
- 1 cup (130g) frozen peas, thawed and drained
- 2 stalks green onions, sliced

1. **Preheat the oven to 400°F (205°C).** Also, prepare a 9 × 13-inch (23 × 33cm) baking dish. If desired, also prepare a piping bag fitted with a large piping tip of your choice for the potatoes. We used a large open star piping tip.

2. **Boil the potatoes.** Add the potatoes to a large pot and cover the potatoes with water. Place it over high heat and bring to a boil. Cook the potatoes until they are fork tender, about 30–35 minutes. Drain well.

3. **Make the cottage pie filling.** While the potatoes are cooking, begin preparing the filling. In another large pot set over medium-high heat, melt the butter. Add the garlic and ginger and sauté until fragrant, about 20–30 seconds. Add the ground beef and cook until no longer pink, breaking it up as it cooks. Stir in the onion and carrots and sauté until the onion begins to turn translucent. Add the mushrooms and cook for a few minutes more. Pour in the beef stock and crushed tomatoes, then add the curry mix, salt, and black pepper. Bring to a simmer and cook for 10–15 minutes, until the curry cubes have dissolved and the filling has thickened. Stir in the peas and green onions, then transfer the filling to the prepared baking dish and set aside.

4. **Prepare the cream and butter for the mashed potatoes.** To a medium saucepan, add the cream and butter. Warm it over medium heat until the butter has melted. Stir occasionally. You can also do this in the microwave in a microwave-safe container.

5. **Make the mashed potatoes.** Pass the potatoes through a sieve or a ricer, into a large mixing bowl. Add the warmed cream with butter and the salt. Gently mix and fold the mashed potato with a rubber spatula until evenly combined. If using a piping bag, transfer mashed potatoes in portions and refill as you go.

6. **Assemble and bake.** Pipe or spread the mashed potato over the cottage pie filling. The potato should reach pretty close to the rim of the baking dish. Place the baking dish on a large sheet pan to catch any drippings. Bake on the middle rack for 20 minutes or until the filling is hot and bubbly. If you want to add some color on top of the potatoes, broil on high until golden brown.

Sichuan Pepper Steak au Poivre

Whether you've had steak au poivre before or not, this is a version you need to try. Start with a cut like hanger, bavette, or New York strip that's well-marbled, and generously season and sear it until it develops a perfect crust. Then, in the fond, cook the Sichuan peppercorns and aromatics in butter, deglazing with Shaoxing rice wine instead of the usual cognac or brandy. Finish it with a splash of cream to create a rich, velvety sauce where the Sichuan peppercorn's numbing heat is gently mellowed, revealing its subtle fruity notes. We love serving it just as is or alongside crispy French fries or golden potato wedges. — Kyong

---

Prep time: **10 minutes**
Cook time: **15 minutes**
Makes: **2 servings**

Steak

- 2 (8oz/227g each) hanger steaks or New York strips
- Kosher salt
- Cracked black pepper
- 1–2 tbsp (15–30ml) neutral oil
- 2 tbsp (28g) unsalted butter
- 4 cloves garlic, crushed

Sauce

- 3 tbsp (42g) unsalted butter
- 1 (3oz/85g) shallot, minced
- 1 tbsp (9g) minced garlic
- 1 tbsp (6g) coarsely ground black peppercorns
- 1 tsp (2g) coarsely ground Sichuan peppercorns
- ¼ cup (60ml) Shaoxing rice wine
- ½ cup (120ml) heavy cream
- ½ tsp kosher salt

1. **Cook the steak.** Generously season the steaks with salt and black pepper. To a large pan over medium-high heat, add the oil. Once the oil is hot, sear the steaks until golden brown then flip to sear the other side. At this point, add the butter and crushed garlic and let the garlic cook in the fat for about a minute while the steaks are searing, then start basting the steaks until they reach your desired level of doneness (see tips). Once done, move the steak aside onto a plate or sheet pan (preferably with a rack) and pour the butter and garlic over the steaks. Let the steaks rest while you prepare the sauce.

2. **Make the sauce.** Wipe the same pan clean with paper towels and heat it over medium heat. Add the butter and once it's hot and melted, add the shallot and garlic. Sauté for a minute or until the aromatics are fragrant and the shallot is translucent, then add the black pepper and Sichuan pepper. Sauté for another 30 seconds to 1 minute. Next, add the Shaoxing rice wine and let it reduce by half, then add the heavy cream and salt. Let the sauce simmer for a minute, stirring occasionally.

3. **Serve.** After the steak has rested, slice it to your desired thickness and transfer onto a serving plate(s). Enjoy the steak while it's hot with the sauce poured over it or served on the side for dipping.

Tips from our kitchen: Here are the cooking temperatures for steak:

125°F (51°C) for rare

135°F (57°C) for medium-rare

145 °F (62°C) for medium

155°F (68°C) for medium-well

165°F (74°C) for well-done

Bibimbap

Bibimbap, which translates to "mixed rice," is one of the most iconic and popular Korean dishes. For us, it's the perfect meal for cleaning out the fridge or an easy way to enjoy a variety of vegetables. We often prepare a quick soy-seasoned ground beef and pair it with vegetables like mung bean sprouts, zucchini, or whatever vegetables and toppings we have on hand. So feel free to substitute any of the vegetables or use more of one than another. The only downside to making bibimbap at home is that it can require quite a few bowls and pans. To reduce the number of dishes, you can store the cooked vegetables on a foil-lined sheet pan or in a heatproof storage container as you prepare them. We prefer using a storage container so we don't have to transfer the vegetables if there are leftovers—which there almost always are when we cook for just the two of us. — Kyong

---

Prep time: **30 minutes**
Cook time: **30 minutes**
Makes: **about 4 servings**

2–3 cups (380–630g) raw white rice (long, medium, or short-grained)
4 large (200g) eggs, for serving (optional)
Neutral cooking oil, as needed for cooking
Toasted sesame seeds, for garnish (optional)

Sauce
½ cup (145g) gochujang
¼ cup (84g) honey
2 tsp (6g) minced garlic
2 tsp (10ml) sesame oil

Vegetables
8 (32g) dried shiitake mushrooms
1 lb (454g) bean sprouts, rinsed
2 ¼ tsp (13g) plus a pinch of fine salt, divided
3 tbsp (45ml) toasted sesame oil, divided
10 oz (284g) baby spinach
1 lb (454g) zucchini, cut into ¼-inch (6mm) half moons
2 large (12oz/340g) carrots, peeled and julienned
⅛ tsp cracked black pepper, divided

Beef
¼ cup (60ml) soy sauce
¼ cup (84g) honey
1 tbsp (9g) minced garlic
2 tsp (10ml) toasted sesame oil
1 tbsp (15ml) neutral cooking oil
1 lb (454g) lean ground beef

1. **Prepare the rice.** Wash and cook the rice using your preferred method. You can also refer to page 22 for rice cooking instructions. Keep warm for serving.

2. **Make the sauce.** Combine all the ingredients for the sauce and mix well. Set aside until ready to use, or cover and keep refrigerated for up to 1 week.

3. **Prepare the shiitake mushrooms.** Place the dried mushrooms into a heatproof bowl and add enough boiling hot water to cover them. Let the shiitake soak for 10–15 minutes until they're rehydrated, then rinse them well to remove any debris. After rinsing, cut and discard the woody stems, then cut the mushroom caps into slices. Set aside.

4. **Cook the beef.** Mix the soy sauce, honey, garlic, and sesame oil in a bowl and set aside until needed. To a large saucepan over medium-high heat, add the cooking oil. When the oil is hot, add the ground beef and cook until no longer pink, about 5 minutes. Make sure to break up the beef while cooking. Once the beef is cooked through, add the prepared sauce and mix well. Bring everything to a simmer and let the beef cook in the sauce for another minute or two. Keep warm for serving.

5. **Blanch the bean sprouts.** Bring a large pot of water to a boil over high heat and have a spider strainer and a large bowl at the ready. Once at a boil, add the bean sprouts and bring the water back to a boil. When it's boiling again, scoop out the bean sprouts with the strainer, making sure to drain well, and place them into the mixing bowl and season with 1 teaspoon of salt and 1 tablespoon (15ml) of sesame oil. Set aside.

6. **Blanch the spinach.** Bring the same pot of water to a boil again, and add the spinach. Cook until wilted, about 30 seconds, then drain immediately and rinse with cold water until the spinach is completely cooled. Holding a small handful of spinach at a time, squeeze firmly to remove excess water. Place the spinach into a bowl and season with ¼ teaspoon of salt and ½ tablespoon (7ml) of sesame oil. Gently break up the clumps as you mix. Set aside.

7. **Sauté the zucchini.** In a large pan over medium heat, add ½ tablespoon (7ml) of sesame oil. Once the oil is hot, add the zucchini and season with ½ teaspoon of salt and a few cracks of black pepper. Sauté until tender, about 5 minutes. Set aside.

8. **Sauté the carrots.** To the same pan over medium heat, add 2 teaspoons (10ml) of sesame oil. When the oil is hot, add the carrots and season with ½ teaspoon of salt and a few cracks of black pepper. Sauté until the carrots are limp and no longer crunchy, about 4–5 minutes. Set aside.

9. **Sauté the shiitake mushrooms.** In the same pan over medium heat, add 1 teaspoon of sesame oil. When the oil is hot, add the shiitake mushrooms and season with a pinch of salt. Sauté for 3–4 minutes or until the mushrooms are lightly golden. Set aside.

10. Fry the eggs (optional). Wipe down the same pan with paper towels. Heat the pan over medium-high heat and add enough oil to cover the bottom of the pan. When the oil is hot and just starts to smoke, crack in the eggs and pan fry for about 3 minutes or until the whites are set with golden brown lacy edges and the yolk is still runny.

11. Assemble. Evenly divide the rice into 4 serving bowls, then top with equal amounts of each topping and a fried egg, if adding. Drizzle on your desired amount of sauce over the top, and garnish with sesame seeds.

12. Serve. To enjoy, stir everything up and mix well. If needed, add more sauce. Leftover toppings can be stored in the refrigerator for up to 3 days.

Tips from our kitchen: You can also serve bibimbap in a hot *dolsot* (a traditional Korean stone or ceramic bowl), which is a popular presentation at Korean restaurants. This version features crispy rice that forms as the dolsot heats up. To serve bibimbap dolsot-style, brush the inside of the bowl with a teaspoon of sesame oil, then add your desired amount of rice. Spread the rice into an even layer and arrange the toppings on top. Heat the dolsot over medium heat until you hear it sizzling. Then increase the heat to medium-high and continue cooking for 5–10 minutes, or until the rice becomes crispy on the bottom. Note that dolsots are best used on gas stovetops.

Not-Your-Average BBQ Shrimp and Grits

Growing up in Louisiana, surrounded by the bold flavors of Cajun and Creole cuisine, BBQ shrimp and grits has always held a special place as one of my all-time favorites. Inspired by those memories, I wanted to put a playful twist on this classic using Asian ingredients. Miso and brown butter is added to make the grits rich and creamy, and the shrimp are coated in a buttery BBQ sauce made from sautéed garlic and ginger, Shaoxing rice wine, Worcestershire sauce, soy sauce, and a few other flavor-packed ingredients. This is such a fun recipe that tastes just like how I remembered shrimp and grits to be. — Kyong

---

Prep time: **10 minutes**
Cook time: **25 minutes**
Makes: **4 servings**

BBQ shrimp

- 1 lb (454g) jumbo shrimp, peeled and deveined
- 1 tsp (6g) kosher salt
- 3 tbsp (45ml) neutral cooking oil, divided
- 2 tbsp (18g) minced garlic
- 2 tsp (7g) minced ginger
- ¼ cup (60ml) Shaoxing rice wine
- ⅔ cup (160ml) water
- ¼ cup (60ml) soy sauce
- ¼ cup (60ml) Worcestershire sauce
- 2 tbsp (25g) granulated sugar
- 1 bird's eye chili, sliced (optional)
- 4 tbsp (57g) cold unsalted butter, cut into smaller pieces
- Sliced green onion, for garnish (optional)

Grits

- 4 tbsp (57g) unsalted butter
- 3 cups (720ml) whole milk
- 2 cups (480ml) water
- 1 cup (185g) stone-ground yellow grits or polenta
- 5 tbsp (90g) white miso

1. **Season the shrimp.** Season the shrimp with salt and set aside until needed.
2. **Make the grits.** To a medium pot over medium-high heat, add the butter. Let the butter melt and cook, stirring occasionally, for about 1–2 minutes or until the butter has browned and smells nutty. Add the milk and water and give it a good whisk to scrape the fond off the bottom of the pot. Bring the milk mixture to a gentle boil, then, while whisking, pour in the grits or polenta. Reduce the heat to medium-low to medium and continue cooking the grits, stirring occasionally, for 8–13 minutes or until soft and creamy. Finish by adding the miso paste and whisk until the paste is dissolved and well combined. Keep the grits warm while you prepare the BBQ shrimp.
3. **Sear the shrimp.** To a pan over medium-high heat, add 2 tablespoons (30ml) of the oil. Once the oil is hot, add the shrimp and sear on both sides until the shrimp are just cooked, about 1–2 minutes per side. Remove the shrimp from the pan.
4. **Make the sauce.** To the same pan over medium-high heat, add the remaining 1 tablespoon of oil. When the oil is hot, add the garlic and ginger. Sauté for about 15–30 seconds or until the aromatics are fragrant, then add the Shaoxing rice wine and let it reduce by half. Next, add the water, soy sauce, Worcestershire sauce, sugar, and sliced chili (if you want it a little spicy). Bring everything to a simmer and let it cook for about a minute so that the flavors can marry.
5. **Finish.** After simmering, turn the heat to low and add the cold butter. Stir constantly until the butter has melted and emulsified into the sauce and the sauce looks glossy. Add the seared shrimp back to the pan to warm them back up. Toss the shrimp to coat them in the sauce.
6. **Assemble.** Give the grits a good whisk and portion your desired amount onto plates. Top with BBQ shrimp and sauce and garnish with sliced green onions, if desired.
7. **Serve.** Enjoy the shrimp and grits while they're hot. Leftover shrimp and grits can be refrigerated in airtight containers for up to 3 days.

Sweet & Sour Fish

I told Mei that if there was one fish recipe we had to include—one that truly hits all the right notes—it had to be our sweet & sour fish. To start, we fry slices of tilapia filet coated in seasoned dredge until golden brown. This alone is already delicious, but the real magic happens when the fried fish is tossed in the sweet and tangy, pineapple juice- and ketchup-based sauce. But don't sleep on the vegetables! They add a nice savory note to the sauce that helps balance the sauce's sweetness. — Kyong

---

Prep time: **30 minutes**
Cook time: **15 minutes**
Makes: **3–4 servings**

Fish
1 lb (454g) tilapia filet (thawed if frozen)
1 tbsp (15ml) Shaoxing rice wine
¾ tsp fine salt
Neutral cooking oil, for frying

Sauce
¾ cup (180ml) pineapple juice
½ cup (100g) granulated sugar
¼ cup (68g) ketchup
3 tbsp (45ml) white vinegar
1 tbsp (8g) cornstarch
1 tbsp (15ml) water
1 tbsp (15ml) neutral cooking oil

Fry batter
½ cup (64g) cornstarch
½ cup (60g) all-purpose flour
½ tsp fine salt
¼ tsp cracked black pepper
2 large (100g) eggs, beaten

Vegetables
1 (7oz/200g) green bell pepper, cut into 1-inch (2.5cm) pieces
¼ large (3.5oz/100g) yellow onion, cut into 1-inch (2.5cm) pieces
½ medium (2oz/57g) carrot, peeled and thinly sliced

1. **Prepare the fish.** Cut the tilapia filet into 2-inch (5cm) pieces and season it with the rice wine and salt. Mix well and set aside to marinate as you prepare the other ingredients.

2. **Prepare the sauce.** In a bowl, make the sauce by whisking together the pineapple juice, sugar, ketchup, and white vinegar until well combined. Also prepare the cornstarch slurry by mixing together the cornstarch and water in a small bowl. Set them aside until needed.

3. **Prepare the dredge and fry station.** In a mixing bowl, mix together the cornstarch, flour, salt, and pepper until well combined. Set it aside for battering, along with the beaten eggs and marinated fish. In a medium or large pot, heat about 2 inches (5cm) of oil to 350°F (175°C). Also, prepare a sheet pan with a rack or line a plate with paper towels and have a spider strainer at the ready.

4. **Fry the fish.** When the oil is ready, add the beaten eggs to the marinated fish and mix well, then dredge each piece of fish in the prepared dredge, making sure to pack the flour mixture onto the fish, then gently shaking to remove any excess dredge. Gently place the battered fish into the hot oil and repeat this process with the remaining fish. Don't crowd the oil, and fry in batches as necessary. Fry the fish for 3–4 minutes or until they are golden and crispy. Remove and let them drain on the prepared rack or plate until needed.

5. **Stir-fry the vegetables.** Heat a well-seasoned wok or large pan over medium-high heat and add the tablespoon of oil. Once the oil is hot, add the bell pepper, onion, and carrot, and stir-fry for a few minutes until fragrant and the onion begins to turn translucent.

6. **Finish the sauce and add the fish.** Add the prepared sauce and bring it to a boil. Reduce the heat to medium and simmer for a couple of minutes, until the vegetables are no longer crunchy and the flavors have melded. Stir the cornstarch slurry again, then slowly drizzle it into the sauce while stirring. Cook for another minute, until the sauce is glossy and thickened. Once the sauce has thickened, add the fried fish and gently mix until everything is well coated.

7. **Serve.** Enjoy it while it's hot, and refrigerate the leftovers in an airtight container for up to 3 days.

Salmon Sushi Bake

We're usually skeptics when it comes to trendy recipes because they often end up being okay at best. But this one is different. It's essentially a casserole of cooked spicy salmon over a bed of sushi rice topped with savory unagi sauce and spicy sriracha mayo. The result isn't very awe-striking, but the flavor will have your taste buds dancing! Not to mention, this is also our favorite way to use up leftover salmon. — Kyong

---

Prep time: **30 minutes**
Cook time: **10–15 minutes**
Makes: **4–6 servings**

Seasoned sushi rice

- 2 cups (400–420g) raw medium or short-grain white rice
- ¼ cup (60ml) rice vinegar
- 1½ tbsp (19g) sugar
- 1 tsp kosher salt
- Toasted sesame oil, for greasing pan

Topping

- 8 oz (227g) cooked salmon, skin removed
- 8 oz (227g) imitation crab meat (thawed, if frozen)
- 4 oz (113g) cream cheese, softened
- ½ cup (120g) sriracha sauce
- ¼ cup (60g) Kewpie mayo
- 1 stalk green onion, sliced (plus more for garnish)

Spicy mayo

- ¼ cup (60g) Kewpie mayo
- 1 tbsp (15g) sriracha sauce

Unagi sauce (or store-bought)

- 2 tbsp (30ml) sake
- 2 tbsp (30ml) soy sauce
- 2 tbsp (25g) sugar
- 1 tbsp (15ml) mirin

To serve

- Furikake
- Seaweed snack
- Ripe avocado, sliced
- English cucumber, sliced

1. **Wash and cook the rice.** Wash and cook the rice using your preferred method. You can also refer to page 22 for rice cooking instructions. Keep warm for serving. For this recipe, it's ideal to make the rice a little drier, as we'll be adding seasoned vinegar to it after it's cooked.
2. **Make the seasoned vinegar.** In a bowl, mix together the rice vinegar, sugar, and salt until dissolved. You can warm the mixture in the microwave or on the stove to help dissolve the sugar and salt faster. Set aside until needed.
3. **Prepare the topping.** To a mixing bowl, add and break up the cooked salmon and shred the imitation crab meat. You can also cut the crab meat in half if you prefer shorter strands. Add the rest of the ingredients for the topping and mix with a gloved hand until well combined. If you prefer the topping less spicy, you can reduce the amount of sriracha used. Set aside until needed.
4. **Season the rice.** Once the rice is cooked, fluff with a rice paddle, then transfer it to a wide heatproof bowl. Drizzle in the seasoned vinegar in 2–3 sessions, while fluffing and mixing the rice with the rice paddle, making sure the vinegar is absorbed before adding more.
5. **Assemble and bake.** Preheat the oven to 425°F (220°C) and lightly grease a 8 × 11-inch (20 × 28cm) or a 9 × 13-inch (22 × 33cm) baking dish with a little sesame oil. Spread the seasoned sushi rice evenly in the baking dish, then top with the salmon and crab mixture. Spread it out evenly. Bake the sushi bake on the middle rack for 10–15 minutes or until everything is hot. Remove from the oven and let it cool for a few minutes.
6. **Prepare the sauces.** While waiting for the mixture to bake, prepare the two sauces. They can be transferred to bags if you want to pipe them later. Make the spicy mayo by mixing the mayo and sriracha sauce in a small bowl until well combined. Make the unagi sauce (if making) by combining all the ingredients in a saucepan and bringing to a simmer over medium heat. Once the sauce is at a simmer, let it cook for about 5 minutes or until it's glossy and has the consistency of a thin syrup. Remove from the heat and let the unagi sauce cool. It'll thicken more once cooled.
7. **Serve.** Add your desired amount of spicy mayo, unagi sauce, and furikake over the sushi bake. Serve while hot and enjoy by placing a spoonful of sushi bake on a sheet of seaweed snack and dressing it with avocado, cucumber, and if desired, more sauce. Leftovers can be stored in an airtight container in the fridge for up to 3 days.

Tips from our kitchen: If you're cooking the salmon from raw, season with salt and pepper, then pan sear in a nonstick pan over medium-high heat with a little oil for about 3–4 minutes per side, or bake in an oven preheated to 425°F (220°C) for about 15–20 minutes.

Meatless Mapo Tofu

We absolutely love classic mapo tofu with ground pork, but this meatless mapo tofu is *seriously* good. So let us show you how mushrooms can surprisingly rock your taste buds! We chose king trumpet mushrooms because they're like little flavor sponges that soak up all that spicy, savory mapo tofu seasoning and give you a satisfying meaty bite. Then you have the shiitake mushrooms that bring out the rich, umami flavor that takes the whole dish to the next level without the need to add meat. Now, all you need is to dig in with a bowl of rice, and this might just become your new favorite mapo tofu! — Mei

---

Prep time: **20 minutes**
Cook time: **10 minutes**
Makes: **2 servings**

- 2 (8g) dried shiitake mushrooms
- 14 oz (397g) soft tofu, cut into 1-inch (2.5cm) cubes and drained
- 3 tbsp (45ml) neutral cooking oil
- 2 tbsp (18g) minced garlic
- 1 tbsp (10g) minced ginger
- 1 tsp Chinese chili pepper flakes or crushed red pepper
- ½ tsp ground Sichuan peppercorn
- 1½ tbsp (30g) Chinese spicy bean paste (spicy doubanjiang)
- 1 medium (5oz/140g) king trumpet mushroom, finely chopped
- 1½ cups (360ml) water
- 1 tsp granulated sugar
- ¼ tsp kosher salt
- ½ tsp mushroom bouillon powder
- 3 tbsp (24g) cornstarch (mixed with 3 tbsp water)
- 1 stalk green onion, sliced
- 1 tsp toasted sesame oil

1. **Rehydrate the shiitake mushrooms.** To a heatproof bowl, add the dry shiitake mushrooms and cover them with boiling hot water. Let the mushrooms rehydrate for 15 minutes as you prepare the other ingredients. Once rehydrated, rinse the mushrooms to remove any debris and gently squeeze to remove extra moisture. Cut and remove the woody stalks, then finely chop the mushroom caps. For extra flavor, the mushroom water can be reserved and combined with more water to equal 1½ cups (360ml) to replace the regular water. Discard the bottom bits if there is debris.
2. **Purge the tofu (optional).** Purging helps to firm up the tofu, get rid of unwanted tofu flavor, and ironically, make the tofu less watery. To do so, bring a pot of water to a boil and season with salt. (We recommend about 2 teaspoons of salt per 4 cups of water.) Once the water is at a boil, gently add the soft tofu and bring it back to a simmer. Let the tofu simmer for about 1 minute, then drain it well gently. Set the tofu aside until needed.
3. **Make the mapo tofu.** To a well-seasoned wok or nonstick sauté pan over medium heat, add the oil. When the oil is hot, add the garlic, ginger, chili pepper, Sichuan peppercorn, and spicy bean paste. Sauté until fragrant, about 30 seconds. Next, add the chopped king trumpet and shiitake mushrooms. Sauté for about a minute or until the mushrooms have softened and wilted, then add the water and season with sugar, salt, and mushroom bouillon powder. Bring everything to a boil, then gently add the tofu. Let everything simmer for 3–5 minutes or until the saltiness is to your liking.
4. **Thicken the sauce.** Once the sauce has reduced to your desired saltiness, give the cornstarch slurry a good stir and drizzle it into the mapo tofu. Gently stir to incorporate the slurry and let the sauce simmer for 15–30 seconds to thicken and become glossy. If you prefer your sauce thinner, use only two-thirds of the cornstarch slurry first. Once the sauce thickens, you can decide whether to add the remaining slurry.
5. **Finish and serve.** Gently stir in the green onion and sesame oil and enjoy while it's hot. Leftovers of this mapo tofu can be refrigerated in an airtight container for 3–4 days.

Tips from our kitchen: To prevent the tofu from breaking too much in the cooking process, always stir the wok/pot in a pushing motion using the back of a spoon or spatula. Start from the edge of the pot and move toward the center while shaking the wok to help move the tofu.

Honey Garlic Tofu

Fried tofu may not be the first thing that comes to mind for most people when they think of something delicious, but tofu is actually a very good canvas for all your favorite sauces since it's so mild. One of our favorite ways to serve fried tofu is coating it in a sticky, sweet-and-savory honey garlic sauce. It's perfect with rice or in a rice bowl when you want a meatless meal. — Kyong

---

Prep time: **10 minutes**
Cook time: **15 minutes**
Makes: **2 servings**

Tofu

14 oz (396g) firm tofu
⅔ cup (85g) cornstarch
Neutral cooking oil, for frying

Sauce

1 tbsp (14g) unsalted butter
2 tbsp (18g) minced garlic
¼ cup (84g) honey
2 tbsp (25g) granulated sugar
2 tbsp (30ml) soy sauce

1. **Prepare the tofu.** Drain and cut the tofu into even cubes about 1 inch (2.5cm) thick, then use paper towels to pat them dry. As they sit, the tofu will release more moisture, so make sure to pat them dry again before coating them with the cornstarch.

2. **Prepare the fry station.** Heat about 2 inches (5cm) of oil to 350°F (175°C). Prepare a sheet pan with a rack or a plate lined with paper towels, and keep a spider strainer nearby.

3. **Coat the tofu.** To a large mixing bowl, add the cornstarch, then add the tofu cubes. Shake and toss the tofu cubes to coat them in the cornstarch. This part can be a little messy, so we recommend doing it over your kitchen sink. If needed, gently toss with your hands to get the tofu coated on all sides.

4. **Fry the tofu.** When the oil is ready, gently drop the tofu into the oil one piece at a time, shaking off excess cornstarch as needed. Fry the tofu for 5–7 minutes or until it's golden and crispy. Use the spider strainer to remove the tofu from the oil and let it drain on the prepared rack or plate.

5. **Make the sauce.** To a well-seasoned wok or large nonstick pan over medium heat, add the butter. Once the butter has melted, add the garlic and sauté until fragrant, about 15 seconds. Then add the honey, sugar, and soy sauce, and mix until well combined. Keeping it on medium heat, bring the sauce to a boil and let it cook for about 30 seconds to slightly thicken.

6. **Finish and serve.** To the sauce, add the crispy tofu and toss until all the tofu pieces are evenly coated. Enjoy it while it's hot with rice or in a rice bowl. Leftovers can be stored in an airtight container and refrigerated for up to 3 days.

Tips from our kitchen: Because tofu contains a lot of moisture, it's best to coat it in cornstarch just before frying to prevent large clumps from forming. However, after coating, let the tofu sit for about 30 seconds so the cornstarch can hydrate and adhere properly before it goes into the oil. For best results, start coating the tofu when the oil reaches about 300°F (150°C).

Pan-Seared Snapper with Pomegranate Persimmon Salsa

We always seem to have persimmons lying around when they're in season, and one of our favorite ways to enjoy them is by making salsa! I know—persimmons and salsa might not sound like a natural pairing, but it's surprisingly delicious, especially when combined with pomegranate. We usually find persimmons and pomegranates more in the fall or winter, so if it's out of season we like to swap it with mango. We like to serve this fruity and slightly tangy salsa with seared red snapper, as the snapper's buttery, crab-like flavor complements it perfectly. — Kyong

---

Prep time: **20 minutes**
Cook time: **about 10–12 minutes**
Makes: **2–3 servings**

Salsa

- 1 small (3oz/85g) ripe Fuyu persimmon, peeled and cut into ¼-inch (6mm) chunks
- ⅓ cup (2oz/57g) pomegranate seeds
- 1 small (30g) shallot, finely chopped
- ¼ cup (8g) roughly chopped cilantro
- 2 tbsp (30ml) lemon juice
- 1 tbsp (15g) packed dark brown sugar
- 1 tbsp (15ml) extra-virgin olive oil
- ½ tbsp (3g) lemon zest

Fish

- 2 red snapper filets (10–11oz/280–315g each)
- ½ tsp kosher salt (per filet)
- ⅛ tsp cracked black pepper (per filet)
- 2 tbsp (30ml) neutral cooking oil
- 1 small lemon, cut into wedges, for serving (optional)

1. **Make the salsa.** Place all the ingredients for the salsa into a medium bowl and mix until the sugar has dissolved. Cover and keep refrigerated until needed.

2. **Prepare the snapper.** Pat the snapper filets dry with paper towels then season with salt and pepper. Gently pat the filet to help the seasonings stick.

3. **Pan-sear the filets.** To a large pan over medium-high heat, add the oil. Once the oil is hot, arrange the filets in the pan skin-sides down and sear until the bottom two-thirds of the filets turn opaque and the skin is crispy. (Our filets are usually about ¾-inch (2cm) thick, so it took about 6–7 minutes.) Also, make sure to press down on the filet with a spatula for the first few minutes to help keep the filet flat and cook evenly, then flip the filets and cook for another 4–6 minutes or until cooked through and the internal temperature registers 145°F (63°C). Once cooked, transfer the filets skin-sides up to a serving plate.

4. **Finish and serve.** Top the pan-seared snapper with the prepared salsa. Enjoy while the fish is hot and, optionally, give the fish a squeeze of lemon juice for extra brightness and tanginess. Store leftovers in a sealed container in the fridge. Leftovers are best enjoyed within 2 days.

Tips from our kitchen: Fuyu (flat-shaped) and Hachiya (acorn-shaped) are the most common varieties of persimmon. The one we want to use for this recipe is Fuyu, and they are ripe when they turn a bright orange. At this point, they are still pretty firm and usually seedless. This is the stage best for our salsa. If you let them ripen longer, they'll turn deep orange and become very soft. Hachiya, on the other hand, will not be ready to eat until they turn deep orange and are very soft.

CHAPTER 6

Noodles + Pasta

Gochujang Pasta

By now, it's probably clear that we love gochujang—especially finding ways to use it in dishes outside of traditional Korean cuisine. My favorite way to incorporate it into a meal is with pasta, which Mei likes to joke is my second love. I particularly enjoy using it in a simple cream-based pasta, which balances the heat of the gochujang while creating a rich sauce in a beautiful shade of orange. — Kyong

---

Prep time: **5 minutes**
Cook time: **15 minutes**
Makes: **2 servings**

Kosher salt, for pasta water
8 oz (227g) dry rigatoni
3 tbsp (42g) unsalted butter
1 tbsp (9g) minced garlic
3 tbsp (54g) gochujang
1 cup (240ml) heavy cream
1 tsp granulated sugar
Parmesan cheese, grated (optional)
Green onions, sliced (optional)

1. **Boil the pasta.** Bring a medium pot of water to a boil over high heat and season with salt. We recommend adding 1 teaspoon of salt per quart of water (about 1L) of water. When the water comes to a boil, add the rigatoni and cook according to package instructions or until al dente. Once the pasta is cooked, reserve ½ cup (120ml) of the pasta water, then drain the pasta well.

2. **Make the sauce.** In a large sauté pan over medium to medium-low heat, melt the butter and add the garlic. Sauté the garlic until fragrant, about 15–20 seconds, then add the gochujang and sauté for another 10–15 seconds. Add the cream and sugar and mix until well combined, then let the sauce simmer for about 30 seconds. Add the pasta to the sauce along with the reserved pasta water, and simmer over medium heat for 3–4 minutes or until the sauce thickens, stirring occasionally.

3. **Serve.** Serve immediately, topped with grated Parmesan and green onion if desired. Store leftover pasta in an airtight container in the refrigerator for up to 3 days.

Tips from our kitchen: Depending on the brand of pasta, your pasta water may not be as starchy, which can make your sauce appear thin. If this happens, simmer and reduce the sauce for about a minute longer to get it to the right consistency.

Creamy Peanut Butter Miso Ramen

In under 30 minutes, you can create a creamy bowl of ramen with a rich broth made with peanut butter, miso, stock, and coconut milk. While the peanut butter dominates with its sweet, nutty flavor, the coconut milk and miso add a nice richness and umami that works well together. We love using instant ramen noodles, but feel free to use whatever noodles you have on hand and you can top it with some Chinese Chili Oil (page 240) to really make the dish shine! — Kyong

---

Prep time: **10 minutes**
Cook time: **10 minutes**
Makes: **2 servings**

- 2 large (100g) eggs
- 2 packs instant ramen noodles (4oz/113g per pack)
- 4 heads Shanghai or baby bok choy, halved and washed (optional)
- Sliced green onion (optional)
- Chinese Chili Oil (page 240) (optional)

Soup base

- 1 tbsp (15ml) neutral cooking oil
- 1 tbsp (10g) minced ginger
- 1 tbsp (9g) minced garlic
- 2 cups (480ml) unsalted chicken stock
- 1 cup (240ml) unsweetened coconut milk
- ¼ cup (64g) creamy peanut butter
- 2 tbsp (36g) white miso
- 1 tbsp (15ml) soy sauce
- 1 tsp sesame oil
- ½ tsp chicken bouillon powder (optional)

1. **Boil the eggs.** Cook the egg to your preferred doneness. (Refer to page 23 for details and cook time.)

2. **Make the soup base.** To a large saucepan over medium-high heat, add the oil. When the oil is hot, add the ginger and garlic and sauté until fragrant, about 15–30 seconds, then add the remaining soup base ingredients. Bring everything to a boil and whisk well to help dissolve the peanut butter and miso paste. Once the soup has come to a boil, reduce the heat to low to keep the soup warm.

3. **Cook the noodles and bok choy.** Bring a medium pot of water to a boil over high heat. Once at a boil, add the instant noodles and cook according to package instructions. (There's no need to add the dried vegetables or seasoning packet.) If using bok choy, add it towards the last 2 minutes of cooking if you want it more tender, or the last 30 seconds of cooking if you want it more crisp. When done cooking, drain the noodles and bok choy well and then portion them into 2 serving bowls.

4. **Finish and serve.** Divide the hot soup base between the bowls of noodles. Add the boiled eggs, and if desired, top each bowl with some green onion and chili oil. Instant noodles can become mushy quickly, so having leftovers is not recommended. However, the soup base can be stored in the fridge for up to 3 days.

Japchae

We love japchae not only because it's delicious, but also because it's incredibly versatile. You can swap in almost any vegetables you like, depending on what you have on hand. Our vegetable mix often rotates between carrots, onion, bell peppers, dried shiitake or other fresh mushrooms, and whatever leafy greens are in the fridge. We sometimes substitute the beef with pork loin or leave out the meat entirely, so feel free to make it your own. Lastly, if you're in a pinch and don't have honey or brown sugar, you can substitute one for the other or use regular granulated sugar in equal amounts—just note that using only honey will give the dish a more pronounced honey flavor. — Kyong

---

Prep time: **20 minutes**
Cook time: **20 minutes**
Makes: **4 servings**

Sauce

3 tbsp (45ml) soy sauce
2 tbsp (30ml) toasted sesame oil
1½ tbsp (32g) honey
1 tbsp (13g) packed dark brown sugar
½ tsp cracked black pepper

Noodles

3 (12g) dried shiitake mushrooms
6 oz (170g) dry sweet potato glass noodles
3 tbsp neutral cooking oil, divided, or as needed
1 large (50g) egg, beaten
8 oz (227g) sirloin steak, cut into ¼-inch (6mm) strips
1 medium (3oz/85g) carrot, peeled and julienned
½ large (7oz/200g) yellow onion, sliced
1 cup (1.5oz/45g) packed baby spinach
1 stalk green onion, cut into 2-inch (5cm) pieces
Kosher salt and cracked black pepper, as needed

1. **Prepare the sauce.** Add all the ingredients for the sauce to a bowl and mix until well combined. Set aside until needed.

2. **Prepare the shiitake mushrooms.** Place the dried mushrooms in a heatproof bowl and add enough hot water to fully cover them. Let the mushrooms soak for about 10–15 minutes or until rehydrated. Once ready, rinse the mushrooms well to remove any debris. Then cut and discard the woody stems and cut the mushroom caps into slices.

3. **Boil the noodles.** Bring a medium pot of water to a boil over high heat. When the water is at a boil, add the sweet potato noodles and cook according to package instructions or until the noodles are tender and easy to chew but still bouncy. Once cooked, drain the noodles and rinse thoroughly with cold water until the noodles are completely cooled, then drain the noodles really well. Optionally, cut the noodles with kitchen shears or on a cutting board with a knife into shorter strands so that it's easier to eat. We usually cut the noodles to around 10 inches (25cm).

4. **Cook the egg.** To a large sauté pan over medium heat, add about 1 tablespoon (15ml) of oil. Once hot, add the beaten egg and tilt the pan around to spread the egg thinly like a crepe. Don't worry if the egg isn't perfectly circular. When the egg has set on the bottom, flip it with a rubber spatula and cook for about 10 seconds, then transfer the egg to a cutting board and let it cool. Once it's cool enough to handle, fold the egg in half and cut it into thin strips. Set aside.

5. **Sauté the beef.** In the same pan over medium-high heat, add 1 tablespoon (15ml) of oil. When the oil is hot, add the beef and sauté until just cooked. Lightly season with some salt and pepper. Remove and set aside.

6. **Cook the vegetables.** Place the same pan (wiped clean with a paper towel, if needed), over medium-high heat and add the remaining 1 tablespoon (15 ml) of oil. When the oil is hot, add the carrot and cook for 2–3 minutes or until they are no longer crunchy. Next, add the onion and shiitake mushrooms and cook until the onion turns translucent, about 1 minute, then add the spinach and green onion and sauté until the spinach is just wilted, about 30 seconds to 1 minute. With each addition, season the vegetables with a pinch of salt and pepper and more oil as needed. Remove all the vegetables and set aside.

7. **Finish and serve.** To the same pan, add the prepared sauce and place over medium-high heat. Bring the sauce to a simmer, stirring to help dissolve the sugar. Once the sugar has dissolved and the sauce is hot, reduce the heat to low and add the noodles back into the pan. Give it a good mix, then add the beef, vegetables, and egg, and mix well. Enjoy the japchae warm, at room temperature, or even chilled. Leftovers can be stored in an airtight container and kept refrigerated for up to 3 days.

Braised Lamb Udon

There's a restaurant near where we live that serves a tomato lamb noodle dish that's absolutely to die for! But ever since they changed the recipe, it was never the same. So we decided to recreate it at home, and we gotta say, we deserve a pat on our backs. The lamb is braised in a savory tomato-soy-based sauce until it's incredibly tender and free of any gamey flavor, and with the mild heat from the addition of some Chinese chili pepper flakes, each bite becomes utterly addictive. We prefer the braised lamb with udon, but you can enjoy it with the noodles you have on hand. — Kyong

---

Prep time: **15 minutes**
Cook time: **1 hour 30 minutes**
Makes: **3–4 servings**

- 3 tbsp (45ml) neutral cooking oil
- 1½ lb (680g) boneless lamb shoulder, cut into ¼-inch (6mm) chunks
- ½ large (7oz/200g) yellow onion, diced
- 1 medium (4oz/113g) carrot, peeled and cut into ¼-inch (6mm) chunks
- 3 garlic cloves (12g), roughly chopped
- 3 cups (720ml) water
- 1 (14oz/397g) can diced tomatoes
- 8 oz (227g) gold potatoes, peeled and cut into ¼-inch (6mm) chunks
- 6 tbsp (90ml) soy sauce
- 4 tsp (17g) granulated sugar
- 2 tsp (4g) Chinese chili flakes or crushed red pepper (optional)
- 1 tsp dark soy sauce, for serving (optional)
- 3–4 bundles frozen udon (8.8oz/250g each)
- Chopped cilantro, for serving (optional)

1. **Braise the lamb.** To a well-seasoned wok or large pot over medium-high heat, add the oil. When the oil is hot, add the lamb and stir-fry until browned, stirring often, then add the onion, carrot, and garlic, and cook until fragrant, about 15–30 seconds. Next, add the water, tomatoes, potatoes, soy sauce, sugar, chili flakes, and dark soy sauce, then give everything a stir. Bring to a boil, then reduce the heat to medium or medium-low to keep the braise at a gentle simmer. Cover and braise for about 1 hour or until the lamb is tender. Stir occasionally.
2. **Reduce.** Once the lamb is tender, remove the lid and increase the heat to medium-high. Continue to simmer, stirring often, until the braise is reduced by about half the original amount and the consistency resembles a thick gravy. Keep it warm while you prepare the udon noodles.
3. **Prepare the udon.** Bring a pot of water to a boil and add the frozen udon. Cook for 40 seconds to 1 minute, or according to package instructions, until the noodles are hot and flexible. Drain well and place them into a serving bowl.
4. **Finish and serve.** Top the udon noodles with the hot braised lamb and some chopped cilantro if desired. Stir well before enjoying. Leftover braised lamb can be stored in an airtight container and refrigerated for up to 4 days or frozen for up to 3 months.

Soondubu Alfredo

One of the first pasta dishes I ever made growing up was Alfredo. I loved the simple, creamy, cheesy flavors, but the cream and milk never agreed with my stomach, so we would rarely eat it. Then, one day we had a light-bulb moment when Kyong and I were watching a Korean show where they made a dipping sauce using silken tofu (soondubu). We thought, "Why not try making Alfredo sauce with that?" And that's how this more lactose-friendly Alfredo recipe came about. It tastes just like traditional Alfredo sauce, and without the fat from the cream, the sauce doesn't break. It stays creamy! It was such an amazing discovery, we had to share it. You can enjoy the pasta as is or top it with your favorite proteins like shrimp, salmon, or chicken. — Mei

---

Prep time: **10 minutes**
Cook time: **20 minutes**
Makes: **4 servings**

- 2 tsp (11g) kosher salt, plus more for the pasta water
- 16 oz (454g) dry fettuccine
- 1 large (14oz/400g) yellow onion, sliced
- ¼ cup (60ml) extra-virgin olive oil
- 4 cloves garlic, sliced
- 16 oz (454g) silken tofu
- 2 cups (6oz/170g) grated Parmesan, plus more for garnish
- 1 tsp cracked black pepper, plus more for finishing
- Crushed red pepper, for finishing (optional)
- Chopped parsley, for garnish (optional)

1. **Boil pasta.** Bring a large pot of water to a boil over high heat and season with salt. We recommend adding 1 teaspoon of salt per quart of water (about 1L) of water. When the water comes to a boil, add the fettuccine and cook according to package instructions or until just al dente. Once the pasta is done cooking, reserve 1 cup (240ml) of pasta water, then drain the pasta.
2. **Sauté the aromatics.** While the pasta is cooking, add the olive oil to a large nonstick pan over medium heat. When the oil is hot, add the onion and cook until it just starts to brown. Add the garlic and cook for a few more minutes or until the onions are brown around the edges and the garlic is golden. Set aside.
3. **Blend.** To a high-power blender, add the silken tofu, the sautéed onion and garlic, and the pasta water. Blend until smooth.
4. **Finish and serve.** Wipe the pan that was used to sauté the onion and add the soondubu Alfredo sauce. Warm up the sauce over medium heat and add the grated Parmesan, salt, and black pepper. Stir until the cheese is melted and the sauce is hot, then add the fettuccine. Mix well until all the pasta is evenly coated. Portion and enjoy while it's hot. Garnish with more Parmesan, black pepper, crushed red pepper, and chopped parsley, if desired.

Perilla Pesto Pasta with Blistered Cherry Tomatoes

When we first started gardening, perilla was one of the first plants we grew. We had no idea it would grow so vigorously—almost like a weed—and we ended up planting nearly a dozen plants. That abundance led us to explore new ways to use perilla leaves beyond their usual role as a wrap for Korean BBQ. As a devoted pasta lover, I created this perilla pesto pasta as a perfect introduction for anyone new to pesto or looking for a milder, more balanced alternative to the classic basil version. — Kyong

---

Prep time: **20 minutes**
Cook time: **15 minutes**
Makes: **4 servings**

Kosher salt, for pasta water
12 oz (340g) dry linguine
1 pint (10oz/280g) cherry tomatoes
Neutral cooking oil, as needed
Grated Parmesan, for garnish (optional)

Perilla pesto
25–30 perilla leaves (about 2oz/57g)
⅓ cup (40g) walnuts
¼ cup (25g) grated Parmesan, tightly packed
2 tbsp (30ml) lemon juice
2 garlic cloves (8g), peeled
½ tsp kosher salt
A few cracks of black pepper
¾ cup (180ml) extra-virgin olive oil, divided

1. **Prepare the perilla leaves.** Cut and discard the thick stems of the perilla leaves, then gently rinse the leaves in a bowl of cold water. Bring a small pot of water to a boil and prepare a bowl of ice water. Add the perilla leaves to the boiling water and blanch for about 5 seconds or until they are wilted and turn bright green. Using tongs or a spider strainer, remove the perilla immediately and shock the leaves in the ice water. Swish the leaves around so that they cool faster. Once cooled, remove the leaves and gently squeeze to remove excess water.

2. **Make the perilla pesto.** To a high-power blender, add the prepared perilla leaves, walnuts, Parmesan, lemon juice, garlic, salt, black pepper, and about half of the olive oil. Turn the blender on low while drizzling in the remaining olive oil in a thin stream. Increase the speed as the pesto becomes smoother. Pause the blender and scrape down the sides, if needed. Once all of the olive oil has been added, gradually increase the blender to high speed to fully emulsify the pesto. Set aside until needed. The perilla pesto should be used immediately after making. If not used immediately, transfer the pesto into an airtight container suitable for the amount of pesto and top with a thin layer of extra-virgin olive oil to keep it from browning. Keep refrigerated for up to 4 days.

3. **Boil the pasta.** Bring a large pot of water to a boil over high heat and season with salt. We recommend adding 1 teaspoon of salt per quart of water (about 1L) of water. When the water comes to a boil, add the linguine and cook according to package instructions or until al dente. Once the pasta is cooked, reserve 1 cup (240ml) of the pasta water then drain the pasta well.

4. **Blister the tomatoes.** While the pasta is cooking, blister the tomatoes. To a large pan over medium-high heat, add enough oil to lightly grease the bottom of the pan. Once the pan is hot, add the tomatoes and cook for a couple of minutes or until you see blistered spots. Shake the pan occasionally. If your tomatoes are really hardy, add a splash of water and cover with a lid so the tomatoes can steam. When the tomatoes are blistered to your preference and have softened, remove the tomatoes from the pan and set aside. Wipe the pan clean with a paper towel.

5. **Finish and serve.** To the same pan over low heat, add two-thirds of the reserved pasta water, the cooked pasta, and all of the pesto. Shake the pan and mix the pasta until the pesto is creamy and the pasta is evenly coated. If needed, add more of the remaining pasta water to thin out the sauce. Add the blistered tomatoes back into the pan and give it a quick mix. Serve the pasta immediately and garnish with more cheese if desired.

Tips from our kitchen: You can usually find perilla leaves in the produce aisles of large Asian markets like 99 Ranch and H Mart. Korean markets will usually have them in stock.

Kimchi Carbonara

Alright, let's nip this in the bud right away: yes, I use whole eggs for this carbonara. Traditionally, carbonara is made with just yolks. So why whole eggs? Simple—I don't want leftover egg whites hanging around, and honestly, the result is just as creamy and satisfying. What really sets this version apart, though, is the kimchi. It's sautéed in the rendered fat from guanciale, infusing it with smoky, savory richness before getting tossed with the creamy egg and Parmesan base to create a bold, tangy, and umami-rich sauce that clings beautifully to the pasta. There's beauty in tradition, and I am not an advocate for breaking traditions. But if it tastes good and you love it, that's what really matters. — Kyong

---

Prep time: **10 minutes**
Cook time: **15 minutes**
Makes: **2 servings**

- Kosher salt, for pasta water
- 8 oz (227) dry spaghetti
- Neutral cooking oil, as needed
- 3 oz (85g) guanciale, diced
- 1 cup (220g) fermented kimchi, roughly chopped
- 2 large (100g) eggs
- 1 cup (60g) grated Parmesan cheese, loosely packed, plus more for garnish
- ¼ tsp cracked black pepper
- Sliced green onions or chives (optional)

1. **Boil pasta.** Bring a medium pot of water to a boil and season with kosher salt. We recommend 1 teaspoon of kosher salt per 1 quart of water. When the water comes to a boil, add the pasta and cook according to package instructions or until al dente. Once the pasta is cooked, reserve ¼ cup (60ml) of the pasta water, then drain the pasta well. Set aside.
2. **Cook the guanciale and kimchi while waiting for the pasta.** To a medium or large pan over medium heat, add enough oil to lightly oil the pan. Add the guanciale and cook until the fat is well rendered, then remove the guanciale from the pan and set aside. Leave about 1 tablespoon (15ml) of rendered fat in the pan and discard the rest. Heat the pan over medium heat and add the chopped kimchi. Sauté for about 5 minutes, stirring often, until most of the kimchi juice has evaporated. Set aside.
3. **Prepare the carbonara sauce.** Crack the eggs into a large heatproof bowl and add the grated Parmesan and black pepper. Whisk until everything is well combined.
4. **Finish and serve.** Add the hot pasta water, pasta, kimchi, and rendered guanciale to the prepared carbonara sauce. Mix with a pair of tongs in a circular direction until the pasta is creamy. Serve the carbonara immediately and top with more grated Parmesan, cracked black pepper, and chopped chives (if using).

Tips from our kitchen: Guanciale can be a little difficult to find and is usually only available at specialty stores. You can substitute with equal amounts of pancetta or thick-cut bacon. If you're using guanciale or pancetta, ask the deli to cut them to ½-inch (1cm) slices.

Kabocha Gnocchi with Brown Butter, Sage, and Ricotta

When we were developing *Fork & Chopsticks*, we wanted to explore creative ways to use kabocha squash. It's become quite a staple in our pantry over the past few years—and the first thing that came to mind was gnocchi. These beautifully orange-colored gnocchi have the pillowy, tender texture of classic potato gnocchi, complemented by the squash's natural sweetness. Paired with fragrant sage, the nuttiness of brown butter, and the creaminess of ricotta, it's a dish that feels both comforting and elevated. — Kyong

Prep time: **1 hour**
Cook time: **15 minutes**
Makes: **3–4 servings**

1 lb (454g) raw kabocha squash, peeled, deseeded, and cut into 1-inch (2.5cm) chunks
1 large (50g) egg
½ tsp kosher salt
Generous dash of ground nutmeg
¾–1 cup (90–120g) all-purpose flour, plus more for dusting
Kosher salt, for pasta water
8 tbsp (113g) unsalted butter
3–4 sprigs fresh sage

For serving
Ricotta
Cracked black pepper

1. **Prepare the kabocha squash.** Use your preferred method to steam the kabocha until tender. A classic steamer setup will take about 15 minutes to cook the squash. Make sure to drain off excess liquid/condensation that collects on the plate. Alternatively, cook the kabocha in the microwave. Place the kabocha in a single layer on a microwavable plate and cover tightly with plastic wrap. Microwave on high for about 7 minutes or until completely tender. Drain any excess moisture if needed. Every microwave is different, so you may need to adjust the time. Once cooked, let the kabocha cool until it's comfortable to handle, then mash it well. You should end up with about 1½ cups (375g) of mashed kabocha. Set aside to cool until needed.

2. **Make the dough.** In a mixing bowl, mix together the mashed kabocha, egg, salt, and nutmeg with gloved hands or a rubber spatula until well combined. Start with ¾ cup (90g) of flour and mix until just combined. The dough should be somewhat tacky but not sticky and can easily hold its shape. You may or may not need a little more flour depending on your kabocha's moisture content and the humidity in your area. Make sure not to overmix the dough. Once no more dry flour is visible, stop mixing.

3. **Shape the gnocchi.** Prepare a sheet pan dusted with flour. Turn your gnocchi dough out onto a floured work surface and divide it into 4 equal-size portions. Working with one portion at a time, roll the dough into a ½-inch (1cm) rope, then cut the rope into 1-inch (2.5cm) pieces. If you'd like to get those classic gnocchi grooves, roll each piece of gnocchi with your palm over the prongs of a fork or a gnocchi board. When making the grooves, make sure to lightly dust your gnocchi as needed and also tap out any excess flour from the gnocchi board when the grooves become less visible. When a gnocchi is done, place it onto the prepared sheet pan. Repeat this process with the remaining dough and apply more flour as needed during the shaping process.

4. **Cook the gnocchi.** Bring a pot of water to a boil and season with salt. We recommend about 1 teaspoon of salt per 4 cups (about 1L) of water. When the water is boiling, give it a good stir, then gently add the gnocchi. Avoid adding any excess flour if possible. Let the gnocchi cook until they start to float. Once floating, let them cook for another 30 seconds or until cooked through, then drain well.

5. **Sauté the gnocchi.** When the gnocchi has been drained, heat a large pan over medium-high heat and add the butter. Let the butter melt, and when it just starts to brown, add the sage and the drained gnocchi. Sauté until the sage is fragrant, the butter smells nutty, and the gnocchi starts to get crispy and golden brown. Gently shake the pan to toss the gnocchi to prevent them from breaking. We recommend sautéing in batches, depending on the size of your pan, so you can get an even color on the gnocchi.

6. Finish and serve. Smear a generous dollop (about 3 tablespoons) of ricotta onto the bottom of each serving bowl, then portion the sautéed gnocchi and sage (optional) on top of the ricotta. Top with a few cracks of black pepper and enjoy while hot. Leftovers can be refrigerated for up to 3 days.

Tips from our kitchen: If a full batch of kabocha gnocchi is more than you need, you can freeze the extra gnocchi. To do so, arrange the shaped (raw) gnocchi in a single layer on a parchment-lined, lightly floured sheet pan. Freeze until solid, then transfer to a freezer-safe bag or container. They will be good for up to 3 months frozen.

Cold Ramen

Cold ramen may sound unusual, as it is traditionally served hot. However, if you've ever enjoyed naengmyeon, a classic Korean cold noodle dish, this preparation will feel familiar. Served cold, the noodles maintain a pleasantly bouncy texture, and the chilled broth is seasoned with your favorite instant ramen packet, a splash of vinegar for brightness, and some sugar and soy sauce for balance. This recipe transforms the instant ramen we grew up eating into something cold and refreshing! You can garnish it with crisp cucumber and a boiled egg to make it a quick, light meal. — Mei

---

Prep time: **10 minutes**
Cook time: **6–12 minutes**
Makes: **1 serving**

1 large (50g) egg
1 (4oz/113g) pack instant ramen noodles
1 cup (240ml) cold water
2 tbsp (30ml) white vinegar
2 tsp (8g) sugar
1 tsp soy sauce
¼ (75g) English cucumber, julienned
Toasted sesame seeds (optional)

1. **Boil the egg.** Cook the egg to your preferred doneness. (Refer to page 23 for details and cook time.)
2. **Boil the noodles.** Bring another small pot of water to a boil over high heat. Set the seasoning packet aside and add the instant noodles to the water along with the dried vegetables. Cook the noodles according to the package instructions until al dente, then drain the noodles and vegetables using a mesh strainer. Rinse the noodles with cold water until completely cooled. Drain well.
3. **Make the cold broth.** While waiting for the noodles to cook, mix together the 1 cup of cold water, white vinegar, sugar, soy sauce, and the entire packet of the ramen seasoning in a serving bowl.
4. **Assemble and serve.** When ready to serve, you can add a small handful of ice cubes to the cold broth to make it extra cold and refreshing, then place the cooled ramen (with the vegetables) into the broth. Top with the cucumber, boiled egg, and sesame seeds, if desired. Enjoy immediately.

Tantanmen Udon

Tantanmen is a Japanese adaptation of Chinese dan dan noodles that's similar yet very different. Dan dan noodles is a dry noodle dish, while tantanmen is a noodle dish served in a creamy broth. In our version of tantanmen, we opted for udon instead of ramen noodles because we love the bouncy, chewiness of udon noodles. We used ground chicken for the ground meat topping but you can swap it for lean ground pork or beef. It's cooked with aromatics and seasoned with doubanjiang—the spicy fermented broad bean paste—to bring a bold balance of heat, saltiness, and umami to the noodle dish. Also, instead of the traditional sesame paste, we use a combination of peanut butter and miso paste to create a nutty, savory broth that's ready for slurping! — Kyong

---

Prep time: **15 minutes**
Cook time: **15 minutes**
Makes: **2 servings**

Toppings

- 2 large (100g) eggs
- 2 bundles frozen udon noodles (8.8oz/250g each)
- 2–4 heads Shanghai or baby bok choy, cut in half and washed
- Sliced green onion (optional)
- Toasted sesame seeds (optional)

Ground chicken

- 1 tbsp (15ml) neutral cooking oil
- ½ tbsp (5g) minced garlic
- ½ tbsp (5g) minced ginger
- 1 tbsp (20g) Chinese spicy bean paste (spicy doubanjiang)
- 8 oz (227g) ground chicken
- 1 tbsp (15ml) Shaoxing rice wine

Soup base

- 1 tbsp (15ml) neutral cooking oil
- ½ tbsp (5g) minced garlic
- ½ tbsp (5g) minced ginger
- 2 cups (480ml) unsalted chicken stock
- 1 cup (240ml) unsweetened coconut milk
- 2 tbsp (42g) creamy peanut butter
- 1 tbsp (18g) white miso
- 1 tbsp (15ml) soy sauce
- 2 tsp (10ml) Chinese Chili Oil (page 240), plus more as desired

1. **Boil the eggs.** Cook the eggs to your preferred doneness. (Refer to page 23 for details and cook time.)

2. **Prepare the udon noodles.** Bring a medium pot of water to a boil and add the frozen udon noodles. Cook for 40 seconds to 1 minute, or according to package instructions, until the noodles are hot and flexible. Drain well and portion them into 2 serving bowls.

3. **Cook the ground chicken.** To a medium nonstick pan over medium-high heat, add the oil. When the oil is hot, add the garlic, ginger, and spicy bean paste. Sauté until fragrant, about 15–30 seconds, then add the ground chicken and cook until it's no longer pink and is cooked through. Make sure to break up the chicken as you cook. Once the chicken is cooked, finish by drizzling in the rice wine and sauté for another 30 seconds to cook off the alcohol. Set aside until needed.

4. **Make the soup base.** To a large saucepan over medium-high heat, add the oil. When the oil is hot, add the garlic and ginger, and sauté until fragrant, about 15–30 seconds, then add the stock, coconut milk, peanut butter, miso, soy sauce, and chili oil, and bring the soup to a simmer. Use a whisk to help dissolve the peanut butter and miso.

5. **Cook the bok choy.** When the soup comes to a simmer, add the bok choy and cook for 30 seconds to 2 minutes, depending on how cooked you prefer the bok choy.

6. **Assemble and serve.** Divide the soup amongst the bowls and top with the cooked bok choy, boiled eggs, ground chicken, and if desired, green onion, sesame seeds, and more chili oil. Enjoy it while it's hot. We don't recommend having leftover udon noodles as they'll bloat, but leftover soup and chicken can be stored in the fridge for up to 4 days.

Tips from our kitchen: We prefer using frozen udon noodles (available at most Asian markets) because they have the best texture. However, you can use dry or vacuum-packed udon noodles or even regular dry wheat noodles as an alternative.

Miso Garlic Mushroom Pasta

This miso garlic mushroom pasta is like an adult version of the butter noodles kids love to order at dine-in restaurants, except it's delightfully garlicky and tastes creamy and rich from the butter and miso. It's a simple pasta dish that really grows on you the more you eat. We also made an unusual discovery—a little side of our Gochujang Bacon Jam (page 38) goes deliciously with this pasta dish! — Kyong

---

Prep time: **10 minutes**
Cook time: **15 minutes**
Makes: **2 servings**

Kosher salt, for pasta water
8 oz (227g) dry fettuccine
4 tbsp (57g) unsalted butter
8 oz (227g) baby portobello mushrooms, sliced
3 tbsp (30g) roughly chopped garlic
¼ tsp crushed red pepper
⅛ tsp cracked black pepper, plus more for finishing
2 tbsp (36g) white miso
Grated Parmesan, for garnish (optional)
Chopped parsley, for garnish (optional)

1. **Boil the pasta.** Bring a medium pot of water to a boil over high heat and season with salt. We recommend adding 1 teaspoon of salt per quart of water (about 1L) of water. When the water comes to a boil, add the fettuccine and cook according to package instructions or until just al dente. Once the pasta is done, reserve ½ cup (120ml) of pasta water, then drain the pasta well.

2. **Start the sauce.** While the pasta cooks, place a large pan over medium-high heat and add the butter. Once the butter has melted, add the mushrooms and sauté until golden brown, about 6–8 minutes. Add the garlic and cook until fragrant, about 15–30 seconds. Stir in the crushed red pepper and black pepper and sauté briefly, about 10–15 seconds, then set aside.

3. **Bring the dish together.** When the pasta water is ready, whisk the miso paste with the reserved pasta water until well combined. Add the mixture to the pan with the mushrooms, along with the fettuccine. Bring to a boil over medium-high heat, stirring constantly, until the sauce slightly thickens and the pasta is evenly coated.

4. **Finish and serve.** Transfer the pasta to serving plates. If desired, top with cracked black pepper, grated Parmesan, and parsley. Enjoy it while it's hot. Leftover pasta can be stored in an airtight container and refrigerated for up to 3 days.

Cumin Lamb Noodles

While we were working in New York, we tried Xi'an Famous Foods and were instantly captivated by the bold flavors, the chewy texture of the hand-pulled noodles, and of course, the free noodle-pulling show while we waited for our food. Their cumin lamb noodles quickly became our favorite, even though the spiciness left us with red-rimmed eyes and tears streaming down our faces. This recipe is our take on that unforgettable dish—with a few personal touches and a more tolerable level of heat. For the lamb, we like to use lamb shoulders and slice it ourselves for the best and most authentic texture, but if you can't find boneless lamb shoulder or have one deboned, you can substitute it with thinly sliced lamb used for hotpot/shabu-shabu. — Kyong

---

Prep time: **35 minutes**
Cook time: **15–20 minutes**
Makes: **4 servings**

Lamb

1 lb (454g) boneless lamb shoulder or thinly sliced lamb for hotpot/shabu shabu
1 tbsp (15ml) Shaoxing rice wine
½ tsp fine salt
½ tsp baking soda
2 tsp (6g) cornstarch
2 tsp neutral cooking oil

Spice mix

1 tbsp (8g) cumin seeds
1 tsp Sichuan peppercorn
½ tsp coriander seeds

Sauce

¼ cup (60g) Chinese Chili Oil (homemade [page 240] or store-bought)
3 tbsp (45ml) Chinese black vinegar
3 tbsp (45ml) soy sauce
1 tsp granulated sugar
1 tsp dark soy sauce

For the rest of the stir-fry

3 oz (85g) Asian chives
1 batch of homemade hand-pulled noodles (page 165) or 8 oz (227g) dry knife-sliced noodles
Neutral cooking oil, as needed
1½ tbsp (14g) minced garlic
1 tbsp (10g) minced ginger root
8 oz (225g) green cabbage, cut into 1-inch (2.5cm) pieces
1 rib (1.5oz/42g) regular or Chinese celery, cut into ¼-inch (6mm) slices
½ large (7oz/200g) red onion, sliced
½ cup (15g) roughly chopped cilantro, divided

1. **Velvet the lamb.** If using lamb shoulder, cut the lamb against the grain into slices no thicker than ¼ inch (6mm). Add the sliced lamb (or thinly sliced lamb for hotpot) to a bowl along with the rice wine, salt, and baking soda. Mix until the rice wine is absorbed, then add the cornstarch and mix until evenly coated. Lastly, mix in the oil until combined. Cover and let the lamb marinate at room temperature for 30 minutes or overnight in the fridge and up to 3 days.

2. **Toast the spices.** Add all the spices to a pan and toast over medium heat until fragrant, about 3–5 minutes. Let the spices cool then transfer to a mortar and pestle or a spice blender and grind finely. Set aside until needed.

3. **Make the sauce.** In a bowl, mix together all the sauce ingredients and set aside. Before use, give it a good stir.

4. **Prepare the Asian chives.** Asian chives can sometimes hold dirt in between the leaves at the bottom of the stalk. Make sure to rinse it well. Also, because the bottom of the Asian chives can be quite woody; cut and discard the bottom 1 inch (2.5cm) of the chive. Cut the chive into 1-inch (2.5cm) pieces.

5. **Boil the noodles.** Bring a medium pot of water to a boil over high heat. If using store-bought noodles, cook according to the package instructions until al dente. If making your homemade hand-pulled noodles, follow the instructions on page 165.

6. **Pan fry the lamb.** To a well-seasoned wok or large pan over medium heat, add enough oil to generously cover the bottom of the wok. When the oil is hot and shimmering, add the lamb pieces and stir quickly to separate them. Pan fry the lamb until it is about 90 percent cooked. Cook in batches, if needed. Remove from the wok and set aside.

7. **Bring the dish together.** To the same wok or a large nonstick pan over medium-high heat, add enough oil so that there's about 2 tablespoons (30ml). Once the oil is hot, add the minced garlic and ginger and stir-fry until fragrant, about 15 seconds. Then add the cabbage, celery, and onion, and stir-fry until the vegetables just begin to wilt, about 1 minute. Add the lamb and toss briefly to combine, then sprinkle in the spice mix and toss again. Add the noodles and sauce, and stir-fry until everything is well combined.

8. **Finish and serve.** Finish by adding the Asian chives and half of the cilantro, tossing well to incorporate. Garnish with the remaining cilantro and refrigerate any leftovers in an airtight container for up to 3 days.

Tips from our kitchen: This recipe is largely dependent on timing so that everything stays hot. Timing the noodles to cook perfectly on time for when you need to add them can be tricky. So, if needed, keep a pot of boiling water hot on your stove after the noodles are cooked, and before you toss your noodles into the stir-fry, give them a dip in the hot water to separate the noodles and re-warm them. But make sure to drain them well before adding to the stir-fry.

1

2

3

4

Homemade Hand-Pulled Wide Noodles

Store-bought noodles are convenient but making hand-pulled noodles at home is a fun experience and doubles as an impressive tableside show for your lucky guests! This is an easy version that makes wide noodles perfect for saucy dishes and stir-fries like our Cumin Lamb Noodles (page 162). This is perfect for days when you're feeling up for a fun challenge. — Mei

---

Prep time: **15 minutes, plus 2 or more hours of resting time**
Cook time: **5 minutes**
Makes: **1 batch (3–4 servings)**

1¼ cup (150g) all-purpose flour
½ tsp fine salt
⅓ cup (80ml) plus 1 tbsp (15ml) water
Neutral oil, for coating

1. **Prepare the noodles.** In a mixing bowl, mix together the flour and salt. Add the water and mix until the dough comes together and no more dry flour is left. Cover and let the dough rest for 10–15 minutes, then knead the dough until smooth. Roll the dough into a long rope about 1 inch (2.5cm) thick, then divide it into 4 even-size pieces. Using a rolling pin, flatten each piece of dough into an oval-ish slab about ⅛-inch (3mm) thick. Generously coat each slab of dough with oil and arrange them on a sheet pan or plate. Cover the dough with cling film, making sure the film is touching the dough, and let it rest at room temperature for at least 2 hours or overnight in the fridge.

2. **Pull the noodles.** When you're ready to use the noodles, bring a medium pot of water to a boil over high heat. When the water starts to boil, start pulling the noodles. Place a slab of the dough flat on your work surface and indent lengthwise firmly across the dough using a flat edge, like a chopstick (photo 1). Next, hold the short ends of the dough in your hands, between your fingers and your palm (photo 2). Pull in one smooth motion until the dough is about as long as your arm span. Feel for the tension, and when the dough starts to feel tight, stop pulling, then give the dough a flick with your wrists to stretch the noodle to its maximum length (photo 3). Finish by splitting the pulled noodle into two strands along the indentation you made with the chopstick (photo 4).

3. **Boil the noodles.** Drop the pulled noodles into the boiling water and quickly repeat with the rest of the dough. Let the noodles cook until they float to the surface and cook for another 30 seconds. Drain well.

Shrimp Red Curry with Noodles

I'm a huge fan of coconut milk and often use it in place of milk and heavy cream, partly because I'm lactose intolerant, but also because I love how it tastes and how creamy it is. So, it's not surprising that this shrimp red curry is one of my favorite recipes. I love that the shrimp are juicy and bouncy while the vegetables add crisp textures to the curry. The soup base is made with red curry, stock, and coconut milk, making it rich, creamy, and fragrant with fish sauce to add extra umami—perfect for noodles to soak up all the flavors! — Mei

---

Prep time: **15 minutes**
Cook time: **10–15 minutes**
Makes: **2 servings**

½ lb (227g) jumbo shrimp, peeled and deveined
¼ tsp kosher salt
6 oz (170g) dry wheat noodles of choice
Roughly chopped cilantro

Soup

2 tbsp (30ml) neutral cooking oil
⅓ cup (80g) Mae Ploy red curry paste
1 tbsp (9g) minced garlic
1 tbsp (10g) minced ginger
2 cups (480ml) unsalted seafood stock or water
1 can (13.5fl oz/400ml) unsweetened coconut milk
2 tbsp (30ml) fish sauce
2 tbsp (25g) granulated sugar
2 heads Shanghai or baby bok choy, halved and washed
½ (3.5oz/100g) red bell pepper, core discarded and cut into 1-inch (2.5cm) chunks
¼ large (3.5oz/100g) yellow onion, cut into 1-inch (2.5cm) chunks
½ medium (1.5oz/43g) carrot, peeled and cut into thin slices

1. **Season the shrimp.** Place the shrimp in a bowl and season with salt. Mix well and set aside until needed.

2. **Make the soup.** To a large saucepan over medium-high heat, add the oil. When the oil is hot, add the curry paste, garlic, and ginger, and sauté for about a minute, then add the stock (or water), coconut milk, fish sauce, and sugar, and bring to a boil. Once the soup is at a boil, add the bok choy, bell pepper, onion, and carrot and bring it back to a boil. Then add the shrimp and cook for 1–2 minutes or until the shrimp are cooked through. The shrimp should turn orange and curl into a tight C shape. Set the soup aside and keep warm.

3. **Boil the noodles.** Bring a medium pot of water to a boil and add the noodles. Cook the noodles according to the package instructions or until just cooked. Drain well and divide the noodles into 2 serving bowls.

4. **Serve.** Evenly divide the soup, vegetables, and shrimp between the bowls of noodles and top with chopped cilantro. Enjoy while it's hot. Leftover soup can be refrigerated for up to 3 days.

Fujianese-Style Creamy Peanut Noodles

Growing up in a Fujianese household, there's one classic dish I always find myself craving: Fujianese-style noodles coated in a creamy peanut sauce. It's classic to pair these noodles with a bowl of tangy wonton soup, but honestly, these noodles are so good, we eat them on their own at least once a week. Kyong likes to top his with extra green onions and a drizzle of chili oil, but feel free to enjoy them however you like.
— Mei

Prep time: **5 minutes**
Cook time: **7 minutes**
Makes: **1 serving**

- 3.5 oz (100g) flat dry wheat noodles
- 2 tbsp (32g) creamy peanut butter
- 1 tbsp (15ml) neutral oil
- ½ tsp dark soy sauce
- ¼ tsp fine salt
- ¼ tsp sugar
- ⅛ tsp MSG
- 1 tsp (4g) lard
- 1 stalk green onion (green parts only), thinly sliced

1. **Cook the noodles.** Bring a small or medium pot of water to a boil over high heat and add the noodles. Cook according to the package instructions or until just cooked, stirring occasionally to prevent the noodles from sticking to the bottom of the pot. Once the noodles are cooked, reserve ¼ cup (60ml) of the noodle water and then drain the noodles well.
2. **Make the sauce.** While the noodles are cooking, make the sauce by combining the peanut butter, oil, dark soy sauce, salt, sugar, and MSG in a serving bowl or plate. Mix until the sauce looks emulsified. Add the lard to the bowl (no need to mix) and set aside.
3. **Mix the sauce and noodles.** When the noodles are ready, add them to the prepared sauce along with 2–3 tablespoons (30–45ml) of the reserved hot noodle water. Mix well until the lard has melted and the noodles are evenly covered with the sauce. If the sauce looks too thick, you can thin it out with additional noodle water.
4. **Finish and serve.** Top with green onions and enjoy while hot.

Tips from our kitchen: We like to use flat wheat noodles for this recipe, but you can use any thin noodles or pasta that are at your disposal. We've tried it using instant ramen noodles, linguine, and both regular and thin spaghetti, and have liked them all. Also, if you prefer, you can omit the lard. It does provide an additional dose of savoriness, but the noodles will still taste delicious without it.

Night Market Spaghetti

While visiting China, we found ourselves dining at street food stalls for dinner quite often because there's almost an endless array of options. But there was one stall we returned to on more than a few occasions, and it was for their black pepper spaghetti. The pasta was made with crisp but cooked onions and tossed in a dark, peppery sauce made with surprisingly familiar ingredients like black pepper, soy sauce, brown sugar, and Worcestershire sauce. It was served on a sizzling hot cast-iron platter, giving the pasta a lovely smoky flavor. Topped with a perfectly fried egg and an order of sizzling steak, each bite captures the vibrant energy and excitement of the bustling night market. — Mei

---

Prep time: **10 minutes**
Cook time: **15 minutes**
Makes: **2 servings**

- Kosher salt, for pasta water
- 6 oz (170g) dry spaghetti
- 2 tbsp (30ml) soy sauce
- 2 tbsp (30ml) Worcestershire sauce
- 2 tbsp (30ml) water
- 1 tbsp (15g) dark brown sugar
- 1 tsp black pepper, preferably coarsely ground
- 2 tbsp (30ml) neutral cooking oil, or as needed
- ¼ large (3.5oz/100g) yellow onion, sliced
- 3 cloves (8g) garlic, sliced
- 2 large (100g) eggs, for serving (optional)

1. **Boil the pasta.** Bring a medium pot of water to a boil over high heat and season with salt. We recommend adding 1 teaspoon of salt per quart of water (about 1L) of water. When the water comes to a boil, add the pasta and cook according to package instructions or until al dente. Drain and set aside.

2. **Make the sauce.** In a bowl, combine the soy sauce, Worcestershire sauce, water, brown sugar, and black pepper. Set aside until needed.

3. **Finish the pasta.** To a large pan over medium-high heat, add the oil. Once hot, add the onion and garlic and sauté until fragrant and the garlic just begins to turn golden. Add the prepared sauce and bring it to a boil. Then add the spaghetti and cook in the sauce, mixing and tossing often, until most of the sauce is absorbed and the pasta is well coated. Transfer to serving plates and enjoy as is, or top with a fried egg.

4. **Make the fried eggs (optional).** In a medium or large frying pan over medium-high heat, add a couple tablespoons of oil, or as needed for frying the eggs. Once the oil is shimmering and just starting to smoke, crack in the eggs and fry until the bottoms are golden brown and the egg whites are set, about 3 minutes.

CHAPTER 7

Soups + Stews + Braises

Gochujang Chicken Stew

This stew is a deeply comforting dish that I grew up eating often. It's loaded with chicken drumsticks and hearty chunks of vegetables, all stewed until the meat is tender and the vegetables are soft. It tastes slightly sweet with a mild heat from the gochujang, making it easily a high-ranking rice thief. Also, like any stew, this is perfect for making a big pot of and enjoying over several days. I understand now why my mom made it so often for dinner when she was busy with work: this recipe is the definition of a super flavorful but minimal-effort one-pot meal. — Kyong

---

Prep time: **15 minutes**
Cook time: **45–50 minutes**
Makes: **5 servings**

- 2 lb (907g) chicken drumsticks
- 2 cups (480ml) water
- ⅓ cup (80ml) soy sauce
- 3 tbsp (21g) coarse gochugaru
- 2 tbsp (36g) gochujang
- 2 tbsp (30ml) Shaoxing rice wine
- 2 tbsp (25g) granulated sugar
- 3 tbsp (27g) minced garlic
- 1 lb (454g) gold potatoes, peeled and cut into 2-inch (5cm) chunks
- 1 large (6oz/170g) carrot, peeled and cut into 1-inch (2.5cm) chunks
- ½ large (7oz/200g) yellow onion, cut into 1-inch (2.5cm) chunks
- 2 stalks green onion, cut into 1-inch (2.5cm) pieces (greens and white pieces separated)

1. **Cook the chicken.** Place the drumsticks, water, soy sauce, gochugaru, gochujang, rice wine, sugar, and garlic into a large pot and bring to a boil over medium-high heat. Reduce the heat to medium-low to low to keep the stew at a simmer, and cover with a lid. Cook for 20 minutes.
2. **Stew with vegetables.** After 20 minutes, add the potatoes, carrot, yellow onion, and the white parts of the green onions. Bring the stew back to a boil over medium-high heat, then once again reduce the heat to medium-low to low to keep the stew at a simmer. Cover and cook for another 25–30 minutes or until the potatoes and chicken are both fork-tender.
3. **Finish and serve.** To finish, stir in the green parts of the green onions and enjoy hot with a side of rice. Leftovers can be stored in an airtight container and kept refrigerated for up to 4 days.

Korean-Style Pot Roast

We love recipes that are very involved, but sometimes we just want a deeply flavorful and comforting dish that we can leave mostly to the oven. This Korean-style pot roast is just that! We love how the onions melt into the sauce as it cooks and add a natural sweetness. We also love the subtle heat gochujang brings to the sauce, and the pairing of soy sauce and brown sugar that thoroughly seasons the incredibly tender beef. Enjoy the pot roast with some rice along with a side of some simple Garlic Bok Choy Stir-Fry (page 66) and some fresh or fermented Kimchi (page 236). — Kyong

---

Prep time: **10 minutes**
Cook time: **3–3½ hours**
Makes: **4–6 servings**

- 4½–5 lb (2–2.3kg) well-marbled chuck roast
- 1 tbsp (16g) kosher salt
- 1 tsp cracked black pepper
- 2 tbsp (30ml) neutral cooking oil
- 1 large (14oz/400g) yellow onion, thinly sliced
- 2 tbsp (36g) gochujang
- 2 tbsp (18g) minced garlic
- 1 tbsp (10g) minced ginger
- 2 cups (480ml) unsalted beef stock
- ¼ cup (55g) packed dark brown sugar
- ¼ cup (60ml) soy sauce
- 1 tbsp (15ml) toasted sesame oil

1. **Preheat the oven to 350°F (175°C).**

2. **Season and sear the chuck roast.** Season both sides of the chuck roast with the salt and pepper, make sure to press the seasoning into the meat to help the seasonings stick. To a 4-quart (3.8L) or larger Dutch oven over medium-high heat, add the oil. When the oil is hot, sear both sides of the chuck roast until golden brown, about 3–5 minutes per side. Remove the chuck roast and set it aside until needed.

3. **Sauté the aromatics.** Reduce the heat to medium and add the onion and sauté until it becomes translucent, about 2–3 minutes. Then add the gochujang, garlic, and ginger and sauté for 1–2 minutes or until the garlic and ginger are fragrant and the gochujang is well combined with the ingredients. If the gochujang starts to turn too dark on the bottom of the pot, add a couple of splashes of stock or water to help deglaze the pot.

4. **Braise the roast.** Add the stock, brown sugar, soy sauce, and sesame oil and give everything a good mix, then add the seared chuck roast and bring everything to a high simmer over medium-high heat. Cover with a lid and place the Dutch oven into the preheated oven on the middle rack, and let it cook for 2½–3 hours or until the roast is fork tender. Midway through, carefully take the Dutch oven out of the oven and flip the chuck roast. Place it back in the oven and continue cooking.

5. **Serve.** When the chuck roast is tender, portion and serve while it's hot. Leftovers can be stored in an airtight container and refrigerated for up to 4 days.

Tips from our kitchen: The most important ingredient for this pot roast, and any pot roast, is a well-marbled cut of meat. Our go-to choice is Angus or prime chuck roast. The fat in the meat really makes a big difference in the flavor, tenderness, and juiciness of the roast.

Coconut Fish Curry

Kyong first made this dish for me when we were in college, and it sparked my love for curry beyond the familiar curry powder I grew up tasting at my parents' restaurant. The red curry paste brings layers of aromatic complexity that blend seamlessly with the creamy coconut milk, and fish sauce adds a deep umami along with a mild seafood flavor that complements the fish. The fish filets cook very quickly, so they are added at the very end of cooking to keep them tender and perfectly cooked.— Mei

---

Prep time: **15 minutes**
Cook time: **15 minutes**
Makes: **4 servings**

1 (7oz/200g) bell pepper of choice, core discarded and cut into 1-inch (2.5cm) chunks

½ large (7oz/200g) yellow onion, cut into 1-inch (2.5cm) chunks

4 oz (113g) baby portobello mushrooms, quartered

4 oz (113g) canned baby corn, drained, rinsed, and cut in half

½ large (3oz/85g) carrot, peeled and thinly sliced

4 oz (113g) sugar snap peas, ends trimmed and cut in half

1 lb (454g) tilapia filet, cut into 1-inch (2.5cm) chunks (thaw if frozen)

Soup base

2 tbsp (30ml) neutral cooking oil

½ cup (120g) red curry paste

1 tbsp (10g) minced garlic

1 tbsp (10g) minced ginger

4 cups (960ml) unsweetened coconut milk

2 tbsp (30ml) fish sauce

2 tbsp (25g) granulated sugar

To serve

Cooked white rice, for serving (page 22)

Chopped cilantro, for serving (optional)

Lime wedges, for serving (optional)

1. **Make the soup base.** To a medium pot over medium-high heat, add the oil. When the oil is hot, add the curry paste, garlic, and ginger, and sauté for about 1 minute. Add the coconut milk, fish sauce, and sugar, and bring to a boil.
2. **Cook the vegetables and fish.** Once the soup base is at a boil, add the bell pepper, onion, mushrooms, baby corn, and carrots, and bring it to a simmer. Let the vegetables cook for 1–2 minutes, then add the snap peas and tilapia. Simmer for another minute or so until the tilapia is cooked. The fish is cooked when the filet is flaky when you break off a piece.
3. **Serve.** Enjoy the fish curry while it is hot with a side of rice. If desired, top the curry with cilantro and a squeeze of lime for some brightness.

Caramelized Gochujang Tomato Soup

There's a restaurant in New Orleans called Café Amelie. It's tucked away, just off Royal Street, and it serves a humble bowl of roasted tomato soup rich with the ripe, sun-soaked flavors of summer. It was actually the first time I've ever tried tomato soup at a restaurant, and since then, I've explored a variety of versions. This recipe is one of my favorite takes and starts with slowly cooking onions in butter, then stirring in gochujang to caramelize the paste's natural sugars. It adds a subtle sweetness and a pleasant lingering heat that keeps you coming back for more. — Kyong

---

Prep time: **5 minutes**
Cook time: **25 minutes**
Makes: **about 6 cups (1.4L)**

- 3 tbsp (42g) unsalted butter
- 1 large (14oz/400g) yellow onion, sliced
- 2 tbsp (18g) minced garlic
- 3 tbsp (54g) gochujang
- 2 cups (480ml) unsalted vegetable stock or chicken stock
- 1 can (28oz/794g) crushed San Marzano tomatoes
- ½ tsp kosher salt

1. **Caramelize the onion and gochujang.** In a large saucepan over medium heat, melt the butter and add the onion. Cook the onions, stirring occasionally, until they are lightly caramelized, about 7–10 minutes, then add the garlic. Sauté the garlic briefly, until aromatic, then add the gochujang. Cook the gochujang for about 3–5 minutes or until it turns a few shades darker.

2. **Simmer the tomatoes.** To the same pan with the onion and gochujang, add the stock, crushed tomatoes, and salt. Mix well and let the soup simmer on medium heat for about 10 minutes.

3. **Blend the soup.** Carefully transfer the hot soup to a high-power blender and blend the soup until smooth. Do not over fill the blender and start at low speed and gradually increase to high speed. Also, make sure to loosen the filler cap of the blender cover, but still keep it on, to release excess pressure created from the heat and blending. Be very careful as the soup is super-hot! You can also blend using an immersion blender if you don't have a high-power blender.

4. **Serve.** Portion the soup into bowls and enjoy while hot. Let leftovers cool completely before storing. Keep refrigerated for up to 4 days.

Tips from our kitchen: I like to serve this soup with crème fraîche, a swirl of EVOO, some cracked black pepper, and a few leaves of fresh basil, or pair it with our Kimchi Grilled Cheese (page 41) that's perfect for dipping.

Restaurant-Style Hot and Sour Soup

I might be biased, but I still believe no one makes hot and sour soup better than my parents. Customers would come into their restaurant and order it by the quarts, sometimes just because they were craving it, other times for a sick friend or family member. It was that kind of soup: comforting but bold. — Mei

---

Prep time: **15 minutes**
Cook time: **10 minutes**
Makes: **about 6 cups**

Soup base

- 3 tbsp (24g) cornstarch
- 3 tbsp (45ml) cold water
- 1 tsp neutral cooking oil
- ½ tsp crushed red pepper
- 4 cups (960ml) unsalted chicken stock
- ¼ cup (60ml) white vinegar
- 1 tbsp (15ml) soy sauce
- 1 tbsp (15ml) dark soy sauce
- 1 tbsp (13g) granulated sugar
- ¾ tsp kosher salt
- ½ tsp ground white pepper
- 1 tsp toasted sesame oil

Add-ins

- 5–6 pieces (5g) dried wood ear mushrooms (optional)
- 7 oz (200g) firm tofu, drained and cut into ½-inch (1cm) cubes
- 4 oz (113g) baby portobello or white button mushrooms, sliced
- 3 oz (85g) canned bamboo shoot strips, drained
- 2 large (100g) eggs, beaten
- 2 stalks green onion, sliced

1. **Rehydrate the wood ear mushrooms (if using).** Place the dried wood ear mushrooms into a heatproof bowl and cover the mushrooms with at least 1 inch (2.5cm) of boiling hot water. Let the mushrooms soak for about 10–15 minutes to rehydrate. Once fully rehydrated, rinse the mushrooms well to remove debris and drain well. Stack the mushrooms, cut them into thin strips, and set aside.

2. **Make the cornstarch slurry.** In a small bowl, stir together the cornstarch and cold water until combined. Set aside.

3. **Make the soup base.** To a large saucepan over medium-high heat, add the oil. When the oil is hot, add the crushed red peppers and sauté until fragrant, about 15 seconds, then add the chicken stock, vinegar, both soy sauces, sugar, salt, and white pepper. Bring the soup base to a boil, then add the tofu, wood ear mushrooms, portobello or white button mushrooms, and bamboo shoots. Bring the soup to boil once again.

4. **Thicken the soup and add egg drop "flowers."** When the soup is back to a boil, reduce it to a simmer. Give the prepared cornstarch slurry a good stir, then drizzle it into the soup while stirring continuously. Let the soup simmer for 30 seconds to 1 minute to thicken, then slowly drizzle the beaten egg into the soup in a thin stream, moving in a circular motion. Let the egg sit for a few seconds then gently stir the soup to create the egg drop "flowers."

5. **Finish and serve.** Finish the soup by stirring in the green onions and sesame oil. Enjoy while hot. Leftover hot and sour soup can be refrigerated in an airtight container for up to 4 days.

Tips from our kitchen: Feel free to adjust the amount of crushed red pepper and vinegar based on your personal preference for spice and tanginess, but note that the soup base should taste much tangier before the add-in ingredients are added. The soup will mellow out after.

Chinese Oxtail Borscht

This is a delicious twist on the classic borscht. Rather than beets, this version uses a tomato base and hearty oxtails. It's one of our favorite soups, packed with vegetables and melt-off-the-bone tender oxtails. The broth itself is perfectly balanced, bright and slightly tangy from the tomatoes, yet rich and savory from the oxtails—making every spoonful irresistible. Plus, this soup is perfect for meal prep; we always keep quarts of it frozen for days when we're too busy to cook. — Mei

---

Prep time: **30 minutes**
Cook time: **2–3 hours**
Makes: **4–6 servings**

- 5 lb (2.2kg) oxtails, fat trimmed if necessary
- 2 tbsp (30ml) neutral cooking oil
- 1 large (14oz/400g) yellow onion, diced
- 4 ribs (7oz/200g) celery, cut into ½-inch (1cm) pieces
- 1 large (7oz/200g) carrot, peeled and cut into ½-inch (1cm) chunks
- 1 tbsp (9g) minced garlic
- 2 tbsp (33g) tomato paste
- 8 cups (1.9L) unsalted beef stock
- 1 (15oz/425g) can crushed tomatoes
- 1¼ lb (567g) beefsteak tomatoes, cut into ½-inch (1cm) chunks
- 4 tsp (21g) kosher salt, divided (or as needed)
- 1 lb (454g) gold potatoes, peeled and cut into 1-inch (2.5cm) chunks
- 6 oz (170g) green cabbage, cut into 1-inch (2.5cm) chunks

1. **Blanch the oxtails.** Place the oxtails into a large pot and fill it with enough water to cover them by about 1 inch (2.5cm). Bring the pot to a boil over high heat and cook the oxtails for about 5–10 minutes. You'll start to see scum float up to the surface. Then drain the oxtails into a colander and rinse well with warm water. The oxtails will be hot, so you may need to run some cold water over them until they are more comfortable to handle. There will likely be stubborn scum stuck on the oxtails. If so, rub it with your fingers while rinsing under the water.
2. **Start the borscht.** To the same pot used for blanching (clean it first, if necessary) or in a clean pot set over medium-high heat, add the oil. Once hot, add the onion, celery, and carrot, and sauté for a few minutes, until the onion begins to soften. Add the garlic and cook until fragrant, then stir in the tomato paste and cook for about 30 seconds.
3. **Simmer the borscht.** Add the stock, crushed tomatoes, beefsteak tomatoes, and 3 teaspoons (16g) of salt. Stir well, then return the blanched oxtails to the pot and bring to a boil. Once boiling, reduce the heat to medium or medium-low to maintain a gentle simmer. Cover and cook for 2–3 hours, or until the oxtails are tender, stirring occasionally. Skim the surface as needed to remove excess fat.
4. **Add potato and cabbage.** During the last 20–30 minutes of cooking, add the potatoes and cabbage and cook until the potatoes are fork-tender. Taste and season with the remaining 1 teaspoon of salt, adding more if needed to suit your preference.
5. **Serve.** Enjoy the oxtail borscht while it's hot. (We like to pre-shred all the meat off the oxtail to keep eating easier and cleaner.) Leftover oxtail borscht can be stored in the fridge for up to 4 days.

Miso Egg Drop Soup

This miso egg drop soup is one that comes to mind when we crave an easy, quick, and comforting soup. Each spoonful is filled with silky, delicate wisps of egg, tender tofu cubes, chopped seaweed, and a savory miso broth, making it a gentle remedy for both the soul on a dreary day and the body when you're under the weather. — Mei

---

Prep time: **10 minutes**
Cook time: **10 minutes**
Makes: **4 servings**

- 4 cups (960ml) water
- 1–2 tbsp (5g) dried seaweed (Japanese wakame or Korean miyeok)
- 1 tsp Hondashi bonito soup stock powder
- 7 oz (200g) soft tofu, cut into ½-inch (1cm) cubes
- 2 large (100g) eggs, beaten
- 4 tbsp (72g) white miso
- 1 stalk green onion, sliced
- 1 tsp toasted sesame oil

1. **Rehydrate the seaweed and start the soup base.** To a medium pot, add the water, dried seaweed, and soup stock powder. If the seaweed is not cut, break it into smaller pieces or use a pair of kitchen shears to cut it. Bring the soup to a gentle boil over medium high heat. Once the soup is boiling, add the tofu and bring the soup back to a boil again. Let the soup simmer for a minute or two or until the seaweed is fully rehydrated.

2. **Adding the egg drop "flowers."** When the seaweed has fully rehydrated, drizzle in the beaten egg in a circular motion. If you like larger egg "flowers," let the egg sit for a few seconds before stirring. If you prefer thinner, smaller egg "flowers," you can stir the soup with a spoon immediately after adding the egg. Bring the soup to a simmer again.

3. **Add the miso.** Take the soup off the heat and dissolve the miso into the soup using a strainer. If you don't have a strainer, add a small amount of soup into a bowl with the miso and mix until the miso becomes a looser paste before adding it back to the soup.

4. **Finish and serve.** Stir in the green onion and sesame oil to finish the soup and enjoy while it's hot. Leftover soup can be stored in the fridge for up to 3 days. When reheating the soup, never bring it to a boil! Just heat it up until hot so that the miso's nutritional benefits are preserved.

Clay Pot Soy-Braised Chicken

We love cooking with our clay pots, and one of the dishes we make regularly is our soy-braised chicken. We use chicken thighs because they're an affordable cut that stays juicy and full of flavor. The chicken is seasoned with a soy marinade and then cooked with shiitake mushrooms and lots of aromatics. As it cooks, the juices from the chicken simmer with the aromatics and get absorbed into the mushrooms, creating a wonderfully delicious and savory sauce. — Mei

---

Prep time: **15 minutes, plus 30 minutes marinating time**
Cook time: **30 minutes**
Makes: **3 servings**

1½ lb (680g) boneless chicken thighs, cut into 1-inch (2.5cm) pieces
¼ cup (60ml) Shaoxing rice wine, divided
1 tbsp (19g) oyster sauce
1 tbsp (15ml) soy sauce
½ tbsp (7ml) dark soy sauce
1 tsp granulated sugar
1 tbsp (8g) cornstarch
3 (12g) dried shiitake mushrooms
2 tbsp (30ml) neutral cooking oil
3–4 (270g) shallots, cut into 1-inch (2.5cm) chunks
2-inch (5cm) (20g) knob of ginger, peeled and cut into smaller chunks
4–6 (16g) garlic cloves, cut in half crosswise
Chopped cilantro or sliced green onion, for garnish (optional)

1. **Marinate the chicken.** In a bowl, season the chicken thighs with 1 tablespoon (15ml) of rice wine, the oyster sauce, both soy sauces, and sugar. Mix well, then add the cornstarch and mix until well combined. Let the chicken marinate for at least 30 minutes, or cover and refrigerate overnight.
2. **Prepare the shiitake mushrooms.** Place the dried mushrooms into a heatproof bowl and add enough boiling water to cover them. Let them soak for 10–15 minutes until they're rehydrated, then rinse them well to remove any debris. After rinsing, cut and discard the woody stems, then quarter the mushrooms. Set aside until needed.
3. **Sauté aromatics.** To a 40 ounce (1.2L) or larger clay pot, add the cooking oil and place over medium to medium-low heat. Once the oil and pot are hot, add the shallots, ginger, and garlic. Sauté for 1–2 minutes or until the aromatics are fragrant, then add the rehydrated shiitake and sauté for 10–15 seconds. Spread the aromatics into a single layer and then arrange the marinated chicken on top of the aromatics.
4. **"Braise" the chicken.** Place the lid on the clay pot and drizzle the remaining rice wine around the lid of the clay pot. Turn the heat to low and let the chicken cook for 20–25 minutes or until the chicken is cooked through and the internal temperature registers 165°F (74°C).
5. **Finish and serve.** Once the chicken is cooked through, uncover the pot and top with cilantro or green onions, if desired. Enjoy while it's hot. Leftovers can be stored in an airtight container and refrigerated for up to 4 days.

Tips from our kitchen: You can use a medium pot or a Dutch oven as an alternative for the clay pot. Follow the instructions as is but drizzle the rice wine around the pot before covering with a lid.

Chicken and Mushroom Dumpling Noodle Soup

Dumplings are great on their own, but we love them even more in a comforting bowl of light broth with noodles. In this recipe, we are serving our Chicken and Mushroom Dumplings (page 56) with some lightly seasoned chicken stock, along with bok choy, green onion and cilantro, and some wonton noodles. Other noodles, such as instant ramen noodles, dry wheat noodles, or even fresh ramen noodles are great choices, too. Top off the soup with some Chinese Chili Oil (page 240) and you've got the ultimate cure for any dreary day. — Mei

---

Prep time: **10 minutes**
Cook time: **15 minutes**
Makes: **2 servings**

Soup base

- 4 cups (1L) unsalted chicken stock
- 1¼ tsp (7g) kosher salt
- 1 tsp chicken bouillon powder
- 1 tsp toasted sesame oil
- A generous dash of white pepper

To serve

- 10 chicken and mushroom dumplings (page 56), fresh or frozen
- 6 oz (170g) thin noodles of choice
- 2–4 heads Shanghai or baby bok choy, halved and washed
- Chinese Chili Oil (page 240)
- Chopped cilantro (optional)
- Sliced green onion (optional)

1. **Make the soup base.** In a large saucepan, combine all the ingredients for the soup base and bring to a boil over high heat. Set aside and keep warm.

2. **Cook the dumplings and bok choy.** Bring a medium pot of water to a boil over high heat and have a spider strainer at the ready. When the water is boiling, add the dumplings. Stir the dumplings occasionally to prevent them from sticking to the bottom of the pot and bring the water back to a boil. Whether using fresh or frozen chicken and mushroom dumplings, let the dumplings cook for an additional 2–3 minutes or after they float to the surface. The dumplings are cooked when juices in the filling run clear or the internal temperature registers 165°F (74°C). Add the bok choy at the latter 30 seconds to 2 minutes of cooking, depending on how cooked you like your bok choy. Use the strainer to remove the dumplings and bok choy, making sure to drain them well. Divide them into serving bowls.

3. **Boil the noodles.** To the same pot of water, add the noodles and cook according to package instructions until just cooked. Once the noodles are cooked, drain well and portion into the serving bowls.

4. **Finish and serve.** Divide the soup between the bowls. Top with your desired amount of chili oil, and if desired, cilantro and green onion as well. Enjoy while hot.

CHAPTER 8

Bakery + Sweet Things

Orange Chocolate Salt Rolls

Salt rolls, also known as shio pan, are croissant-shaped breads with a crunchy exterior and a soft, fluffy interior. The crisp crust is largely created by the small log of salted butter wrapped inside the dough; as the rolls bake, the butter melts and seeps out, gently "frying" the bottoms and forming a beautifully crispy, golden-brown crust. A well-developed gluten structure is key to achieving their fluffy interior, which is why we use ice-cold water in the dough: a small portion is warmed to dissolve and activate the yeast, while the remaining cold water keeps the dough cool to maximum gluten development and prevents the yeast from working too quickly during kneading. To skip having to divide the water and needing to dissolve and activate the yeast, you can use the same amount of instant dry yeast instead of active dry yeast. Use the full amount of water but the instant yeast can be added directly into the dry flour.

We've added a twist to these salt rolls by stuffing them with dark chocolate for a rich, decadent surprise and incorporating orange zest into the dough for bright, sunny citrus notes. With their irresistible contrast of textures and flavors, they're truly delicious—just watch out for the melted chocolate if you enjoy them warm! — Mei

---

Prep time: **1 hour, plus 2½ hours of resting and proofing**
Cook time: **14 minutes**
Makes: **12 salt rolls**

Dough

- 1 cup (240g) ice-cold water, divided
- 2 tsp (6g) active dry yeast
- ¼ cup (50g) granulated sugar, divided
- 2 cups (270g) bread flour (fluffed, spooned, and leveled)
- 1 cup (120g) all-purpose flour (fluffed, spooned, and leveled), plus more for dusting
- 2 tbsp (12g) milk powder
- 2 tbsp (28g) unsalted butter, softened
- 2 tbsp (12g) orange zest
- 1 tsp (7g) fine salt

Filling and garnish

- 6 tbsp (84g) cold salted butter, divided into 12 equal-size (7g) logs
- 2 oz (60g) dark chocolate, divided into 12 equal-size (5g) pieces
- Coarse salt or kosher salt, for garnish

1. **Activate the yeast.** Add 2 tablespoons (30ml) of the water to a microwave-safe bowl and microwave it for a few seconds or just until lukewarm. Add the yeast and a generous pinch of the sugar. Stir well then set it aside in a warm area to let the yeast activate. After a few minutes, the yeast should be foamy and have formed a cap.

2. **Make the dough.** While waiting for the yeast to activate, add both flours, the remaining sugar, and milk powder to the stand mixer bowl and mix until well combined. When the yeast is ready, add it to the dry ingredients along with the remaining cold water. Using the dough hook attachment, mix on low speed until the dough comes together, then increase the speed to medium-high and knead the dough until it's almost at the window-pane stage (page 21), about 10 minutes. Then add the softened butter, orange zest, and salt and knead on medium-low speed until everything is incorporated, then increase to medium-high speed and knead until the dough is supple, smooth, and passes the window-pane test, about 5–10 minutes.

3. **Perform the first proof.** With the dough in your hands, fold the edges of the dough to the bottom, turning between each fold, until the dough is a nice, smooth ball. Place the dough back into the bowl and cover the bowl with plastic wrap or a clean kitchen towel. Let the dough proof in a warm area until it has doubled in size, about 1 hour. In the meantime, prepare a couple sheet pans and line time with parchment paper.

4. **Perform the initial shaping.** When the dough has doubled in size, punch it down to deflate and degas it. Turn the dough out onto a lightly floured surface, then divide the dough into 12 equal-size pieces (photo 1). For each piece of dough, round it into a ball with your palm (photo 2) then shape them into long raindrops (photo 3). To make raindrop shapes, first roll the ball into a thick log then taper one end of the log. The dough should be about 5 inches (12.5cm) long. Repeat with all the dough balls and keep them covered with plastic wrap while you work. Dust lightly with flour as necessary during this whole process. Once done, let the dough rest for 10–15 minutes to let the gluten relax.

Initial Shaping

Second Shaping

5. **Perform the second shaping and proofing.** For this part of the shaping process, we find the tackiness of the dough helpful when rolling out the dough. But if needed, lightly dust the top of the dough with some flour. Using a rolling pin, roll out each raindrop-shaped dough to about 16–18 inches (40–45cm) long (photo 4). The trick here is to roll the top third up, then lift the bottom two thirds of the dough as you gently pull and roll downward (photo 5). The top should be about 3 inches (7.5cm) wide, and it will taper at the end. Place a piece of salted butter and a piece of chocolate about 1 inch (2.5 cm) from the top of the dough (photo 6). Pull the dough over the butter and chocolate, then roll it downward all the way to the tapered tip (photo 7). Keep the dough centered as you roll and pull lightly for tension (photo 8). At the end, try to keep the tapered tail end sitting on the bottom of the roll. Arrange the finished roll on the prepared sheet pan, keeping each roll about 3 inches (7.5cm) apart. Repeat with the remaining. Then cover and let the rolls proof in a warm area until doubled in size, about

Recipe continues...

45 minutes to 1 hour. The dough should slowly spring back and leave a light indentation if you gently press it.

6. Bake. Start preheating the oven to 450°F (230°C) about 15–30 minutes ahead of time. When the rolls are nearly ready to bake, lightly spray the rolls with water and top with a light sprinkle of coarse salt for garnish. Right before ready to bake, *very* generously spray the rolls with water. This is to recreate that steam function in commercial bakery ovens. Alternatively, you can preheat the oven with a sheet pan on a lower rack, and right before you're ready to bake, throw a handful of ice cubes onto the hot tray. (If using this method, make sure to move fast so you don't lower the oven temperature too much.) Place the tray of salt rolls in the oven on the center rack and immediately lower the oven temperature to 425°F (220°C). Bake for 13–14 minutes or until the rolls are evenly golden brown. Turn the tray midway for even browning.

7. Cool and enjoy. Remove the salt rolls from the oven and repeat the process with the second tray. Let the rolls cool until they are comfortable to handle before enjoying.

8. Storage. They are best enjoyed freshly baked, but can be stored at room temperature for up to 1 week or frozen for up to 2 months.

Tips from our kitchen: To revive leftover salt rolls (thaw if frozen) so they are soft and chewy on the inside and crispy on the outside again, give the roll(s) a quick rinse with water and then shake off the excess. Bake at 370°F (190°C) for about 10 minutes or air fry at 350°F (175°C) for 3–5 minutes.

Yuzu Cream Cheese Bread

These vibrant yuzu cream cheese breads are made with soft, fluffy milk bread dough and topped with some sweet and tangy cream cheese filling that's full of yuzu's citrusy flavor. Whether they're sprinkled with the buttery crumble topping or left plain, each bread tastes light yet indulgent. They are best enjoyed slightly warmed, when the citrus aroma is most expressive. — Mei

---

Prep time: **50 minutes, plus 2 hours 10 minutes proofing time**
Cook time: **20–25 minutes per batch**
Makes: **12 bread**

Dough

- 2 tsp (6g) active dry yeast
- 1 cup (240ml) whole milk, warm (around 105°F/40°C)
- 5 cups (600g) all-purpose flour (fluffed, spooned, and leveled), plus more for dusting
- ½ cup (100g) granulated sugar
- ½ cup (120ml) boiling hot water
- 3 large (150g) eggs, divided
- 4 tbsp (57g) unsalted butter, softened
- 2 tsp (14g) fine salt

Yuzu cream cheese

- 8 oz (226g) full-fat cream cheese, softened
- ½ cup (60g) powdered sugar
- 2 tbsp (30ml) yuzu extract (juice)

Crumble (optional)

- 1 tbsp (14g) unsalted butter, softened
- 1½ tbsp (15g) powdered sugar
- A dash of vanilla extract
- 2 tbsp (15g) all-purpose flour

1. **Activate the yeast.** Sprinkle the yeast over the warm milk and give it a good stir. Set it aside in a warm area to let the yeast dissolve and activate, about 5 minutes. It should form a foamy cap. Give it another stir before use.

2. **Make the dough.** To a mixing bowl, add the flour and sugar and mix to combine using the dough hook attachment. While stirring, drizzle in the boiling water, then add the milk-and-yeast mixture along with 2 eggs. Mix on low to medium-low speed until the dough comes together, then increase the speed to medium to medium-high and knead for about 10 minutes, until the dough is nearly at the window-pane stage (page 21). Add the softened butter and salt, and continue kneading on medium-low to medium speed until the butter and salt are fully incorporated and the dough is smooth and passes the windowpane test, about 5–10 minutes.

3. **First proof.** With the dough in your hands, fold the edges of the dough to the bottom, turning between each fold, until the dough is a nice, smooth ball. Place the dough back into the bowl and cover the bowl with plastic wrap or a clean kitchen towel. Let the dough proof in a warm area until it has doubled in size, about 1 hour.

4. **Initial shaping.** Prepare a few sheet pans and line them with parchment paper. After the dough has doubled in size, punch it down to deflate and degas it. Turn the dough out onto a lightly floured surface and divide it into 12 equal-size pieces. Shape each piece of dough into a ball by pulling the edges of the dough to the bottom, then round it out with your palm. Cover with plastic wrap and let the dough rest for about 10 minutes so the gluten can relax.

5. **Final shaping.** After 10 minutes, flatten each dough ball into a 4-inch (10cm) circle using a rolling pin, lightly dusting with flour as needed. Arrange the dough discs on the prepared sheet pan, keeping them at least 3 inches (7.5cm) apart. Using the base of a flat object about 2½ inches (6.5cm) wide—such as a dry measuring cup or drinking glass—press firmly into the center of each disc to create a well. Dust the bottom of the cup with flour as needed, and brush off any excess flour from the dough with a pastry brush.

6. **Second proof.** Once all the bread has been shaped, cover and proof in a warm place until nearly doubled in size, about 45 minutes to 1 hour. While the dough is proofing, prepare the yuzu cream cheese filling and the crumble (if using). When the dough is about halfway to doubled, begin preheating the oven to 350°F (175°C).

7. **Prepare the yuzu cream cheese.** To a mixer bowl fitted with the paddle attachment or a large mixing bowl with a hand mixer, add the cream cheese and powdered sugar. Mix on medium-low speed until the powdered sugar is no longer visible, then increase to medium-high speed and mix until well combined. Add the yuzu extract and mix on medium speed until fully incorporated. Scrape down the sides of the bowl as needed throughout the process. Once finished, cover and keep refrigerated until needed.

8. Prepare the crumble (if using). To a small or medium mixing bowl, add the butter, powdered sugar, and vanilla extract. Use a fork to mix until well combined, then add the flour. Mix with the fork until the mixture looks crumbly. Cover and set aside until needed.

9. Assemble. Whisk the remaining egg in a small bowl to make an egg wash. Once the dough has nearly doubled in size, gently re-indent each well with the back of a spoon. Lightly dust the spoon with flour as needed to prevent sticking. Brush the puffed edges of the dough with the egg wash, then fill each well with about 2 tablespoons of the yuzu cream cheese, spreading it evenly to fill the well. If using, sprinkle some crumble over each bread. We like to keep the crumble on the egg-washed edges, but feel free to sprinkle it over the entire surface if you prefer.

10. Bake and enjoy. Place a tray of the bread in the oven on the middle rack and bake for 20–25 minutes or until the breads are golden brown on the outside (the crumbles will be slightly lighter in color) and the internal temperature registers 190°F (88°C). Once baked, remove the tray and let the breads cool until warm to the touch before enjoying. Repeat with remaining bread, but make sure the oven is back at 350°F (175°C) before baking the next batch.

11. Storage. Leftover bread should be stored in an airtight container and kept refrigerated for up to 3 days, or individually wrapped and frozen for up to 2 months. Refrigerated bread can be baked in the oven at 325°F (160°C) for about 5–10 minutes for best texture. Frozen bread should be thawed overnight or at room temperature before reheating.

Leek and Mushroom Miso Galette with Buttery Sesame Crust

One of my favorite flavor combinations is leek and mushroom. I remember the first time I used this pairing was in a puff pastry tart before I started culinary school, and I was hooked. Over time, I made some tweaks, and now it's even more delicious—even my cousin who isn't a mushroom lover loved it! The puff pastry tart has been turned into a galette with a nutty, double sesame crust that's rustic but still buttery and flakey, and the leek and mushrooms are cooked down in butter and miso to replace the salt for extra umami, along with a healthy spread of ricotta in between to add creaminess. — Kyong

---

Prep time: **40 minutes, plus 30 minutes or more chilling time**
Cook time: **45–50 minutes**
Makes: **8 servings**

Sesame crust

- 1½ sticks (170g) cold unsalted butter
- 1¾ cup (210g) all-purpose flour (fluffed, spooned, and leveled), plus more for dusting
- ½ tsp fine salt
- 1 tbsp (9g) toasted white sesame seeds
- 1 tbsp (9g) toasted black sesame seeds
- ¼ cup (60g) cold water
- 1 egg, beaten for egg wash

Leek-and-mushroom filling

- 3 tbsp (42g) unsalted butter
- 6 oz (170g) leek, thinly sliced (whites only)
- 1 lb (454g) baby portobello mushrooms, sliced
- 1 tsp fresh thyme, plus more for garnishing
- 2½ tbsp (45g) white miso
- ½ cup (130g) ricotta

1. **Make the dough for the sesame crust.** Onto a plate or a bowl, grate the cold butter using a coarse grater. Keep the butter refrigerated until needed. In a large bowl, mix together the flour, salt, and both sesame seeds, then add the cold, grated butter. With your hands, work the butter into the flour mixture with a rubbing motion. We're aiming for pea-size to half-pea-size butter pieces. Once you've got the butter worked in, add the cold water and mix until just combined. *Do not overwork the dough!* Just mix until no more dry flour is visible. This dough will be slightly on the sticky side but don't be tempted to add more flour. Flatten the dough into a disc and wrap it with cling film. Refrigerate for at least 30 minutes to 1 hour or overnight.

2. **Make the leek-and-mushroom filling.** To a large sauté pan over medium heat, add the butter. Once the butter has melted, add the leek and cook for about 3 minutes until wilted, then add the mushrooms and sauté for another 5–7 minutes or until the mushrooms are tender and any excess moisture is cooked out. Add the thyme and cook for a minute until aromatic. Finish by adding the miso, stirring until it has dissolved into the leek and mushrooms. Remove and set aside to cool completely before using.

3. **Preheat the oven to 400°F (205°C).** Also, prepare a large sheet pan lined with parchment paper.

4. **Roll out the crust.** If you refrigerated your dough overnight, take it out 30 minutes ahead of time so that it can soften a bit. Lightly dust your clean work surface with flour and roll out the sesame dough into a circle, about ⅜ inch (9mm) thick. Lightly dust your dough and work surface as necessary, and make sure to move the dough around to prevent it from sticking to your work surface. Transfer the rolled out dough to the prepared sheet pan.

5. **Assemble and bake.** Spread the ricotta evenly across the crust, but leave 1½ inches (4cm) of the crust along the edges clean. Top the ricotta with the now-cooled leek-and-mushroom filling. Gently fold the edge of the dough over the filling, overlapping itself at each new fold. Brush the folded edge of the crust with egg wash and bake on the center rack for 35–40 minutes, until the crust is golden brown and crispy.

6. **Cool and enjoy.** Remove the galette from the oven and let it cool for 5–10 minutes. Cut into desired size and enjoy while warm.

7. **Storage.** Leftovers can be stored in an airtight container and refrigerated for up to 4 days. Reheat refrigerated galette in the oven at 350°F (175°C) for about 10–15 minutes or until warmed through.

Milk Bread Rolls

For the holidays, we *always* make a batch of my milk bread rolls for the dinner spread. They're soft, fluffy, and just a little sweet—the kind of rolls that disappear before anything else on the table. The secret? A magical little ingredient called *tangzhong*. Tangzhong is a cooked paste made from flour and milk (sometimes water) that gets mixed into the dough. It allows the bread to hold more moisture *without* turning into a sticky, unmanageable mess. That extra hydration is the key to soft, pillowy rolls every time.
— Mei

Prep time: **30 minutes, plus 2 hours proofing time**
Cook time: **20–25 minutes**
Makes: **16 small or 9 large rolls**

Tangzhong

6 tbsp (90ml) whole milk
2½ tbsp (21g) bread flour

Dough

1 tsp (3g) active dry yeast
¾ cup (180ml) whole milk, warm (around 105°F/40°C)
2⅔ cups (360g) bread flour, (fluffed, spooned, and leveled), plus more for dusting
¼ cup (50g) granulated sugar
½ tsp fine salt
4 tbsp (57g) unsalted butter, softened (plus more for greasing)
1 egg, beaten (for egg wash)

1. **Make the tangzhong.** Combine the milk and flour in a small bowl and whisk until well mixed. Pour the mixture into a nonstick pan placed over medium heat and cook, stirring constantly with a rubber spatula, until the mixture thickens to the consistency of soft putty. Once the consistency is right, transfer the tangzhong onto a plate, spread, and cover with plastic wrap, making sure the plastic is touching the tangzhong. Let it cool in the fridge until needed.

2. **Activate the yeast.** Sprinkle the yeast over the warm milk and give it a good stir. Set it aside in a warm area to let the yeast dissolve and activate, about 5 minutes. It should form a foamy cap. Give it another stir before use.

3. **Make the dough.** To a stand mixer bowl, add the flour, sugar, and salt. Give it a good mix with the dough hook attachment, then add the prepared tangzhong along with the butter and the milk-and-yeast mixture. Mix on low speed until the dough comes together, then increase the speed to medium to medium-high and knead the dough until it becomes smooth and passes the window-pane test (page 21), about 10–15 minutes.

4. **First proof.** With the dough in your hands, fold the edges of the dough to the bottom, turning between each fold, until the dough is a nice, smooth ball. Place the dough back into the bowl and cover the bowl with plastic wrap or a clean kitchen towel. Let the dough proof in a warm area until it has doubled in size, about 1 hour.

5. **Shape and second proof.** Lightly grease a 9 × 9-inch (23 × 23cm) baking pan with butter. After the dough has doubled in size, punch it down to deflate and degas it. Turn the dough out onto a lightly floured surface and divide the dough into either 16 or 9 equal-size pieces. Working with one piece of dough at a time, shape the dough into a taut ball by pulling the edge of the dough to the bottom, then round it out in your palm. Arrange the dough ball in the prepared baking pan and repeat with remaining dough pieces. Once finished, cover the pan with plastic wrap or a clean kitchen towel and let the dough proof in a warm area, until doubled, about 45 minutes to 1 hour.

6. **Bake.** Preheat the oven to 350°F (175°C). Before baking, brush the top of the rolls with egg wash. Bake the milk bread rolls on the middle rack for 20–25 minutes or until the tops are golden brown and the internal temperature reaches 190°F (88°C).

7. **Cool and enjoy.** Remove the rolls from the oven. Let them cool at room temperature for 5–10 minutes, then flip them out of the baking pan. You can serve them warm or let them cool completely at room temperature.

8. **Storage.** Although it's best to enjoy these rolls within 3 days for best flavor and texture, they can be stored in an airtight container at room temperature for up to 1 week or frozen for up to 2 months.

Pork Sung Scallion Loaf

Kyong absolutely loves the pork sung bread from the bakery near us, which inspired me to create this pork sung scallion loaf. The loaf is soft and tender, loaded with pork sung and scallion, and has Kyong's stamp of approval. We like to have a thick slice for breakfast with some hot tea or soy milk. If you're new to pork sung, it's essentially seasoned pork that's stewed then dried or fried and shredded. It's a pantry staple in Chinese cuisine and usually served with or used in breakfast food and baked goods. You can often find them packaged with blue or red labeling. The blue-label pork sung is less-fried, slightly chewier, and has longer fibers than the crispier, red-label version. — Mei

---

Prep time: **50 minutes, plus 2 hours proofing time**
Cook time: **25–30 minutes**
Makes: **2 loaves**

Dough

- 4 tsp (11g) active dry yeast
- ½ cup (120ml) whole milk, warm (around 105°F/40°C)
- 4 cups (500g) bread flour (fluffed, spooned, and leveled), plus more for dusting
- ¼ cup (50g) granulated sugar
- ⅔ cup (160ml) ice-cold water
- 2 large (100g) eggs, beaten (reserve 2 tbsp/30g for egg wash)
- 4 tbsp (57g) unsalted butter, softened
- 1 tsp fine salt

Filling

- ¼ cup (60g) Kewpie or regular mayonnaise
- 1½ cups (3oz/85g) pork sung (blue label)
- 4–5 stalks scallion, sliced

1. **Activate the yeast.** Sprinkle the yeast over the warm milk and give it a good stir. Set it aside in a warm area to let the yeast dissolve and activate, about 5 minutes. It should form a foamy cap. Give it another stir before use.

2. **Make the dough.** To a mixer bowl, add the flour and sugar, and give it a good mix with the dough hook attachment. When the yeast is ready, add the milk-and-yeast mixture, water, and eggs. Mix on low to medium-low speed until the dough comes together, then increase the speed to medium to medium-high. Knead the dough until it's nearly at the window-pane stage (page 21), about 10–15 minutes. To the dough, add the softened butter and salt. Knead on medium-low to medium speed until the butter and salt have been absorbed and the dough is smooth and supple and passes the window-pane test, about 5–10 minutes.

3. **First proof.** With the dough in your hands, fold the edges of the dough to the bottom, turning between each fold, until the dough is a nice, smooth ball. Place the dough back into the bowl and cover the bowl with plastic wrap or a clean kitchen towel. Let the dough proof in a warm area until it has doubled in size, about 1 hour.

4. **Shape and fill.** Prepare two lightly greased 8 × 4-inch (20 × 10cm) loaf pans. When the dough has doubled in size, punch it down to deflate and degas it. Turn the dough out onto a lightly floured surface and roll it into a ¼-inch-thick (6mm-thick) rectangle that is about 11 × 16 inches (28 × 40cm). Thinly spread the mayo onto the dough, then top it with pork sung and sliced scallions. Give the layer of filling a firm press to help adhere it to the dough. Next, roll the dough into a log, starting from one of the longer edges then pinch the seam together to seal. Use a knife to cut the log in half so that you have 2 equal-size logs, then split each log lengthwise, all the way through. Working with one piece at a time, position the split sides facing up and twist the two halves together to form a braid. Fold both ends underneath so they meet in the middle, then place the braided loaf split-side up into a prepared pan. Repeat with the remaining piece.

5. **Second proof.** Cover the loaf pans with plastic wrap or a kitchen towel and let the loaves proof in a warm area until nearly doubled in size, about 1 hour. Midway through the proofing time, start preheating the oven to 350°F (175°C).

6. **Bake.** When the loaves have doubled in size, brush the tops with the reserved egg, then place the loaves into the preheated oven on the middle rack and bake for 25–30 minutes or until the loaves are golden brown on top and the internal temperature registers 190°F (88°C). Towards the last 10 minutes of baking, cover the loaves with aluminum foil if they start to get too dark.

7. Cool and enjoy. When the loaves are done baking, remove them from the oven and give them a firm tap on a cooling rack. Take the loaves out of the pans and let them cool completely before cutting and enjoying. For day 2 and older bread, we like to briefly heat it up in the microwave, like 5–10 seconds, just to slightly warm it up for best taste and texture.

8. Storage. To store, wrap the loaves really well with plastic wrap and keep at room temperature for up to 3 days or freeze for up to 2 months.

Tips from our kitchen: If you are limited in space, you can divide the dough into two equal-size portions and roll each into a rectangle about 11 × 8 inches (28 × 20cm). After spreading on the filling, roll it up into a log from one of the short edges.

Osmanthus Black Tea Cookies

These shortbread-style cookies are a twist on a classic favorite, with crispy edges and buttery centers. They are delicately perfumed with the fruitiness of osmanthus and the malty notes of black tea, making them, ironically, perfect accompaniments for a cup of hot tea. (Not to discredit how delicious they are on their own!) — Mei

---

Prep time: **30 minutes, plus 1 hour of chilling time**
Cook time: **14–16 minutes per batch**
Makes: **32 cookies**

- 1 tbsp (2g) osmanthus tea
- 1 tbsp (4g) black tea (like Assam or English breakfast)
- 1 stick (113g) unsalted butter, softened
- ½ cup (60g) powdered sugar
- ½ tsp fine salt
- 1 large (17g) egg yolk
- 1½ cups (180g) all-purpose flour (fluffed, spooned, and leveled)
- ¼ cup (55g) turbinado sugar (optional)

1. **Prepare the teas.** Grind the osmanthus tea and black tea as fine as possible using a mortar and pestle or a blender.
2. **Make the cookie dough.** In the mixer bowl or a large mixing bowl, beat the butter, ground teas, powdered sugar, and salt on medium-high speed using the paddle attachment or a hand mixer until pale and fluffy. Next, add the egg yolk and beat on medium speed until well combined. Scrape down the sides of the bowl as needed. Then add the flour and mix on low speed until just combined and no more dry flour is visible. If your kitchen is cold, the dough may stay crumbly and not come together. In this case, you may need to give the dough a couple of kneads with your hands to help warm up the butter and soften the dough.
3. **Shape and chill.** Transfer the cookie dough onto a sheet of parchment paper or plastic wrap and roll the dough into a 1½-inch (4cm) thick log. Wrap the dough in the parchment paper or plastic wrap and refrigerate it for at least 1 hour or overnight, and up to 3 days. The dough can also be frozen for up to 3 months and thawed overnight in the fridge before use.
4. **Preheat the oven to 350°F (175°C).** Preheat the oven 20–30 minutes before baking, and Prepare a couple of sheet pans lined with parchment paper.
5. **Cut and bake.** Unwrap the log of cookie dough and place it onto a cutting board. If decorating with sugar, very lightly wet the log of cookie dough by brushing it with water then sprinkle the turbinado sugar along the length of the log. Firmly roll the log in the sugar then discard the excess sugar. Cut the cookie dough into ¼-inch (6mm) slices and arrange them about 1 inch apart on the prepared sheet pans. Place the tray of cookies in the oven on the middle rack and bake for 14–16 minutes or until the edges of the cookies just start to turn golden brown.
6. **Cool and enjoy.** Remove the tray of cookies from the oven and let them cool for 10–15 minutes before enjoying. Repeat with the other tray of cookies.
7. **Storage.** After the cookies are completely cooled, they can be stored at room temperature in an airtight container for up to 1 week.

Kkwabaegi (Korean Twisted Donuts)

As a child, road trips to Houston were always an exciting adventure, especially because they meant a visit to H Mart—specifically to Tous les Jours, a French Asian bakery located inside the grocery store, where I would make a beeline to these twisted donuts called *kkwabaegi.* They're light and airy, fried to golden perfection, and coated in a generous layer of cinnamon-sugar. We've long since recreated them at home, and I'm not bragging, but I think we've surpassed those donuts I've always looked forward to on our Houston road trips. — Kyong

---

Prep time: **45 minutes, plus 2 hours proofing time**
Cook time: **3–4 minutes per batch**
Makes: **12 donuts**

Dough
- 2¼ tsp (7g) active dry yeast
- ⅔ cup (160ml) whole milk, warm (around 105°F/40°C)
- 3 cups (360g) all-purpose flour (fluffed, spooned, and leveled)
- ⅓ cup (65g) granulated sugar
- ½ tsp fine salt
- 2 large (100g) eggs
- 4 tbsp (57g) unsalted butter, softened
- Neutral cooking oil, for frying

Cinnamon-sugar coating
- ⅔ cup (130g) granulated sugar
- ½ tbsp (4g) ground cinnamon

1. **Activate the yeast.** Sprinkle the yeast over the warm milk and give it a good stir. Set it aside in a warm area to let the yeast dissolve and activate, about 5 minutes. It should form a foamy cap. Give it another stir before use.

2. **Make the dough.** To the bowl of a stand mixer, add the flour, sugar, and salt, and give it a good mix with your dough hook attachment. When the yeast is ready, add it to your flour mixture along with the eggs. Mix on medium-low speed until no more dry ingredients are visible then increase the speed to medium or medium-high and knead until the dough is almost at the window-pane stage (page 21), about 10–15 minutes. If your dough is really tacky at this point and your mixer is having a tough time picking up the dough, cover and let the dough rest for 30 minutes instead. Then add the butter and return to kneading on medium-high speed until the dough passes the window-pane test, about 10 minutes.

3. **First proof.** With the dough in your hands, fold the edges of the dough to the bottom, turning between each fold, until the dough is a nice, smooth ball. Place the dough back into the bowl and cover the bowl with plastic wrap or a clean kitchen towel. Let the dough proof in a warm area until it has doubled in size, about 1 hour.

4. **Shape the donuts.** Prepare 12 (3 × 8-inch/8 × 21cm) pieces of parchment paper. When the dough has doubled, punch the dough down to deflate and degas it. Turn the dough out onto a lightly floured surface and divide the dough into 12 equal-size pieces, then roll each piece into a ball. Working with one dough ball at a time, roll it into a ¼-inch (6mm) thick rope that's about 12 inches (30cm) long. When the rope is long enough, twist the rope by placing your palms on each end of the rope and rolling in opposite directions (photo 1). With the rope twisted, pick it up from both ends so that they twist together to make the twisted donut shape (photo 2). Gently pinch the ends to stick them together and place the donut on a prepared sheet of parchment (photo 3). Repeat with the remaining dough and lightly dust with flour as needed during the entire process. Make sure to also keep all the working dough and shaped donuts covered as you work.

5. **Perform the second proof.** Once all the donuts are shaped, cover and let them proof in a warm area until doubled in size, about 45 minutes to 1 hour.

6. **Make the cinnamon-sugar coating.** In a wide bowl or coupe dish, combine the sugar and cinnamon and mix well. Set aside until needed.

7. **Set up the frying station.** When the donuts are almost doubled in size, start heating the oil. In a wide pot, heat 2–3 inches (5–7cm) of oil to 325°F (165°C). While the oil is heating, prepare a sheet pan with a rack or line a plate with paper towels. Also have a pair of tongs and a spider strainer at the ready.

8. **Fry the donuts.** When the oil is hot, pick up the donut using the parchment paper and carefully put it into the oil. After a few seconds, use tongs to give the parchment a jiggle and

remove it from the oil. You may need to splash some oil on the parchment to help release it. Fry the donut for 1–2 minutes per side until it's a light golden brown with an internal temperature of 190°F (88°C). Remove promptly and let it drain on the prepared rack or plate. Repeat with remaining donuts, frying as many as you can comfortably fit in your pot.

9. Finish and enjoy. After the donuts have cooled a little but are still warm, dust and roll them with the cinnamon-sugar. Enjoy while they are warm or at room temperature.

10. Storage. Leftovers can be stored at room temperature in an airtight container for up to 3 days.

Tips from our kitchen: If 12 donuts are too much for you, you can definitely cut the recipe in half, but if your mixer is like ours, you'll likely have trouble kneading the dough because there's not a whole lot. In this case, we like to make it by hand, and it's actually quite easy! Just mix your dry ingredients in a bowl, then mix in the egg and milk once the yeast is ready. Mix until no more dry ingredients are visible and a rough dough comes together. Cover and let the dough rest in a warm area for 30 minutes, then add the butter and knead until the butter is absorbed. Cover the dough again and rest for another 30 minutes, then give the dough a couple minutes of kneading. The dough should be smooth, supple, and have passed the window-pane test at this point. If not, knead it for a few more minutes, then continue with the recipe as written.

CHAPTER XLIII
CREOLE COOK BOOK

Korean-Style Sausage Bread

Sausage bread is easily one of my favorite breads growing up. Every time we go grocery shopping, I would ask Mei to swing by the bakery section so I can pick some up. It's a soft bread that has alternating slices of sausages and a mound of corn and melted cheese mixture baked on top. I love eating them warmed up with a drizzle of ketchup. Knowing that, Mei made it her mission to perfect it for me, and I have to say, she nailed it! It was so good, in fact, it was our most popular baked item sold when we catered.
— Kyong

Prep time: **50 minutes, plus 2 hours proofing time**
Cook time: **18–22 minutes**
Makes: **6 sausage bread**

Sausage bread

- 1 tsp active dry yeast
- ½ cup (120ml) whole milk, warm (around 105°F/40°C)
- 2½ cups (300g) all-purpose flour (fluffed, spooned, and leveled), plus more for dusting
- 3 tbsp (38g) granulated sugar
- 1 tsp fine salt
- ¼ cup (60ml) boiling hot water
- 2 large (100g) eggs, divided
- 2 tbsp (28g) unsalted butter, softened
- 6 hot dogs
- Dried parsley flakes, for garnish (optional)
- Ketchup, for serving (optional)

Topping

- ¾ cup (3oz/85g) shredded mozzarella
- ⅓ cup (5oz/142g) canned sweet corn, drained
- ¼ large (3.5oz/100g) yellow onion, diced
- 2 tbsp (30g) mayonnaise
- 1 stalk green onion, sliced

1. **Activate the yeast.** Sprinkle the yeast over the warm milk and give it a good stir. Set it aside in a warm area to let the yeast dissolve and activate, about 5 minutes. It should form a foamy cap. Give it another stir before use.

2. **Make the dough.** In a mixer bowl, combine the flour, sugar, and salt, and give it a good mix with the dough hook attachment. When the yeast is ready, drizzle the boiling hot water into the flour mixture while mixing with the dough hook, then add one egg and the milk-and-yeast mixture. Mix on low to medium-low speed until the dough comes together, then increase the speed to medium to medium-high and knead until the dough is almost at the window-pane stage (page 21), about 10–15 minutes. If your dough is really tacky at this point and your mixer is having a tough time picking up the dough, cover and let the dough rest for 30 minutes instead. Then add the butter and return to kneading on medium-high speed until the dough passes the window-pane test, about 10 minutes.

3. **First proof.** With the dough in your hands, fold the edges of the dough to the bottom, turning between each fold, until the dough is a nice, smooth ball. Place the dough back into the bowl and cover the bowl with plastic wrap or a clean kitchen towel. Let the dough proof in a warm area until it has doubled in size, about 1 hour.

4. **Initial shaping.** Prepare a sheet pan lined with parchment paper and pat dry the hot dogs. When the dough has doubled in size, punch it down to deflate and degas it. Turn it out onto a lightly dusted work surface, then divide the dough into 6 equal-size pieces and round each piece of dough into a ball. Working with one piece of dough at a time, roll the dough out into an oval about 2 inches (5cm) longer than the hot dog. Place a hot dog in the center of the dough and fold the ends of the oval over the hot dog, then bring the long edges of the dough together and pinch along the entire edge to seal it. Give the dough log a little roll with your palm to even it out. Arrange the log onto the prepared sheet pan and repeat with remaining dough and hot dogs. Leave about 4 inches (10cm) between each log.

5. **Shaping (part two) and second proof.** Using a pair of kitchen shears or a sharp knife, make 8–9 evenly spaced cuts in each log. Be sure to cut all the way through the hot dogs, but not all the way through the dough. To shape the sausage bread, gently pull open each sliced section (the hot dog with the dough) in alternating directions (i.e., one section left then the next section right) (photos 1–3). Repeat with the remaining logs, then cover and let them proof in a warm area until doubled in size, about 45 minutes to 1 hour.

6. **Make the topping.** While the breads are proofing, combine all the ingredients for the topping in a medium bowl and mix well. Cover and keep refrigerated until needed.

7. **Bake.** Preheat the oven to 350°F (175°C). Whisk the remaining egg in a small bowl to create an egg wash. Brush the dough parts of the sausage bread with the egg wash and top the center area of each bread with an equal amount of the prepared topping. When the oven is ready, bake on the middle rack for 18–22 minutes or until the sausage breads are golden brown and the center of the dough registers 190°F (88°C).

8. **Cool and enjoy.** Once cooked, remove the breads from the oven and let them cool until warm to the touch. If desired, top with parsley flakes and enjoy with ketchup.

9. **Storage.** Leftovers can be stored in an airtight container and refrigerated for up to 4 days. To reheat, zap them briefly in the microwave until warm.

Tips from our kitchen: Because this dough is wetter and stickier, we sometimes prefer to make it by hand rather than with a mixer. To do so, combine the dry ingredients in a heatproof bowl, then drizzle in the hot water and mix with chopsticks or a fork. Add the egg and milk mixture and mix with your hands until well combined. Cover and let the dough rest for about 30 minutes. Then add the butter and knead until it is fully absorbed. Cover again and let the dough rest for another 30 minutes, then knead for a few minutes more, until the dough passes the windowpane test. From there, proof and shape as usual.

Miso Banana Bread

Miso in banana bread might sound like an unusual combination, but trust us—the results are undeniably delicious. The natural sweetness of ripe bananas paired with the salty, savory depth of miso creates a flavor that feels both unexpected and familiar. Rather than overpowering the loaf, the miso adds a subtle twist that makes this classic treat pleasantly surprising in the best way. — Mei

---

Prep time: **20 minutes**
Cook time: **65–75 minutes**
Makes: **1 loaf**

- 2 cups (240g) all-purpose flour (fluffed, spooned, and leveled)
- 1 tsp ground cinnamon
- 1 tsp baking soda
- 1 tsp baking powder
- 1 stick (113g) unsalted butter, softened (plus more for greasing)
- 3 tbsp (55g) white miso
- ¾ cup (165g) packed dark brown sugar
- 2 large (100g) eggs
- 2 cups (500g) mashed, overripe bananas (about 4 bananas)
- 1 tsp vanilla extract
- ¾ cup chopped nuts, chocolate chips, or dry fruits (optional)
- 1 just-ripe banana, peeled and split in half lengthwise, for garnish (optional)

1. **Preheat the oven to 350°F (175°C).** Lightly grease an 8 × 4-inch (20 × 10cm) loaf pan with butter or nonstick spray.
2. **Prepare the dry ingredients.** In a medium bowl, whisk together the flour, cinnamon, baking soda, and baking powder until well combined. Set aside until needed.
3. **Make the batter.** In a large mixing bowl, using a hand mixer, or in a stand mixer fitted with the paddle attachment, beat the softened butter, miso paste, and brown sugar on medium speed until well combined. Increase the speed to medium-high and cream the mixture until light, fluffy, and pale, about 2–3 minutes. Scrape down the sides of the bowl as needed. Add the eggs one at a time, mixing on medium speed and allowing each egg to fully incorporate before adding the next. Mix in the mashed bananas and vanilla extract until well combined. Add the prepared dry ingredients and mix on low speed until just combined—do not overmix. Scrape down the sides of the bowl as needed. If using nuts, chocolate, or dried fruit, add it now and gently fold them in with a rubber spatula.
4. **Bake.** Pour the batter into the prepared loaf pan and spread it out evenly. Optionally, arrange the two halves of banana on top of the batter, cut side up. Bake the banana bread on the middle rack for 65–75 minutes or until a toothpick inserted into the center comes out clean or with just a few crumbs. During the last 10–20 minutes of baking, cover the top of the banana bread with a sheet of aluminum foil if the top starts to get too dark.
5. **Cool and enjoy.** Remove the banana bread from the oven and let it cool on a rack until it is comfortable to handle. Then remove it from the loaf pan and let it cool completely or until just warm. Cut into slices of your desired thickness. (This banana bread is great while it's still warm, but it's even better the next day!)
6. **Storage.** Keep it in an airtight container at room temperature for up to 3 days or refrigerate for up to 1 week. If refrigerating, warm it up briefly in the microwave for best texture and flavor.

Tips from our kitchen: We buy bananas probably once a week and always end up with a couple overripe ones we never get to. So, we freeze 4–5 bananas per batch as we collect them, and when we're in the mood for banana bread, we just defrost a batch overnight or on the counter. These frozen bananas give so much banana flavor! Just make sure to drain most of the excess liquid that comes from the freezing and thawing process.

Chai Spice Loaf Cake

This loaf cake is pure indulgence. It's moist and tender, generously swirled with chai spice to layer in even more of that warm, aromatic flavor, then finished with a classic vanilla glaze. The rich, comforting spices shine through in every bite, making it the perfect treat to savor with a cup of hot tea or coffee. — Mei

---

Prep time: **20 minutes**
Cook time: **55–60 minutes**
Makes: **1 loaf**

Homemade chai spice (if making)
2 tbsp (12g) ground cinnamon
1½ tbsp (9g) ground ginger
1 tbsp (6g) ground cardamon
½ tbsp (3g) ground clove or allspice
½ tbsp (3g) ground nutmeg

Chai spice sugar mix
¼ cup (50g) granulated sugar
2 tsp (4g) chai spice
1 tsp all-purpose flour

Batter
2 cups (240g) all-purpose flour (fluffed, spooned, and leveled)
1½ tbsp (9g) chai spice (homemade or store-bought)
1½ tsp (6g) baking powder
½ tsp baking soda
½ cup (110g) packed dark brown sugar
¼ cup (50g) granulated sugar
½ tsp fine salt
1 large (50g) egg
⅓ cup (80ml) neutral cooking oil
½ cup (120g) full-fat sour cream
¾ cup (180ml) whole milk
1 tsp vanilla extract

Glaze
½ cup (60g) powdered sugar
1 tbsp (15ml) whole milk
¼ tsp vanilla extract

1. **Make the chai spice (if making).** Combine all the spices in a small bowl and mix well. Store in an airtight container in a cool, dry place.
2. **Prepare the chai spice sugar mix.** Combine all the ingredients for the chai spice sugar mix in a small bowl and mix well. Set aside until needed.
3. **Preheat the oven to 350°F (175°C).** Also, prepare a 8 × 4-inch (20 × 10cm) loaf pan and lightly grease it with oil or butter, or line it with a sheet of parchment paper with extra paper hanging off the edge. If using parchment paper, the short ends of the pan can be left unlined.
4. **Make the batter.** In a large mixing bowl, whisk together the flour, chai spice, baking powder, and baking soda. To another mixing bowl, add both sugars, salt, the egg, and oil. Whisk until well combined, then add the sour cream, milk, and vanilla extract. Mix until well combined. Pour the wet mix into the bowl of dry flour mixture, and whisk until just combined. Do not overmix!
5. **Bake.** Pour half of the batter into the prepared loaf pan, then sprinkle all the chai spice sugar mixture evenly over the surface of the batter. Pour the remaining batter into the loaf pan and evenly spread the batter with a spoon or spatula to level it out. Use a butter knife to draw swirls in the batter. Place the loaf pan into the oven on the middle rack, and bake for 55–60 minutes or until a toothpick inserted in the middle of the loaf cake comes out clean or with just a few crumbs.
6. **Cool.** When the loaf cake is done baking, remove it from the oven and let it cool for 10–15 minutes, then remove it from the loaf pan. If you lined the loaf pan with parchment, you can use the edges of the paper to lift the loaf cake out of the pan and then peel it off. Let the loaf cake cool on a wire rack until completely cooled.
7. **Glaze.** When the loaf cake has completely cooled, make the glaze by mixing together all the glaze ingredients in a small bowl until well combined and smooth. Drizzle the glaze over the top of the loaf cake, and let it dry for a few minutes until it's no longer wet to the touch. We recommend placing the loaf cake on parchment paper or a cutting board for the glazing.
8. **Slice and enjoy.** Cut the loaf cake into slices of your desired thickness, and enjoy at room temperature, chilled, or slightly warmed. If you don't plan on serving all the loaf cake, we recommend only cutting as many slices you're serving to keep the loaf moist.
9. **Storage.** Leftover loaf cake should be tightly wrapped with plastic wrap or stored in an airtight container and kept refrigerated for up to 7 days.

Tips from our kitchen: If you have time and good self-control, you can make the loaf cake a day before, wrap and refrigerate overnight, and glaze the next day for an extra-moist loaf. We like to wrap and refrigerate the loaf cake while it is still slightly warm to trap extra moisture.

Honey Osmanthus Ice Cream

Osmanthus tea has a delicate, sweet floral aroma with a hint of honey and subtle notes of apricots and peaches. Steeping it in an ice cream base and then sweetening it with honey creates a super creamy ice cream that's fruity and slightly floral, with honey flavors and a malty undertone. It's such a delicious ice cream and honestly probably our favorite flavor so far! — Mei

---

Prep time: **30–35 minutes, plus 2 or more hours for cooling, churning, and freezing**
Cook time: **none**
Makes: **about 1½ qt (1.4L)**

2 cups (480ml) whole milk
2 cups (480ml) heavy cream
½ cup (18g) osmanthus flower tea
6 large (105g) egg yolks
¾ cup (255g) good quality honey

1. **Prepare your ice cream churner.** If needed, place your ice cream churner in the freezer the night before so that it's frozen and ready for churning.
2. **Steep the tea.** Combine the milk, heavy cream, and osmanthus flower tea in a large saucepan. Heat the mixture over medium heat until it just starts to simmer, then remove it from the heat and let the osmanthus steep for 5–10 minutes. Make sure to keep an eye on the mixture while it's heating and stir occasionally.
3. **Temper the egg yolks.** Place the egg yolks in a large heatproof mixing bowl and give them a whisk to break up the yolks. After the osmanthus is done steeping and while the milk mixture is still hot, stream the hot milk mixture, a little at a time, into the bowl of egg yolks while continuously whisking. After a quarter of the milk mixture is added, you can pour faster.
4. **Cook the ice cream base.** Strain the ice cream base into a clean saucepan using a mesh strainer and cook it over medium to medium-low heat until it becomes thick, almost as thick as gravy. Make sure to stir the mixture constantly with a rubber spatula and scrape the bottom and sides of the saucepan during the whole process. Because of the tea, the ice cream base may look slightly curdled, but don't worry—it isn't. Just be careful not to overcook it, or the base may scramble.
5. **Cool and finish the ice cream base.** Transfer the ice cream base to a heatproof bowl or container. Cover it with plastic wrap, making sure it's touching the surface of the ice cream base to prevent it from forming a skin. Chill it in the fridge until completely cooled. When the ice cream base has completely cooled, stir in the honey until well combined.
6. **Churn the ice cream.** Transfer the chilled ice cream base to your ice cream churner and churn the ice cream until it's a soft-serve consistency. Transfer the ice cream to a freezer-safe container with a lid or a loaf pan tightly wrapped with plastic wrap. We recommend also freezing the containers ahead of time so that your ice cream doesn't melt. Freeze the ice cream for at least an hour, or until solid, before serving.
7. **Serve.** Enjoy the ice cream as is or give it a light drizzle of honey and a sprinkle of osmanthus flower tea for garnish.

Tips from our kitchen: To make this ice cream without a churner, pour the chilled ice cream base into a metal mixing bowl and freeze it for 30 minutes to 1 hour. Once the edges start to freeze, use a hand mixer to beat the mixture, breaking up the frozen portions and incorporating them into the still-liquid center. Repeat this freezing and mixing process until the ice cream becomes mostly solid. Alternatively, you can freeze the base in ice cube trays, then blend the cubes in a high-powered blender, like in our Mandarin Orange Calpico Sorbet (page 231).

Matcha Strawberry Cake Roll

This fluffy matcha cake roll is soft and tender and filled with lightly sweetened whipped cream and fresh strawberries. It's one of our favorite desserts, especially with our afternoon tea. For the matcha, you can use either culinary-grade powder, which is more widely available and affordable, or, if your budget allows, barista/cafe matcha, which is more expensive but will produce a more vibrantly colored cake. — Mei

Prep time: **40 minutes, plus 3–4 hours for chilling**
Cook time: **25–30 minutes**
Makes: **1 cake roll (6–8 servings)**

Cake batter

- 5 large (250g) eggs, egg whites and yolks separated
- ¼ cup (60ml) neutral cooking oil, hot (around 165°F/74°C)
- 2 tbsp (10g) matcha powder
- ¼ cup (60ml) whole milk, lukewarm
- ½ cup (60g) cake flour (fluffed, spooned, and leveled)
- ⅓ cup (67g) granulated sugar
- 1 tsp lemon juice or white vinegar

Filling

- 1¼ cup (300ml) heavy cream
- ⅓ cup (67g) granulated sugar
- 1 tsp vanilla extract
- 8 oz (227g) strawberries, plus more for garnish
- Powdered sugar, for garnish (optional)

1. **Preheat the oven to 325°F (160°C).** Also, prepare a 10 × 15-inch (25 × 38cm) jelly roll pan lined with parchment paper.

2. **Chill the egg whites (optional).** Place the egg whites into the mixer bowl or a large mixing bowl and place it into the freezer to chill for about 15 minutes or until the edges of the egg whites start to form frozen shards. This step is not necessary but will help you whip up a more stabilized meringue with better volume.

3. **Make the batter base.** When the egg whites are nearly ready, start making the batter base. To a medium or large mixing bowl, add the oil and matcha powder and whisk until well combined and no more matcha clumps are visible. Next, add the milk and whisk until roughly emulsified, then add the cake flour and whisk until no more dry flour is visible. To finish, add the egg yolks and mix until well combined and smooth. The batter should be smooth with a consistency that's a little thinner than pancake batter. Cover the bowl and set aside until needed.

4. **Make the meringue.** To the slightly frozen egg whites, add all the sugar and lemon juice. With the whisk attachment or a hand mixer, beat the mixture on medium-high to high speed until the meringue starts to show ripples and is able to form a soft peak when you lift up the whisk. Continue beating on low speed until the meringue is shiny and reaches medium-stiff peak, where a sharp, small hook forms when you lift up the whisk.

5. **Incorporate the meringue.** Transfer a third of the meringue into the prepared batter base and gently mix with a whisk using a "J" motion while turning the bowl until the batter is mostly even in color. Pour the batter into the bowl of the remaining meringue and mix gently with the whisk in a "J" motion until mostly combined. Then switch to a rubber spatula and fold the batter using the same "J" motion until the batter is even in color. Don't overmix.

6. **Bake.** Pour the batter into the prepared jelly roll pan and gently level it out with the rubber spatula. Firmly tap the pan on the countertop to pop any remaining large bubbles, and place the pan into the oven on the middle rack. Bake the cake for about 25–30 minutes or until a toothpick inserted into the center of the cake comes out clean and the top of the cake is a light golden color.

7. **Cool the cake.** Once the cake is done, remove it from the oven and give it a firm tap on the countertop. Cut along the edges of the cake to separate it from the pan and slightly lift the cake out of the pan then slide it off onto a wire rack to cool. Let the cake cool completely then flip it onto a sheet of parchment paper. Peel off the bottom parchment.

8. **Make the whipped cream.** To the mixer bowl or a large mixing bowl, add the heavy cream, sugar, and vanilla extract. Using the whisk attachment or the hand mixer, beat the cream until it reaches a stiff peak, starting from low speed then increasing to medium-high speed once the cream starts to thicken. Cover and keep the whipped cream refrigerated until needed.

9. Prepare the strawberries. If possible, choose small or medium strawberries of similar size. Wash the strawberries and thoroughly dry them with paper towels. Trim and discard the ends where the leaves are. Cover and keep refrigerated until needed.

10. Prep and assemble the cake roll. Trim off all the sides of the cake and follow the assembly instructions for the cake roll.

11. Chill the cake roll. When you're finished rolling up the cake, tightly wrap the cake roll with the parchment paper and secure it with tape if necessary. Refrigerate the cake roll with its seam side down for at least 3–4 hours or overnight to set the whipped cream.

12. Garnish and serve. Cut the cake roll into 6–8 slices with a serrated knife, and, if desired, top each slice with a dollop of the remaining whipped cream, a light dusting of powdered sugar, and half of a strawberry. Enjoy immediately or keep it refrigerated in an airtight container for up to 3 days.

Assembling the cake roll

1. First, decide which side of cake you'd like as the presentation side. With the presentation side facing down on the parchment paper, evenly spread about half of the whipped cream over the top of the cake, but leave about ½-inch (1cm) border on both of the short edges.

2. About 4 inches (10cm) from one short edge of the cake, arrange the strawberries in a vertical line (photo 1).

3. Top the strawberries with half of the remaining whipped cream and even it out across the strawberries (photo 2).

4. Using the parchment paper to help you lift and roll the cake, begin working from the short edge of the cake closest to the strawberries (photo 3). Roll the cake up to form a log (photo 4).

Tips from our kitchen: To upgrade your cake roll from good to great, you can swap the parchment paper for reusable Teflon mats to line your jelly roll pan. The Teflon mats will prevent waves and crinkling on the bottom of the cake, and it keeps the cake moist on the bottom and edges so that the cake has an even "spongy" appearance.

Roasted Rice Tiramisu

During the pandemic, after we were let go from our restaurant jobs, we started our catering gig and had time to tell stories and reminisce about our childhoods. One of Kyong's childhood memories had us set out to recreate the nostalgic flavor of a scorched rice candy that he loved, which turned into this tiramisu. To replicate the scorched rice flavor, we used Korean morning rice drink (available at most Asian markets and online) instead of coffee, made a cream with the rice drink as well, and topped it with some roasted soybean powder. This tiramisu has all the classic creamy richness of the Italian dessert but tastes nutty and has a lovely roasted flavor throughout instead of the traditional bitterness of coffee. — Mei

---

Prep time: **40 minutes, plus at least 4 hours chilling time**
Cook time: **none**
Makes: **1 (8 × 8-inch/20 × 20cm) baking dish**

Tiramisu cream
- 2 large (30g) egg yolks
- ⅓ cup (67g) granulated sugar
- ¼ cup (60ml) Korean Morning rice drink (Woongjin brand)
- 1 cup (240ml) heavy cream
- 8 oz (227g) mascarpone cheese, softened

For assembling
- 1 (7oz/200g) pack ladyfingers (about 24 pieces)
- 1–1¼ cup (240–300ml) Korean Morning rice drink (Woongjin brand)
- Roasted soybean powder, for dusting

1. **Make the egg yolk base.** Bring 1 inch (2.5cm) of water to a simmer in a pot over medium-high heat, then reduce the heat to low to keep the water hot. To a large heatproof mixing bowl that can sit over the pot but doesn't touch the water, add the egg yolks, sugar, and rice drink. Using a whisk, mix well and set the bowl over the pot of water. Gently but constantly whisk the mixture until it reads 145°F (63°C) on a kitchen thermometer, then immediately remove the bowl, but keep whisking for a few more seconds to prevent the mixture from scrambling (see note). Dry the outside of the bowl with a towel and beat the mixture with a hand mixer on medium-high speed until it's pale, fluffy, and at least doubled in volume. It should also be cooled at this point. Clean the mixer attachment for the whipped cream.

2. **Make the mascarpone whipped cream.** In another mixing bowl, add the heavy cream. Using the hand mixer, beat the cream on medium-low to medium speed until the cream reaches soft peak (the cream starts to show ripples). Then add the softened mascarpone and beat on medium speed until the mixture reaches medium firm peak and is well combined. Make sure to scrape the bowl with a rubber spatula as needed.

3. **Finish the tiramisu cream.** Add half of the whipped cream mixture to the cooled egg yolk base and incorporate using a whisk with a gentle whisking motion. Fold in the remaining whipped cream using a rubber spatula and "J" motion until well combined. Cover and keep chilled until needed.

4. **Assemble.** Prepare a 8 × 8-inch (20 × 20cm) baking dish and a spoon or small offset spatula. Soak the ladyfingers in the rice drink, one at a time, for about 3–4 seconds, letting any excess liquid drip off, and arrange them in the baking dish. Repeat this process until there's an even layer of ladyfingers. If needed, break a few ladyfingers into smaller pieces before soaking to fill the baking dish. Top the layer of ladyfingers with half of the tiramisu cream and level it out with the spoon or spatula. Repeat this layering process again, then cover and refrigerate for at least 4 hours or overnight before serving.

5. **Serve.** Before serving, generously dust the top of the tiramisu with roasted soybean powder. Scoop with a spoon and enjoy it chilled.

6. **Storage.** Leftover tiramisu should be stored in an airtight container or tightly wrapped with plastic wrap and kept refrigerated for up to 3 days.

Tips from our kitchen: While heating the egg yolk base over the pot of water, it is very important to not to scramble the mixture, so make sure to keep the mixture moving by whisking, and take the bowl off and on the pot if the bowl ever feels too hot.

Spiced Kabocha Madeleines

Back in France, Kyong and I were enjoying a rare break together from Institut Paul Bocuse and decided to go bakery hopping to taste all the flavors the local patisseries had to offer. We sampled everything from bright citron pastries to tarts in every shape and flavor imaginable. Although everything tasted good, there was one pastry from a small boulangerie that stood out—perfectly baked pumpkin madeleines. Inspired, we decided we'd recreate it when we got back to the States, thinking maybe we could sell it at our bakery someday when we retired. This version was developed using kabocha squash to give these madeleines a beautiful yellowish-orange color with crispy edges and a moist yet characteristically delicate crumb, which are perfect with a cup of chamomile tea. Each madeleine is tossed freshly in a cinnamon-spice sugar coating that pairs beautifully with the natural, mild flavors of the kabocha. — Mei

---

Prep time: **30 minutes, plus 30 minutes of resting time**
Cook time: **15 minutes**
Makes: **16 pieces**

Madeleine batter

- 3 oz (85g) peeled and deseeded raw kabocha squash, cut into 1-inch (2.5cm) chunks
- 1¼ cup (150g) all-purpose flour (fluffed, spooned, and leveled)
- 1½ tsp (6g) baking powder
- 1 tsp pumpkin spice
- ½ tsp fine salt
- 2 large (100g) eggs
- ½ cup (100g) granulated sugar
- 2 tbsp (30ml) milk (whole or skim)
- 1 tsp vanilla extract
- 8 tbsp (113g) unsalted butter, melted and cooled
- 2 tbsp (28g) unsalted butter, softened

Cinnamon sugar coating

- ¼ cup (50g) granulated sugar
- ½ tsp ground cinnamon

1. **Prepare the kabocha squash.** Steam the kabocha using your preferred method until tender. A classic steam basket setup will take about 10–15 minutes to cook the squash. Make sure to drain off excess liquid or condensation that collects on the plate. Alternatively, you can steam the squash in the microwave. Place the kabocha on a microwave-safe plate and drizzle a little water over the squash. Cover and microwave on high-power for about 2–3 minutes or until completely tender and can be easily pierced with a knife without resistance. Once cooked, let the kabocha cool until it's comfortable to handle, then mash it well. You should end up with about ¼ cup (65g) of mashed kabocha. Set aside until needed.

2. **Prepare the dry ingredients.** In a bowl, combine the flour, baking powder, pumpkin spice, and salt. Mix well and set aside.

3. **Make the batter.** In a large bowl with a hand mixer or a stand mixer fitted with the whisk attachment, beat the eggs and sugar on medium-high speed until pale and fluffy, about 3 minutes. Add the mashed kabocha, milk, and vanilla and beat on medium-high speed until well combined. Using a rubber spatula, fold in the dry ingredients until just combined and no more dry flour is visible. *Do not* overmix the batter! Add the melted butter and fold gently until just combined. Cover and set the batter aside to rest at room temperature for at least 30 minutes and up to 2 hours. If your kitchen is cold, keep the batter in a warm area.

4. **Make the cinnamon-sugar coating.** While waiting, combine the sugar and cinnamon and mix well. You can make this ahead of time and keep it stored in a cool, dry place for whenever you need it.

5. **Preheat the oven to 400°F (205°C)** and generously brush your madeleine pan (see note) with the softened butter, paying special attention to grease up the corners and edges of each cavity.

6. **Bake the madeleines.** After resting, gently fold the batter a couple of times to ensure everything is evenly incorporated, then fill each buttered madeleine pan cavity about three-quarters full. Give the pan a gentle tap on both sides to level out the batter and bake on the middle rack for about 15 minutes or until the edges of the madeleines are golden brown and crispy and a toothpick inserted into the center of a madeleine comes out clean or with just a few crumbs.

7. **Pop out the madeleines.** Remove the pan from the oven then tilt and tap the madeleine pan at an angle to pop the madeleines out of the pan. They should slide right out with a couple of firm taps if the madeleines are baked well and the pan is generously buttered.

8. **Bake the second batch (if needed).** If your madeleine pan is like ours with only 12 cavities, here's how you can ensure your second batch is just as good as your first. Once the first batch of madeleines have been popped out and the pan has cooled enough so that it is comfortable

to handle bare-handed, wash and scrub the cavities well, then dry thoroughly and chill the pan in the fridge. Once cold, brush the center few cavities with butter and repeat the baking process.

9. Cool and enjoy. Let the madeleines cool until comfortable to touch but still warm and then dust them in the prepared cinnamon-sugar.

10. Storage. These madeleines are best freshly made while they're still warm and crispy around the edges, but can be stored at room temperature in an airtight container for up to 3 days. Uncoated ones can be reheated in the oven for about 5 minutes at 350°F (175°C) to revive their former freshness. Enjoy by itself or with tea or coffee.

Tips from our kitchen: If you don't have a madeleine pan, you can use mini muffin pans instead. Generously butter each cavity and fill them about three-quarters full with batter. Bake at 400°F (205°C) for 11–13 minutes, or until golden brown and crisp around the edges and a toothpick inserted into the center comes out clean or with just a few crumbs. This recipe makes about 40 mini muffin-shaped madeleines.

Vietnamese Coffee Crème Brûlée

This recipe marries the creamy richness of classic crème brûlée with the bold flavors of Vietnamese coffee. To impart as much flavor of Vietnamese coffee into the crème brûlée as possible, sweetened condensed milk is used in place of sugar, and a good dark roast ground coffee is important. We like to use Cafe Du Monde's dark roast grounds (the yellow can), but your favorite dark roast coffee works too. The strong coffee flavor along with the smooth, silky custard and crunchy, caramelized sugar crust, really brings the Vietnamese coffee experience to another level. — Mei

---

Prep time: **20 minutes, plus at least 6 hours of chilling time**
Cook time: **40–55 minutes**
Makes: **5 servings**

- 2 cups (480ml) heavy cream
- 1 cup (240ml) whole milk
- ½ cup (50g) Cafe Du Monde dark roast ground coffee
- 6 large (100g) egg yolks
- ¾ cup (240g) sweetened condensed milk
- 2–3 tbsp (25–38g) granulated sugar, for brûléeing

Tips from our kitchen: If you don't have a kitchen torch, you can caramelize the sugar using the oven's broil function. To do so, preheat the oven on the high broil setting. Arrange the custards on a sheet pan and place it into the oven on the top rack, and broil until caramelized. Make sure to check every 15–30 seconds in the beginning, then every 5–10 seconds as the sugar caramelizes.

1. **Preheat the oven to 300°F (150°C).** Also, prepare four 8-fluid ounce (240ml) oven-safe ramekins, a baking dish that can hold all the ramekins with sides as tall as the ramekins (like a brownie pan), and a pot of hot water.

2. **Steep the coffee.** To a large saucepan, add the cream, milk, and ground coffee. Bring the mixture to a simmer over medium heat, stirring occasionally. When the mixture starts to simmer, turn off the heat and let the coffee steep for 10–15 minutes.

3. **Make the custard base.** When the coffee is nearly done steeping, whisk together the egg yolks and condensed milk in a large heatproof bowl until well combined. While whisking the egg yolk and condensed milk mixture, slowly drizzle in the hot coffee and cream mixture. Once a third of the hot coffee cream mixture has been added, you can pour more generously, but keep whisking.

4. **Strain the custard base.** Strain the custard base through a fine-mesh strainer into another heatproof bowl. To remove the finer bits of the coffee ground, you can line the strainer with a couple layers of cheesecloth or use a nut milk bag. You may still see some super fine bits of coffee grounds, but it shouldn't affect the custard's texture.

5. **Portion the custard base.** Divide the custard base evenly among the ramekins and place the ramekins into the prepared baking dish. Carefully pour the prepared hot water into the baking dish until the water is halfway up the ramekins. Be careful not to splash water into the custard base.

6. **Bake the custard.** Carefully place the baking dish with the ramekins in the oven on the middle rack and bake for 30–40 minutes or until the custard only wobbles at the center when you jiggle the ramekin.

7. **Cool and set the custard.** Carefully remove the baking dish from the oven and remove the ramekins from the baking dish. Let the custard cool completely on a wire rack or a kitchen towel, then cover and refrigerate for at least 6 hours, preferably overnight, and up to 3 days.

8. **Brûlée and serve.** When ready to serve, top each ramekin of custard with about ½ tablespoon of sugar. Roll the sugar around by tilting the ramekin until there's an even, generous layer. You can tap out the extra sugar and discard. Using a kitchen torch, brûlée the top of the custard until the sugar is a caramel color.

Black Sesame Mochi Cookies

These black sesame mochi cookies are inspired by my favorite black sesame glutinous rice balls usually eaten during the Lantern Festival and Winter Solstice to symbolize family unity, reunion, and happiness. In this re-edition, the rice ball is basically turned inside out. The nutty, black sesame filling becomes the soft, chewy cookie with crispy edges, while the glutinous mochi rice ball gives each bite a soft, chewy surprise inside. — Mei

---

Prep time: **30 minutes, plus 30 minutes chilling time**
Cook time: **13–15 minutes per batch**
Makes: **10 large cookies**

Cookie dough

- ½ cup (65g) toasted black sesame seeds
- 1½ cup (180g) all-purpose flour (fluffed, spooned, and leveled)
- ¼ tsp baking soda
- ¼ tsp baking powder
- 1 stick (113g) unsalted butter, softened
- ½ cup (100g) granulated sugar
- ¼ cup (55g) packed dark brown sugar
- ½ tsp fine salt
- 1 large (50g) egg
- ½ tsp vanilla extract (optional)

Mochi

- ½ cup (60g) glutinous rice flour
- 2 tbsp (25g) granulated sugar
- ½ cup (120ml) milk (preferably whole)
- ½ tbsp (7g) unsalted butter

1. **Make the black sesame powder.** Place the black sesame seeds into a high-power blender and blend them as fine as possible. Set aside.

2. **Prepare the dry ingredients.** In a medium bowl, mix together the all-purpose flour, baking soda, and baking powder until combined.

3. **Make and portion the cookie dough.** In a mixer bowl fitted with the paddle attachment or a large mixing bowl with a hand mixer, beat the butter, both sugars, and salt on medium-high speed until light and fluffy. Next, add the egg and vanilla and beat on medium speed until well combined, making sure to scrape down the sides of the bowl as necessary. Add the black sesame powder and mix on medium-low speed until combined, then add the dry ingredients and mix on low speed until just combined and no more dry flour is visible. Portion and roll the cookie dough into 3 tablespoon-size (about 2-inch/5cm) balls, then arrange them on a plate or small sheet pan. Cover and chill the cookie dough in the fridge for about 30 minutes.

4. **Make the mochi.** In a microwave-safe bowl, whisk together the rice flour, sugar, and milk until no more rice flour is visible and the batter is smooth. Tightly wrap the bowl with plastic wrap, then poke a few holes all over the plastic wrap. Place the bowl in the microwave and heat on high power for about 1½ minutes or until the center of the mochi is no longer liquid. Add the butter and microwave for another 15–30 seconds or until the butter has melted.

5. **Knead and portion the mochi.** Prepare a plate lined with plastic wrap. Put on a pair of winter gloves or other heatproof gloves, and then cover those with disposable gloves so you can work with the hot mochi. With double-gloved hands, knead the hot mochi until the butter is absorbed and the mochi is stretchy. After kneading, and with your gloves still on, evenly divide the mochi into 10 equal-size portions with your hands and arrange them on the prepared plate. Cover the mochi and let it cool to room temperature before using.

6. **Preheat the oven to 375°F (190°C).** Also, prepare a couple of sheet pans lined with parchment paper.

7. **Assemble.** Working with a ball of cookie dough at a time, flatten the cookie dough with your palm. Place a portion of mochi on the flattened cookie dough then wrap the cookie dough around the mochi. Don't worry about fully sealing the mochi in the cookie dough or making the ball perfect. The cookies will actually look better if the dough looks shaggy. Place the mochi-filled cookie on the prepared sheet pan and flatten it so that it's about an inch (2.5cm) thick. Repeat with remaining cookie dough and mochi and keep the cookies at least 2 inches (5cm) apart.

8. Bake and cool. Place a tray of cookies in the oven on the middle rack and bake for 13–15 minutes or until the edges of the cookies just start to turn brown. Once baked, remove the cookies from the oven and let them cool for 5–10 minutes. The cookies will be soft at first and will harden a bit more as they cool. Repeat with the other tray of cookies.

9. Enjoy. The cookies are great both while they're still warm or when they're completely cooled.

10. Storage. Leftover cookies can be stored at room temperature for up to 3 days.

Tips from our kitchen: The cookies will spread a little as they bake, so here's a tip to help make them round and prettier: First, find a cup, cookie cutter, or anything round and wide enough to fit over one of the cookies. About 2–3 minutes before the cookies are done, take them out of the oven. Place the cup or cookie cutter over a cookie and gently shake it left to right and up and down to shape the cookie into a more even circle. Repeat with the remaining cookies, working quickly so they don't cool too much, then return them to the oven to finish baking.

Mandarin Orange Calpico Sorbet

I'm a firm believer that it's important to have a sorbet recipe in your back pocket for when you need a palate cleanser or just something refreshing and icy for a hot summer day. So, when we were brainstorming for a sorbet idea for this cookbook, I couldn't pass up on making a sorbet out of Calpico since it's one of my favorite drinks I grew up on. We chose the mandarin orange-flavored Calpico and combined it with fresh mandarin orange juice and zest to enhance the drink's original sweet mandarin flavor and also added lime juice for extra brightness. — Kyong

---

Prep time: **15 minutes, plus 4 or more hours for freezing time**
Cook time: **none**
Makes: **about 1½ qt (1.4L)**

- 3 cups (720ml) mandarin orange-flavored Calpico non-carbonated beverage
- 1 cup (240ml) mandarin orange juice
- 1 cup (200g) granulated sugar
- 6 tbsp (90ml) lime juice
- 2 tbsp (12g) mandarin orange zest

1. **Make the sorbet mixture.** In a large mixing bowl, combine all the ingredients for the sorbet and mix until the sugar has dissolved.
2. **Freeze.** Transfer the mixture into ice cube trays or gallon-size freezer safe bags and freeze for at least 4 hours or overnight until they are frozen solid. If using a gallon-size bag, make sure to store it laying down flat. Also freeze a loaf pan or a freezer-safe airtight container for storage.
3. **Blend.** Release the frozen sorbet mix from the ice cube trays, or, if you froze it in bags, break it up into smaller pieces using a rolling pin or something sturdy. Transfer the frozen mix into a high-power blender and blend it as smooth as possible. If your blender comes with a tamper stick, use that to help move the mixture along while it blends. If your blender does not come with a stick, take the blender off the base as needed and mix up the sorbet with a spoon so that everything gets evenly blended.
4. **Serve or freeze.** It's best to freeze the sorbet right after making it, but you can enjoy it immediately if you can't wait (that's us!). To freeze, transfer the sorbet to the prepared loaf pan or airtight container and freeze for a few hours or overnight. If using a loaf pan, wrap well with plastic wrap.
5. **Storage.** This frozen sorbet can be stored in the freezer in an airtight container for up to 3 months.

Yuzu Basque Cheesecake

Being big fans of yuzu in desserts, we had to test it in the form of a Basque cheesecake because, as much as we love a classic New York style cheesecake, the deeply caramelized, "burnt" top and silky smooth, custard-like interior of a Basque cheesecake pairs really well and adds depth to yuzu's flavor. This recipe is one of the trickier ones that we've been testing on and off for a couple of years, and we finally got it right after about a dozen fails. The result: a perfectly creamy, silky interior balanced with a beautifully charred top and just enough yuzu to brighten your taste buds without feeling overwhelming. If you love cheesecake and citrus, this one's for you. — Mei

---

Prep time: **15 minutes**
Cook time: **35–40 minutes**
Makes: **1 (6-inch/15cm) cake**

- 1 lb (454g) full-fat cream cheese, softened and cut into smaller pieces
- 1 cup (200g) granulated sugar
- 2½ tbsp (20g) cornstarch
- 3 large (150g) eggs
- 1¼ cup (300ml) heavy cream
- 6 tbsp (90ml) yuzu extract (juice)

1. **Preheat the oven to 425°F (220°C).** Also, line a 6-inch-wide × 4-inch-tall (15cm-wide × 10cm-tall) round cake pan with parchment paper. Make sure to use a whole sheet of parchment to line the pan and leave about 1 inch (2.5cm) of extra parchment hanging over the edges of the pan to make removing the cheesecake easier after baking.

2. **Make the batter.** In a large mixing bowl with a hand mixer or a stand mixer fitted with a paddle attachment, beat the cream cheese, sugar, and cornstarch on medium-low speed until well combined and smooth. Add the eggs and beat on medium speed until combined. Add the cream and yuzu extract and mix on low speed until fully combined. Make sure to scrape down the sides of the bowl as necessary during the whole process.

3. **Bake.** To ensure your cheesecake has the smoothest texture, you can strain the cheesecake batter through a mesh strainer into the prepared cake pan to remove any stubborn lumps and bubbles. Then give the pan a few firm taps on the counter to pop any remaining large bubbles. Bake the cheesecake on the middle rack for about 35–40 minutes or until the center of the cheesecake is wobbly when you jiggle it and the edges are puffed up and golden brown. If you'd like the classic burnt look, keep the cheesecake on the middle rack and broil it until the top is to your desired color. Make sure to keep an eye on it! The cake will caramelize very fast once it gets going.

4. **Cool.** Remove the cheesecake from the oven and let it cool completely on a rack. Once cooled, cover with plastic wrap and refrigerate for at least 4 hours or overnight. When ready to enjoy, lift the cake from the pan using the parchment paper. Then peel off the parchment and cut the cake into your desired serving size. Enjoy chilled.

5. **Storage.** Leftover cheesecake can be kept refrigerated for up to 3 days or frozen in airtight containers for up to 2 months. Thaw overnight to enjoy.

CHAPTER 9

Sauces + Condiments

Kimchi

My earliest memories of kimchi go back to when my grandma lived with my parents. She'd fill a large plastic tub with salted cabbage, squat down, and use the hose from the backyard to rinse them off. She would spend hours hunching over old newspapers scattered on the floor, chopping vegetables and rubbing the marinade onto each leaf with her long rubber gloves that were stained bright red from the marinade. When the kimchi was ready, she would smile as she held out a piece of rolled up kimchi for one of us to taste. Her kimchi was undeniably the best. While the way we make kimchi may have changed a little over the years, the love and joy of making it remains just as strong as when Grandma made it for us. — Kyong

---

Prep time: **45 minutes, plus 1–2 hours salting time**
Cook time: **none**
Makes: **1½–2 gallon jars (5.7–7.6L)**

- 8 lb (3.6kg) napa cabbage (about 2 medium heads)
- 2 cups (500g) kosher salt, more or less as needed

Kimchi marinade

- 1½ cups (360ml) water
- ⅓ cup (40g) regular or glutinous rice flour
- 1 large (14oz/400g) Fuji apple or Korean pear, peeled and cut into chunks (discard core)
- 1 large (14oz/400g) yellow onion, cut into chunks
- 3 oz (85g) garlic cloves (about 20)
- 2-inch (5cm) (20g) knob of ginger, peeled and cut into smaller chunks
- ½ cup (120ml) fish sauce
- 2 cups (225g) coarse gochugaru

Optional vegetables

- 3 oz (85g) Asian chives
- 8 oz (227g) Korean radish, peeled and julienned
- 1 large (6oz/170g) carrot, peeled and julienned

1. **Prepare the cabbage.** Remove any undesirable outer leaves from the cabbage and trim the root, then quarter the cabbage lengthwise and rinse each quarter well to remove debris and dirt (photo 1). Pay special attention to the outer few leaves. After rinsing, drain well and salt each quarter of napa cabbage in a sanitized area by sprinkling salt between each layer of leaves (photo 2). Make sure to salt more generously around the stems. Repeat with all the cabbages.

2. **Let the cabbage salt.** After all the cabbages are salted, arrange and stack them in a large mixing bowl. Cover and weigh down the cabbages with something heavy, and let them salt for 1–2 hours. Rotate the cabbages every 30 minutes, moving the ones on the top to the bottom. Check to see if the cabbage is ready after 1 hour. To check if the cabbage is ready, rip off a small leaf of cabbage and rinse it a couple of times with water (photo 3). The cabbage should be flexible and taste well-seasoned at the stem. The leafy part will be saltier but not unbearable. If they're not ready, rotate and check again in another 30 minutes. Prepare the marinade and other ingredients while waiting.

3. **Make the rice flour paste.** Whisk together the water and rice flour and pour the mixture into a small nonstick pan. Heat the mixture over medium-high heat, stirring occasionally. When the mixture starts to bubble and thicken, stir constantly and make sure to scrape the bottom and sides of the pan. Once the mixture thickens into a semi-translucent, slightly runny paste, set it aside to cool.

4. **Prepare the Asian chives (if using).** Asian chives can sometimes hold dirt between the leaves at the bottom of the stalk. Make sure to rinse them well. Also, because the bottom of the Asian chives can be quite woody, cut and discard the bottom 1 inch (2.5cm) of the chives. Cut the chives into 2-inch (5cm) pieces.

5. **Make the marinade.** To a blender, add the apple or pear, onion, garlic, ginger, and fish sauce. Blend until smooth and transfer it to a large stainless steel or glass mixing bowl. Add the gochugaru and the cooled rice flour paste and mix well, then add the chives, radish, and carrot and mix well. Set aside until the cabbage is ready.

1

2

3

4

6. Rinse the cabbage. When the cabbage is done salting, rinse it in a large bowl of water, making sure to get between each leaf. Drain and repeat with fresh water a couple more times. We recommend tasting after the first two rinses to determine if the cabbage requires another round or two of rinsing. After the final rinse, firmly squeeze each quarter of cabbage to remove most of the excess water, especially the leafy parts. Be careful not to squeeze too hard, so that the stems don't get bruised or damaged.

7. Marinate the cabbage. Working with one quarter of cabbage at a time, and with gloved hands, place a quarter of cabbage in the bowl of marinade and generously slather each leaf of cabbage with some marinade (photo 4). After all the leaves of the quarter of cabbage have been slathered with marinade, fold the cabbage over itself to keep it tight. Repeat with all the cabbages.

8. Store. When all of the cabbages are coated in the marinade, pack the kimchi into BPA-free plastic kimchi totes or sterilized glass jars. You can refer to our Kimchi Pickles (page 239) for instructions on sanitizing glass jars. Make sure the kimchi is tightly packed in the containers, but leave about 1 inch (2.5cm) of space between the top of the kimchi and the lid. As the kimchi ferments, it will release juices and produce gas, so the extra room will help prevent the kimchi from overflowing.

9. Enjoy immediately or ferment. You can enjoy the napa cabbage kimchi immediately if you like fresh kimchi. Mei especially loves freshly made kimchi, so we'd set a small container aside to eat within a week or two. If you prefer your kimchi fermented and sour, leave the freshly made kimchi at room temperature (not in direct sunlight) for 2–3 days or even up to 1 week before refrigerating. This speeds up the fermentation process. Let the kimchi ferment for a couple of weeks or longer until it's to your preference. Feel free to eat it during the whole process, but remember to always use clean utensils when taking kimchi out of the container. This kimchi can be stored in the fridge for up to a year or even longer, but it will become more and more sour, which is great for cooking! Also, in the first couple of weeks of the fermentation process, you may need to open the lid or loosen the lid of your kimchi containers to release gas.

Tips from our kitchen: Many Korean households prefer using *saeujeot* (fermented salted shrimp) or a mix of saeujeot and fish sauce in their kimchi marinade for more of that briny, funky flavor. You can find it at most Asian markets in the refrigerated aisles. If using saeujeot, substitute 1½ tablespoons per 1 tablespoon of fish sauce.

Sesame Ginger Slaw

This slaw is a quick and simple side dish, tossed in a creamy sesame-ginger dressing. It's perfect on its own or alongside other dishes. Our favorite way to enjoy it is with Soy-Glazed Pork Bao (page 44) or sandwiched between some soft Milk Bread Rolls (page 202) and Korean BBQ Pulled Pork (page 107).
— Kyong

Prep time: **15 minutes**
Cook time: **none**
Makes: **4–5 servings**

2 cups (6oz/170g) red cabbage, thinly sliced and core discarded
1 cup (3oz/85g) napa cabbage, thinly sliced
1 medium (3oz/85g) carrot, peeled and julienned
1 stalk green onion, sliced
¼ cup (32g) crushed peanuts (optional)
1 tbsp (10g) toasted sesame seeds (optional)

Dressing
2 tbsp (30ml) rice vinegar
2 tbsp (30ml) soy sauce
2 tbsp (30g) Kewpie or regular mayonnaise
1 tbsp (21g) honey
1 tbsp (15ml) toasted sesame oil
2 tsp (7g) grated ginger
¼ tsp cracked black pepper

1. **Make the slaw.** In a large bowl, whisk together all the ingredients for the dressing until well combined. Add both of the cabbages, carrot, and green onion, and toss well with the dressing. If desired, mix in some crushed peanuts and sesame seeds. Enjoy immediately or refrigerate for 30 minutes to serve chilled.
2. **Store.** Leftovers can be refrigerated for up to 2 days.

Kimchi Pickles

I was sitting with Mei, eating BBQ and snacking on a bowl of kimchi and some dill pickles, when it hit me—why not make a pickle that tastes like kimchi? Both were delicious on their own, but together they didn't quite satisfy the craving. So I headed to the kitchen to experiment. I started with a brine inspired by classic kimchi flavors, blending apples and ginger into a juice and combining it with a traditional pickle brine. I poured it over sliced cucumbers with gochugaru and garlic, and just like that, kimchi pickles were born. They're mildly spicy, tangy, a little funky, and ridiculously good with BBQ—or honestly, straight out of the jar. — Kyong

Prep time: **20 minutes, plus 4 or more hours for pickling**
Cook time: **5 minutes**
Makes: **2 quart jars (about two 1-liter jars)**

- 1½ lb (680g) pickling cucumbers or English cucumbers
- 2 tbsp (14g) coarse gochugaru
- 8 (27g) garlic cloves, smashed
- 2 cups (480ml) water
- 1 large (400g) Fuji apple, cored and cut into small chunks
- 2-inch (5cm) (20g) knob of ginger, peeled and cut into small chunks
- 2 cups (480ml) white vinegar
- 3 tbsp (38g) granulated sugar
- 2 tbsp (32g) kosher salt

1. **Sanitize the pickling container.** We recommend this step and using durable glass jars for pickling if storing the pickles for more than 1 week. Bring a large pot of water to a boil over high heat then reduce the heat to medium-low. Gently submerge washed containers into the water and let them simmer for 10 minutes. Drain well and remove. If using mason jars, simmer the lids for 5 minutes. Set the jars aside to cool while you prepare the pickles.
2. **Prepare the cucumbers.** Wash and cut the cucumbers into ¼-inch (6mm) round slices. You can cut them thinner if you prefer more traditional thin-cut pickles. Transfer the cucumbers to the cooled containers and add the gochugaru and garlic. If using more than one container, split the gochugaru and garlic evenly.
3. **Juice the apple and ginger.** Prepare a mesh strainer double-lined with fine cheesecloth or a nut milk bag. To a high-power blender, add the water, apple, and ginger. Blend until smooth. Drain the mixture through the prepared strainer and into a saucepan. Squeeze the cloth to get as much juice out of it as possible and then discard the leftover pulp.
4. **Make the pickling liquid.** To the saucepan with the strained juice, add the vinegar, sugar, and salt. Bring the mixture to a boil over high heat. Immediately pour the hot liquid into the jars of cucumbers, making sure the cucumber slices are fully submerged in the liquid.
5. **Pickle.** Loosely cover the jars with the lids and let the pickles cool completely at room temperature before tightening the lid and refrigerating. Let the cucumbers pickle for at least 4 hours before using. The flavor and texture will be better after 24–48 hours.
6. **Store.** Keep refrigerated and use clean utensils each time when removing pickles from the jar. The pickles will last 3–4 months.

Chinese Chili Oil

This chili oil is our all-purpose condiment and something we always keep in our pantry. It's super aromatic, flavorful, and has the perfect amount of heat, so you can drizzle it on anything. Whether you need to add a kick to your dumplings or a salad dressing or just to add an extra dose of love to a dish, it'll deliver. — Mei

---

Prep time: **5 minutes**
Cook time: **30 minutes**
Makes: **about 2½ cups (600ml)**

- 2 cups (480ml) neutral cooking oil
- 1 (2oz/57g) shallot, peeled and cut in half
- 1-inch (2.5cm) (10g) knob of ginger, cut into thick slices
- 4–5 (15g) garlic cloves
- 3 tbsp (12g) Sichuan peppercorns
- 3 star anise
- 8 green cardamon pods, cracked (optional)
- 2 bay leaves
- 1 cinnamon stick
- 1 cup (100g) Chinese chili flakes
- 2 tbsp (20g) toasted white sesame seeds (optional)
- 1 tsp fine salt

1. **Infuse the oil.** To a saucepan, add everything *except* the chili flakes, sesame seeds, and salt. Heat the oil over medium-low to low heat, keeping the oil to between 230–240°F (110–116°C). There should be thin streams of bubbles coming from the aromatics and spices. Let the aromatics fry in the oil for 25–30 minutes.

2. **Finish the chili oil.** After 25–30 minutes, strain the aromatics and spices out of the oil. The oil should be very fragrant, and the shallot and ginger should be golden brown. Keeping the oil at the same temperature, add the chili flakes and sesame seeds and cook for about 30 seconds while stirring. Finish by taking the chili oil off the heat and stirring in the salt.

3. **Storage.** Let the chili oil cool completely before transferring into a sterilized container. Store the chili oil in a cool, dark place and always use a clean utensil. It will last for up to 6 months.

5-Minute Chili Oil

This chili oil may not be as aromatic and flavorful as our all-purpose Chinese Chili Oil (page 240), but it's perfect for when you're in a pinch. — Mei

---

Prep time: **5 minutes**
Cook time: **none**
Makes: **about 2 cups (480ml)**

1 cup (240ml) neutral cooking oil
½ cup (50g) Chinese chili flakes
2 tbsp (20g) toasted white sesame seeds
½ tbsp (8ml) Chinese black vinegar
½ tsp fine salt

1. **Heat the oil.** In a saucepan, heat the oil over medium heat to 350°F (175°C), then take it off the heat.
2. **Finish the oil.** Immediately add the chili flakes and sesame seeds, and give the oil a good stir, then add the black vinegar and salt. Stir to combine.
3. **Storage.** Let the chili oil cool completely before storing in a sterilized container. Keep it in a cool, dark place and it will stay good for up to 3 months.

Tips from our kitchen: If you're in a rush and don't have a thermometer, you can roughly gauge the temperature of the oil by using a wooden chopstick. The oil should sizzle gently around the chopstick when the temperature is between 325–350°F (163–177°C).

Dumpling Dipping Sauce

This is our go-to dumpling dipping sauce. It's quick to make and uses only four simple ingredients you'll likely already have on hand. — Mei

---

Prep time: **5 minutes**
Cook time: **none**
Makes: **about ⅓ cup (80ml)**

- 2 tbsp (30ml) soy sauce
- 2 tbsp (30ml) rice vinegar
- 2 tbsp (30ml) water
- 2 tsp (8g) granulated sugar
- ¼ tsp coarse gochugaru (optional)
- 1 stalk green onion, thinly sliced (optional)
- 1 tsp toasted sesame seeds (optional)

1. **Make the sauce.** In a bowl, combine all the ingredients and stir until the sugar has dissolved.

2. **Store.** Use immediately or keep refrigerated for up to 1 week without green onions and up to 3 days with green onions.

Quick Kimchi

Sometimes I crave kimchi but don't have the time to make a large batch. So, I'd make this quicker version that's seasoned similarly to our traditional Kimchi (page 236) but without the heavy salting or long fermentation, as it is meant to be enjoyed in a shorter amount of time. Mei loves this version because we go through it much faster, meaning it stays fresh and less sour. — Kyong

Prep time: **30 minutes, plus 1 hour of salting time**
Cook time: **none**
Makes: **about 2 quarts (1.9L)**

- 2 lb (907g) napa cabbage (about half of a large head)
- 2 cups (480ml) water
- ¼ cup (64g) kosher salt

Marinade

- ⅓ cup (37g) coarse gochugaru
- 3 tbsp (27g) minced garlic
- 3 tbsp (45ml) fish sauce
- 1 tbsp (13g) granulated sugar
- ½ medium (1.5oz/43g) carrot, peeled and julienned
- ¼ large (3.5oz/100g) yellow onion, thinly sliced
- 3 stalks green onion, cut into 2-inch (5cm) pieces

1. **Prepare the cabbage.** Remove and discard any undesirable leaves and check the stalk areas of the outer few leaves of the cabbage to see if there's a lot of dirt or grime. If so, give those stalks a good rinse and rub them down with your fingers. Next, cut the cabbage into 2-inch (5cm) bite-size pieces and discard the root. Transfer the cut napa cabbage to a large mixing bowl and rinse it with water a couple of times, then drain well.

2. **Salt the cabbage.** Keep the napa cabbage in the bowl and add the water and the salt. Give the cabbage a good mix and set it aside for about an hour. Midway through, rotate the cabbage on the top to the bottom. When the hour is up, rinse a piece of cabbage stalk with fresh water and taste for the saltiness. The cabbage should be just salted, not too salty. If needed, let the cabbage salt for another 30 minutes.

3. **Rinse the cabbage.** When the cabbage is ready, drain the salt water then fill the bowl with fresh water. Swish the cabbage around to rinse off the excess salt. Drain the cabbage well then taste to make sure the cabbage isn't too salty. If it is, rinse it again. After the final rinse, squeeze a handful of cabbage at a time to remove excess moisture, but don't squeeze too hard so that the cabbage doesn't become bruised.

4. **Make the marinade.** While waiting for the cabbage to salt, make the marinade by mixing the gochugaru, garlic, fish sauce, and sugar in a large stainless steel or glass mixing bowl until well combined. Then add the carrot, onion, and green onion and mix until combined. Set aside until the cabbage is ready.

5. **Finish and store.** When the cabbage is done salting and has been rinsed, add it to the prepared marinade and mix until evenly combined. The kimchi can be enjoyed immediately if you like the flavor of freshly made kimchi. If you prefer fermented kimchi, you can store it in BPA-free plastic kimchi totes or sterilized glass containers or jars. See the Kimchi Pickles recipe (page 239) for jar sterilizing instructions. Keep it at room temperature but out of direct sunlight for 1–2 days to speed up the fermentation process, then transfer it to the fridge to ferment for 1–2 weeks or longer for more fermented flavor. Make sure to use clean utensils each time you take kimchi out of the container and it can last up to 6 months. Also, in the first couple weeks of the fermentation process, you may need to open the lid or loosen the jar of your kimchi containers to release gas.

Bulgogi Sauce

This bulgogi sauce also doubles as a marinade. It's perfect for beef, as you can see in our Bulgogi Meatballs (page 34) and Bulgogi Mandu (page 57).

Prep time: **5 minutes**
Cook time: **none**
Makes: **about 3 cups (0.7L)**

1 large (8oz/227g) Fuji apple, peeled, cored, and cut into chunks
8 (27g) garlic cloves
2-inch (5cm) (20g) knob of ginger, peeled and cut into small chunks
¾ cup (165g) packed dark brown sugar
¾ cup (180ml) soy sauce
½ tsp black pepper

1. **Make the sauce.** To a high power blender, add all of the ingredients and blend until smooth.

2. **Store.** Use the sauce immediately or keep refrigerated in an airtight container for up to 4 days or frozen for up to 3 months.

Gochujang BBQ Sauce

This is a great sauce to add to your pantry. It hits all your classic sweet and tangy BBQ sauce flavors, plus a nice mild kick from the gochujang. The best part about this BBQ sauce is that you don't have to cook it at all! Just mix it up and you're ready to go. — Kyong

---

Prep time: **5 minutes**
Cook time: **none**
Makes: **about 4 cups (about 1 liter)**

2 cups (440g) packed dark brown sugar
1½ cup (408g) ketchup
1½ cup (360ml) white vinegar
½ cup (145g) gochujang
2 tsp (10g) kosher salt
2 tsp (4g) cracked black pepper

1. **Make the sauce.** In a bowl, mix together all the ingredients until well combined and the sugar has dissolved completely.

2. **Store.** Store the BBQ sauce in a sealed container and refrigerate for up to 1 month.

Acknowledgments

First and foremost, THANK YOU, our Two Plaid Aprons community—our followers, our supporters, and everyone who has welcomed us into their kitchens and lives! We couldn't have come this far, restarted our lives, and had the chance to write this cookbook without your kindness and unwavering support. Every message, comment, and photo of our recipes coming to life in your kitchens reminded us that this journey was never ours alone—it's a shared experience. Thank you for trusting us with your time, your ingredients, and your kitchen. It means so much more to us than words can fully express. This book exists because of you, and we hope that these pages give back, even if it's just a fraction of the love and joy you've given to us. Thank you for being the best part of our story!

Noah—you are the best manager we could have ever asked for! Since the moment we met, you saw potential in us beyond what we saw in ourselves. Being the recovering micromanagers that we are, you and the team at Underscore Talent made us feel comfortable with delegating managerial tasks so that we have more time to create content. It may not seem like much, but what you do has made our lives so much better. We're able to enjoy our weekends properly and even went on our first vacation in a long time. Meeting you has also opened us to new opportunities we never dreamed of, like writing this cookbook! You've been there since day one of our cookbook planning and have continued to encourage us even when we were on our fifth round of proposal revision and feeling like writing was not in our destiny. Thank you for never losing hope in us and for helping us turn this dream into a reality. We look forward to working with you for many more years.

Our agent, Charlie, for believing in us and for representing us better than we could've represented ourselves! Thank you for always working around our time zone and sacrificing hours in your evening to answer our questions. We are so grateful for the wisdom you've shared along the way and feel so fortunate to have worked with you.

To Brook, our editor, for your endless patience, especially through the many changes and revisions we put you through. When we first met, we were beyond nervous and excited that a senior editor from DK was interested in working with us and were more than pleasantly surprised when you told us that you were already following us even before then. Thank you for being a big supporter of ours even before we met and an even bigger one while you took us under your wings. You made our first cookbook, which could have been a much more intimidating and daunting process, into something enjoyable and more manageable. You were the driving force behind this book, and there is no way we could have done this without you.

To William, our art & design director, we are so grateful for your patience and quick turnaround even when we were behind schedule, and your creative brain is so awe-inspiring —like the cute little tips icons you came up with. (We love them!) We had no idea that a design so wowing could be the face of our cookbook! When we first saw the final design, it truly felt like all the hard work from everyone involved had come to life. So, thank you for adding life and color, literally, to our cookbook!

Joanne—You were one of our biggest inspirations when we first started our social media account, and still are today. We love the vibes of your videos, the art you always create with your photos, and the stories you tell that we've resonated with. When Noah connected us, we were actually doing air-pumps because it was like getting a chance to meet one of our favorite celebrity chefs! But when we met you for the first time, you were like the unnie/noona that we just got to meet. We really appreciated the time you took out of your already busy schedule to share with us your cookbook writing and photo shoot experience. You even went out of your way to share with us your photography tips and contacts to source photography props. We really can't thank you enough. Speaking with you really made us feel more confident and ultimately helps us decide to self-shoot this cookbook. So, thank you!

To our family and friends, thank you for always having our backs and showing your support from hundreds of miles away! Our family and friends in the Dallas area—thank you all for being our willing guinea pigs and food tasters! Sometimes we can be biased toward the food we've made, but you always stayed open-minded and offered us your honest thoughts that helped us make the dishes in this cookbook the best versions they can be.

Ms. Rhoda and Ms. Marie—you have been our biggest fans since before we even started Two Plaid Aprons. Thank you both for always welcoming us into your home and giving us a space that feels safe to completely unwind and recharge. When we shared with you our plans to pursue a career in the digital space that's full of uncertainty, you never discouraged us. Instead, you offered encouragement, reminded us to have fun on the journey, and celebrated our milestones. When we told you that we're writing this cookbook, you both were so excited for us that you even started making plans to purchase copies as Christmas gifts when it's published. Although we can't fully express how blessed we feel to have you in our lives, being able to share this cookbook with you both feels like the most meaningful way we can show it.

To our parents, thank you for giving us homes filled with culture and love, even if the "L" word is rarely spoken in our homes but proven loudly through your actions. When we were younger, we didn't understand the sacrifices you all made to give us better lives, from moving to a new country and leaving everything familiar behind to working long hours toiling from morning to night. Now that we're older, we understand all the times you nagged us, or when we butted heads (like when we decided to pursue blogging and content creation as our career). You were just worried for us—worried that we may be tossing away the stability we had in front of us. Thank you for always staying by our sides at the end, even if we're in disagreement. Maybe it's because you know we're stubborn and will probably never change our minds, but nevertheless, we are grateful that you ultimately still supported us in all that we do. We hope we've made you proud and that you know every success and milestone we've achieved are because of the foundations you built for us, shaping us into who we are today.

Index

— E —

— F —

— G —

About the Authors

Mei Liu and Kyong Han are the culinary duo behind Two Plaid Aprons, a widely loved food blog and social media brand known for its approachable content and thorough instructions on making traditional Asian and Asian fusion dishes at home.

Kyong is Korean and was born and raised in Louisiana. As a teenager, he traveled extensively, developing a deep appreciation for global cuisines. These experiences shaped his curiosity and love for food, both as a window to its culture and as a craft. After formally training as a chef, Kyong went on to work under the guidance of several highly respected chefs, including Certified Master Chef Moosmiller at Southern Hills Country Club, and Chef Aaron Bludorn at Chef Daniel Boulud's Michelin-starred Café Boulud.

Mei is Chinese and grew up immersed in food from an early age. Starting with watching her grandmother make batches of spring rolls in China while standing tip-toed on a step stool, she learned the flavors and techniques of traditional Chinese cuisine. Later, when she moved to America, she worked at her parents' Chinese restaurant after school, where she learned how to make Chinese takeout recipes, which she later adapted for home cooking and now are some of the most popular recipes shared on Two Plaid Aprons. Working at her parents' restaurant also made her understand the significance of nourishment through food and the joy food can bring to people. This inspired and started her pursuit in culinary arts.

Since their time working in the professional kitchen, Mei and Kyong have transitioned to sharing their knowledge and passion for food in the digital space. Today, they have reached millions of followers through their blog and social media channels, where they break down techniques, demystify ingredients, and celebrate the flavors of their heritages. Their work has been featured across local and national food media outlets, newspapers, and television programs, as well as through collaborations with major brands.

Through Two Plaid Aprons, Mei and Kyong have built a vibrant, engaged community rooted in authenticity, education, and joy. Their work reflects their beliefs that cooking should be fun, exciting even, because the kitchen is where some of the most meaningful memories are made—from the kitchen to the table and from one generation to the next.